# FROM 0 TO 130 PROPERTIES IN 3.5 YEARS

## Steve McKnight

**Wrightbooks**

"*From 0 to 130 Properties in 3.5 Years* is simply the best property investing book I have read so far. Thanks!"

- **Shane M. (NSW)**

"I'm halfway through the book and WOW! I can understand it! Thanks for keeping it simple and plain. I'm excited about possessing it and your principles. An extra bonus was to find your website and newsletters."

- **Christine McL. (Qld)**

"This book is truly amazing!! I have been carrying it with me to work and even quoting from it to family and friends! Will we act on the information? We already have!! We have now developed a strategy for positive cashflow properties thanks to this book."

- **Con V. (NSW)**

"This is a wonderful book, it's the first book I've ever started to read and finish. I'm one of those kids that hates reading but I couldn't help myself but to finish your book because I know knowledge is power. I have told countless friends about your book and the strategy of positive gearing but they all seem to say I'm nuts, but I don't care what anyone else thinks... I can't stand the 9 to 5 routine and I believe that I will retire before I'm 30 which is nine years from now."

- **Peter K. (SA)**

"Why do I like the book so much? It's not theory and hot air, it's written by someone who has done it outlining how they did it. It's an excellent book and I thoroughly recommended it as now I feel I know how to start."

- **Lyn C. (NSW)**

First published 2003 by Wrightbooks
an imprint of John Wiley & Sons Australia, Ltd
33 Park Road, Milton, Qld 4064

Offices also in Sydney and Melbourne

Typeset in AGaramond 12/14.4 pt

Reprinted August, September (three times), October (twice), November 2003, January (twice), February, April and October 2004, February and April 2005.

© Steve McKnight 2003

National Library of Australia
Cataloguing-in-Publication data:

McKnight, Steve.

From 0 to 130 properties in 3.5 years.

Includes index.

ISBN 0 731400 77 1

1. Real estate investment.  2. Real estate business.
I. Title.

332.6324

Cover design by Alister Cameron, Element Media Group (www.emg.com.au)

Illustrated by Paul Lennon

Printed in Australia by Griffin Press

20 19 18 17 16

**Disclaimer**

The material in this publication is of the nature of general comment only, and neither purports nor intends to be advice. Readers should not act on the basis of any matter in this publication without considering (and if appropriate taking) professional advice with due regard to their own particular circumstances. The author and publisher expressly disclaim all and any liability to any person, whether a purchaser of this publication or not, in respect of anything and of the consequences of anything done or omitted to be done by any such person in reliance, whether in whole or part, upon the whole or any part of the contents of this publication.

# Contents

# ACKNOWLEDGMENTS

While I offer sincere thanks to everyone who has had a hand in making this book possible, I'd like to make several specific acknowledgments.

First and foremost, I'd like to recognise my belief and faith in Jesus Christ, my personal Lord and Saviour who said "All things are possible for the one who believes" – Mark 9:23.

To my wife and life partner Julie – thank you for your support. I'm delighted to now be able to hold up my end of the bargain. Thanks to my business partner Dave – a more loyal and trustworthy friend you could not find.

Special thanks also to Tony Barton, Brian Cavill, Andrew Deering and Bruce Innocent for their contributions, as well as Charlie Lear, Jon Stuckey, Carmel Drovandi, Marlene Nothling, Karen Lucas, Leslie Howard and Mark Davis.

Further thanks to Les Benbrook, Brent Hodgson and Sooshie for their help in proofing and to Alister Cameron for his excellent cover design. Thank you to Louise Bedford for recommending me to Wrightbooks.

I'd also like to express my appreciation for Robert G. Allen and his priceless advice about real estate investing.

And finally to you the reader – I'm delighted that you chose to invest in this book. It's now time for you to take advantage of the information I've written by using it to transform your life.

## Proverbs 3, verses 13 and 14

*"Blessed is the one who finds wisdom, and the one who obtains understanding. For her benefit is more profitable than silver, and her gain is better than gold."*

# It's More than a Dream...

Not long ago my wife, Julie, decided to advise her employer that from now on she'd only be available to work four days a week, as opposed to the usual five days. Her boss sat there a little dumbfounded while Julie explained that, as our investment income had grown, we were now far less reliant on her salary.

Whilst Julie's boss wasn't exactly doing cartwheels at the idea, he was nevertheless happy about our success and agreed to cut back her hours. If push had come to shove, and her request had cost her the job, it would have been regrettable, but we no longer need Julie's salary in order to live the lifestyle we desire; our positive cashflow investments earn more than enough to cover her wages.

Today Julie *chooses* to work because she finds her employment rewarding. She describes this choice as "amazingly empowering – like a huge burden has been lifted".

As Julie mentioned to her friends and co-workers that she'd decided to no longer work Fridays, it dawned upon her that she was now able to enjoy a permanent long weekend for the rest of her life. As could be expected, the people she told responded with comments like "Wow – that's my dream, you're so lucky", and "Isn't that great! I'd love to do that too and spend the time with my kids, rather than having to leave them in day care".

When Julie explained that it was possible for them to do it too, her friends and co-workers dismissed the idea as impossible and gave excuses like:

⇨ "Are you kidding? I'm too busy to invest"

⇨ "I'm not smart enough"; and

⇨ "I don't know how".

If you'd like to work less and want to discover the way my wife and I achieved financial independence in three and a half years, then this book is for you.

The upcoming pages contain detailed, specific, challenging, honest and thought-provoking information about how to use positive cashflow property to build enough passive income to allow you to gradually work less and then, finally, no longer at all.

## HOW CAN I HELP YOU?

Acting as a mentor, I derive enormous personal satisfaction from helping people, just like you, improve their financial and life position. My expertise is developing strategies to break the shackles of 21st century slavery – the obligation to work. Over several years I've been able to help many people – students while lecturing at RMIT (one of Melbourne's largest educational institutions), aspiring chartered accountants through the Institute of Chartered Accountants' CA program, and my clients while I worked as an accountant. More recently I've shown thousands of investors how buying property for capital gains doesn't necessarily deliver the wealth-building outcomes that are so easily promised and why negative gearing is often a money trap.

The positive gearing model (as outlined in Chapter 11) that I've pioneered looks at property from a different perspective – one that values cashflow returns above capital appreciation in order to gradually scale back your need to work without suffering a drop in your lifestyle. Nothing in this book requires you to be an accountant, economist, rocket scientist or brain surgeon in order to understand what's written. My methodology (refreshingly) is based on common sense.

Since May 1999, my business partner (Dave Bradley) and I have acquired 130 properties, which is quite a remarkable achievement. On average we have acquired a new positive cashflow dwelling every eight and a half days. Yet Dave and I don't normally keep a day to day tally of the number of houses we own. Instead we focus on the net cashflow that our properties deliver, which is currently well in excess of $200,000 per annum.

It's my sincerest wish that this book will help you to achieve your life goals. In order for this to happen you must accept responsibility for turning theory into practice. It will be relatively easy to read this book, but the challenge will be to move out of your comfort zone and take action.

If you believe you deserve the freedom that financial independence delivers, then this book definitely has a lot to offer. I've shown many people how to use positive cashflow property investing to build a lifetime of wealth and now, if you have a mind eager to learn, then I'd like to show you too. I invite you to join me as I outline what works, and what doesn't, in the world of real estate investing. I promise it will change the way you invest in property forever.

Regards,

**Steve McKnight**
**Melbourne**
**August, 2003**

## FREE BONUS CHAPTER

Since the first printing of the book, I've received many requests for more information about the risks of property investing. As a result, I've written a bonus chapter titled 'Managing the Risk of Investing', which is available for free via the internet. To access this bonus chapter outlining more information on avoiding vacancies, managing interest rate fluctuations, how to avoid structual defects and more, go to: www.PropertyInvesting.com/bonuschapter

# PART I:

# Making a Start

# Humble Beginnings

I'm sure that many readers will find this book thought provoking, but I doubt anyone will be more shocked by its existence than my Year 10 maths teacher. He was certain that I'd never amount to anything, and he once wrote on my end-of-term report card; "Always pleasant and amiable, Stephen has much difficulty with even the most basic of maths problems."

Today, at age 31, I co-own (with my business partner Dave), a significant multi-million dollar international property portfolio spanning single (stand-alone or detached) family homes, blocks of units and also commercial real estate. On reflection, I'd have to say that the kid who struggled with algebra managed to at least gain a good appreciation of the maths involved in making money.

However, please don't think this is a rags to riches story, or that I have some supernatural ability that only the truly blessed receive. Neither is the case. My upbringing was decidedly middle-class, neither flush with money, nor crying poor. Working hard in the one job for 40 years, my father abandoned a lot of his own ambition so that his wife and three children would never go without food, shelter and the occasional luxury. For this I love and respect him deeply. Mum never worked in a paid, full-time position, instead she showered her children with delicious home cooking and cuddles. As a gifted musician, Mum would teach piano after school for extra housekeeping money when time allowed.

I'm the youngest of three children and the only one to buck the system and consciously seek a way to quit work as soon as possible. At high school I was the fat kid bereft of any sporting ability, except useful as a defender in basketball because I had (as my coach put it) a "huge presence" on the court. A lack of ability might not be an issue at some schools, but when you attend an all-boys institution where sporting achievement goes hand-in-hand with academic excellence, the unco-ordinated and less athletic students are cast to the bottom of the social pecking order.

## DANGEROUS ASSUMPTIONS

In fact, it wasn't until very, very late in high school that I started to figure the whole academic game out. I'd discovered a rote learning strategy that allowed me to retain a few learning threads, which I wove together as best I could. Faced with the real possibility of not being able to study anything other than horticulture at University (a course which allowed you to fail your final year and still get in!) I knuckled down and hit the books for hours on end.

Looking back it's clear that I was never shown how to study effectively. Instead, it was just assumed that everyone could do it – like reading and counting to ten. A similar problem exists today in that property investors are never taught how to invest profitably. It's just assumed that all of us will be able to invest successfully once we have the finances to start, but no-one ever explains how we should go about it.

Having languished at the bottom of the social and academic pecking order for most of high school, I feel compelled today to do what I can to right the wrongs caused by dangerous assumptions. In terms of property investing I will show you how to make a profit from day one. But more on that later.

My choice of career was made with little forethought. I always wanted to be a physiotherapist, but I was deemed too mathematically challenged and my high school forbade me to do maths in Year 12 – a prerequisite for the course of my dreams.

So, what does someone who is hopeless at maths do? I became an accountant of course! Now, please don't make the mistake of thinking that accountants need to be savvy with maths – that's what they invented calculators for. All that's needed is a solid grasp of how to push buttons, a callused index finger, and a good understanding of your times tables.

I bumbled my way through an RMIT accounting degree with mainly passes and the odd credit. While not counting for much, my crowning achievement was that I was recognised by my peers as a pinball wizard – a poor accolade, but something nevertheless.

Somehow I talked my way into a job in the midst of the early 1990s recession. Turning up for work in a suit that looked uncomfortably like plush-pile carpet, with a pink shirt and tie that I'd be embarrassed to give away today, I began my accounting apprenticeship completing simple tax returns and running errands. Still, much to my Dad's surprise, I never had to make the coffee.

Before long my career took a turn for the better and I secured a job with one of the big six (now big four) international accounting firms. The only cause for concern was that I worked in audit. Unfortunately, audit is not the most exciting of fields, especially at the junior level. But I had a bout of late-onset work ethic (inherited from my father) and worked exceptionally hard. I was regularly promoted and, having already completed the necessary prerequisites, I began to study to become a chartered accountant. This was not an easy thing to do as the postgraduate exams are notoriously difficult to pass. I'd work long hours during the day and then come home to many long nights of study. You could accurately say that I had absolutely no social life. Such was my lot until I succeeded in gaining the status of a chartered accountant, at which point I immediately suffered a massive meltdown.

Disillusioned with my chosen career, I tried in vain to study physiotherapy at Sydney University. It was the only course that would even consider me, and I did exceptionally well to get number 17 on the second round offers (which meant I was 117th out of thousands of applications), but the cold, hard fact was that I was not offered a place.

Shattered, I realised I needed a change and made a career blunder by accepting a job in industry (as opposed to public accounting), more because I felt wanted than because it was a match to my skill set. In between roles I took a holiday and met a woman, Julie, who captured my attention, and my heart. The only problem was I lived in Melbourne and she lived in Mackay – 2,500 kilometres away. Lasting only two months in the new job, I used the excuse of moving to Mackay to be closer to Julie to save face when resigning. Luckily, accounting skills are portable and I had no trouble finding yet another position as an audit manager, with yet another firm of chartered accountants.

By this point in my life I was certain that I'd shaken off the shackles of my high school limitations. I'd gone to Weight Watchers and lost 16 kilos, I'd worked hard and achieved membership to what many regard as the peak accounting body in Australia, and I'd found a woman whom I loved. Yet this new-found self-confidence was to come crumbling down when I was sacked after nine months, and told I was someone who overpromises and underdelivers. This left my confidence savagely beaten and those nasty self-doubts that I thought I'd buried began to resurface again.

Luckily, Julie was a rock of stability. We became engaged and then moved back to Melbourne. Once again, I found work in a small accounting firm, again as an audit manager, and soon I was working harder than ever in an effort to resurrect my career.

I remember my office well. It was long, flat and oddly shaped. A glass partition separated me from the only other manager, Dave Bradley, with black Venetian blinds providing limited privacy. What I remember best were the thick iron bars on the windows, which I'd regularly joke were there to keep the employees in rather than the burglars out.

By late 1998 Julie and I were married and I was still working, working, working. I'd regained my confidence and was beginning to branch out into teaching too. I'd taken on a lecturing role at my old stomping ground, RMIT, and was also, ironically, mentoring other aspiring chartered accountants to manage the art of studying effectively.

I wouldn't say that I ever felt truly settled though. I'd dread Sunday nights and the thought of having to iron five work shirts for the week ahead. I was certainly someone working five days to fund two days off. I was a rat taking my place in the race.

## My Wake Up Call

You might be able to ignore the warning signs, but when you're not happy, your body will eventually give you a wake up call you can't ignore. Some people are unlucky and suffer crippling or fatal injuries, like heart attacks or strokes. For me it was ulcers on... well, 'unusual' body parts.

I raced off to see the doctor, who happened to have a surgery next door, and I was lucky to get an immediate appointment. The doctor was perplexed at my condition and suggested I needed some time off work. Later that afternoon after returning from a walk, I found a piece of paper in the letterbox. It was a photocopy from a medical journal explaining my condition. The doctor had written in large print "Take a holiday!" and also highlighted some text outlining that the ulcers were caused by stress. It was my wake up call telling me to change my lifestyle or suffer the consequences. The lack of career planning and job satisfaction had chipped away over the course of several years and had finally caused my health to suffer.

I talked my situation over with friends and was surprised to learn that other people felt the same way. The obvious common theme was that while we all wanted to be wealthy, what we wanted more was to be free from the obligation to have to work – a concept that someone called 'Financial Independence'.

I spent some quiet time reflecting and decided one thing was for certain... when I looked up the corporate ladder all I could see was the backside of the guy in front of me and I didn't like the view. So, when I received a flyer in the letterbox outlining how I could discover the secrets to retiring a multi-millionaire in five years, you could say that it looked like the opportunity I'd been searching for – the chance to exit the rat race forever. The flyer was an A4 photocopy on white paper and it promised (in large print) to show me the way to a lifetime of riches through the power of the tenant and the taxman. It concluded with a 1800 number for me to call and book my strictly limited seat at an upcoming no-cost, no-obligation 'wealth creation extravaganza'. Since the event was free, and since I might have actually discovered some amazing secret that only the rich knew, I booked two tickets – one for me and the other for Julie.

## The 'All-Hype, No-Substance' Seminar

The seminar was held the following week at a local motel conference centre. The room was quite professionally arranged with 100 seats neatly set out in rows of ten by ten. There was a data projector and a large screen to cater for a computer slide-show presentation. We arrived early and were amongst the first in the room. By the time the presenter – a 40-something balding executive wearing a power suit and matching tie – was ready to begin, the room was three-quarters full with a good cross-section of the community. Most were young or middle-aged workers, tired after a long day at the office. Others were tradespeople – as evident from their overalls. The remainder appeared to be retirees, or soon-to-be retirees. These seemed the best prepared as they brought pads and paper to write down ideas.

A hush came over the audience as the presenter indicated he was ready to begin. "Raise your right hand if you think you pay too much tax", he said. There was a shuffle as the entire room raised their right hands.

"Good. Later I'll show you how you can eliminate your tax bill. Now raise your left hand if you want to be rich." There was more noise as pads and pens were placed on the floor, followed by more hand raising.

"Excellent", the presenter said with a beaming smile. "You folks are in the right place at the right time because I'm going to reveal how the tenant will make you rich, and the taxman will fund your financial independence."

Over the next hour or so we were shown slides of graphs and tables outlining how property only increases in value, and why now was an excellent time to buy. The presentation was a carefully scripted and much practised sales pitch leading to a critical question.

"Now, who'd like to discover where the great growth properties are located and how to purchase them at a bargain price?" A large number of hands went into the air.

"Wonderful!" the presenter exclaimed. "In that case, let's take a short break, and when we come back I'll outline an exciting opportunity to buy property below cost."

My wife and I, sensing that this was a sham marketing scheme selling overpriced out-of-town property to unwitting investors, decided to leave, and I couldn't help but wonder whose best interests the presenter had in mind. Being an auditor, I was highly suspicious of the presenter's lack of independence as it turned out he was being paid a commission for each property sold to a person attending the seminar.

**Steve's Investing Tip**

A good rule of thumb is to always be on guard when your adviser – whether a sales agent, a financial planner or otherwise – is paid a commission for his or her recommendation.

I only lasted a few more months in my job before failing health and continuing frustration forced yet another career move. This time I thought I'd try a different take on the old accounting theme. Instead of being an employee for someone else, I joined forces with the other manager in my office – tax expert Dave Bradley. We were both disillusioned with our managerial roles and decided that we could work less and earn the same amount of money by going into business for ourselves.

Dave was someone who I thought I could trust, but more importantly, he had different skills that would broaden the expertise of our business. Even more critical though was that we shared a common goal – to work hard now and then spend more time with our families later.

In January 1999, the chartered accounting firm of Bradley McKnight opened its doors for business. In an attempt to keep overheads as low as possible, Dave worked from his home and I worked from mine. We'd meet a couple of times a week to talk through issues and to ensure we remained focused. Dave did the lion's share of the work as he already had a number of clients which followed him from our previous employer. My role was to source new business and to handle the administration.

Still not settled, by April I'd finally decided a more substantial change was needed. While I enjoyed the flexibility of working from home, I just hated working in accounting. With some reflection I realised that all I'd managed to do was to trade-in those bars on the windows of my old office for invisible handcuffs to my new clients.

## A NEW DIRECTION

At our next meeting I dropped a bombshell by telling Dave that I didn't want to be an accountant any more. "That's great", he said "but what do you plan to do in our accounting partnership then?"

"I don't know", I replied, "but something other than accounting... give me some time to think about it."

A week or so later I attended an introductory event that contained a good mix of information about alternative wealth creation ideas. I was impressed with the speaker (Robert Kiyosaki) and was eager to hear more about his upcoming two-day intensive training seminar. Even the price tag – $2,000 per seat – didn't seem completely unreasonable. The intro event finished at 10 pm and, as there was only a strictly limited number of seats left and the real possibility of the upcoming seminar being sold out quickly, I immediately phoned Dave to convince him that we both had to attend. I was understandably hyped-up after coming straight from the introductory seminar, while Dave was preparing for bed. After I gave him my best pitch, Dave replied with a sleepy, "Mate, that's great, but at $2,000 a pop, the presenter gets rich off people like you".

"No, no", I said. "We really have to go!"

Wanting to go to sleep, Dave said "Look, go home, cool down and we'll talk about it in the morning. Bye". As I began to frame a counter argument, I heard the phone hang up. Not to be put off, I called him straight back.

"Look," I said, "we don't want to miss out on this opportunity."

"Steve. We've only been in business three months", Dave said. "We can't afford to go. First you say you don't want to be an accountant and now you want to spend money we don't have going to a seminar in Sydney. Mate, get a grip and we'll talk tomorrow. Good night." Click – down went the phone again.

Still undaunted, I rang back only to find that Dave had taken his phone off the hook. Ah ha! A challenge. I called him on his mobile. Expecting him to be irritated, I tried to head him off at the pass by saying, "Do you trust me?"

"Of course I trust you", Dave replied.

"Well then, trust me on this. We won't be disappointed."

That night I booked and paid for two seats to the impending Sydney wealth creation seminar. It was a decision that Dave and I have never regretted, not so much because of the mind-blowing content of the event but because we gleaned one revelation. We found that some of the attendees were investing in property in such a way as to earn immediate passive income. This could then be used as a replacement for salary, allowing the recipient to work less without taking a lifestyle cut. This discovery was to change our lives, and our career prospects, forever.

## Chapter 1 Insights

### Insight #1:

We all have our own story of where we've come from. The truth is your history isn't as important as your future and your future is what *you* make of it.

### Insight #2:

Don't fall into the trap of thinking that because I have an accounting background I'm better qualified than you to invest. You can pay a good accountant to be on your team and access the same skill set that I take for granted.

### Insight #3:

You need to expect to pay for your education, either directly, by attending seminars, or indirectly through making mistakes and paying to fix them. I recommend attending seminars provided you're committed to implementing what you discover – otherwise they're a waste of valuable time and money.

### Insight #4:

Financial independence is not just a dream that only a select few can achieve. It's a matter of making a series of choices that are consistent with moving you closer to your goal.

# The Money Mindset Needed for Success

While the majority of this book is focused on how to use real estate to make money, the journey you must travel, in order to achieve financial independence, begins well before you will inspect your first property.

**Steve's Investing Tip**

It requires less effort to *save* a dollar than it does to *earn* a dollar.

Surprisingly simple, the secret to creating a lifetime of unending wealth is to spend less than you earn and invest the difference.

Lots of books have been written on how to get rich by earning more money, but the truth is your capacity to attract and keep wealth has little to do with how much money you earn, and a lot to do with how much you spend.

## BEING A GOOD NEIGHBOUR

One day, early in the life of our business, Bradley McKnight – Chartered Accountants, I was working from home when there was a loud knock at the back door. Putting down my trusty green audit pen for a few moments, I went to see who was there, only to hear the muffled sounds of sobbing. Opening the door I found my neighbour in tears. Putting my arm around her and trying to comfort her, I said "Jackie, what's wrong?"

"Steve, I can't do it any more – it's just too hard."

"What?" I replied in a confused tone.

"My financial situation is crippling me."

A short time later I was over at Jackie's house sorting through a great wad of pay slips, bills and letters demanding payment. Trying to make sense of the chaos, it was quickly evident that I was working with a financial time-bomb of unpaid bills and mounting debts – and the bomb was about to explode.

Now, you or someone you know might be in some financial trouble, but Jackie was the closest I've ever seen to someone on the brink of financial collapse. It wasn't that she didn't earn enough money; she was a well-paid sales executive on a salary package of $60,000 per annum. What was crippling her was her lavish lifestyle, which was funded by debt. She had a mortgage, a car loan for her BMW, a maxed out Amex, a Visa card which she used to pay her monthly Amex bill, a personal loan, and a few store-issued credit cards with nasty interest rates in excess of 24% per annum. The interest and loan repayments on this debt meant that my unfortunate neighbour had many more expenses in the month than her money could ever cover. How could this have occurred?

Managing your money effectively is simple enough – the secret is to only spend what you earn. But there are two tricks that catch many people out. You must:

1.  Remember that you earn less than you think you earn, because what you receive is eroded by tax and superannuation; and

2.  Learn to equate the joy of spending with the effort of earning.

Let's expand on these two points.

## 1: The Erosion of Your Pay Packet

If you don't know how much money you have available to spend then it's easy to live beyond your means. Working out how much you have to spend is not necessarily easy because you'll need to deduct tax and superannuation (which can be complicated) to accurately quantify. Let's use my neighbour as an example.

Jackie made the fundamental error of believing that a salary package of $60,000 per annum meant that she had $60,000 (or thereabouts) to spend. Sure, she may have been a little financially naive, but she would certainly not be alone. From her salary I deducted her superannuation ($3,925), her PAYG income tax instalments ($16,957) and the Medicare levy ($841). The result was that all Jackie actually had available to spend was $38,277. The breakdown of her salary is illustrated in Figure 2.1 below.

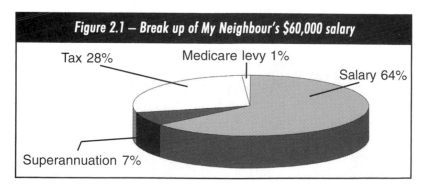

Figure 2.1 – Break up of My Neighbour's $60,000 salary

Where my neighbour really came unstuck was that she enjoyed a $60,000 plus lifestyle, but only had $38,277 available to pay for it. Can you imagine how the shortfall between what she earned and what she spent was funded? Yes, by debt – principally personal loans and credit cards.

As I explained to Jackie exactly how and why she didn't actually have $60,000 to spend, I saw the flicker of understanding in her eyes as she remarked "Why doesn't anyone tell you this?"

"Well", I replied, "usually it's just assumed that you know these things but, in reality, it's a poorly disclosed phenomenon that's keeping many people poor."

My neighbour's recipe for financial disaster (i.e. spending more than she earned) is becoming an everyday occurrence. For the first time since figures were recorded, in March 2003 the Australian Bureau of Statistics reported that household spending had outstripped household incomes[1].

### Keeping Control Over What You Spend

I couldn't find a quick fix for my neighbour. I tried to roll all of her credit card and personal loan debt into her home mortgage to reduce the interest bill, but the bank refused, as it considered her a poor credit risk. The only answer I could come up with was to lock away her credit cards and provide a cash budget to spend each week that would leave extra to begin repaying her debts, starting with the debts that attracted the highest interest rates.

My efforts to turn my neighbour's finances around also hinged on getting her to face up to her obligations.

# The W.E.A.L.T.H. Approach to Controlling Spending

In order for Jackie's financial situation to improve it was critical that she become a much better custodian of her money and the

---

1 – Horan, Matthew, 'Nation Spends Beyond Means', *Sunday Telegraph*, 9 March 2003.

credit cards in her purse. What had happened was that my neighbour had gradually developed enough poor financial habits to make her totally **money repellent**.

### Steve's Money Tip

If you're having trouble making debt repayments then don't be an ostrich and stick your head in the sand. Pick up the phone and ask for a repayment plan. Control your money or it will control you!

Instead of building wealth, money repellent people act as clearing houses where 100%, and more, of the dollars they earn at work are exchanged for lifestyle related goods and services. The source of the problem is inevitably not earning too little – it's spending too much. Trying to put the clamps on a financial haemorrhage is next to impossible for people who are addicted to spending. So instead of lecturing my neighbour about the evils of unnecessary shopping, I went for the reverse psychology approach and encouraged her to buy whatever she liked, *provided* she could satisfy six criteria that I turned into the acronym W.E.A.L.T.H.

### Steve's W.E.A.L.T.H Acronym

| | |
|---|---|
| W: | Wise |
| E: | Economical |
| A: | Accountable |
| L: | Liable |
| T: | Thorough |
| H: | Honest |

See Appendix A (page 339) for more information on my W.E.A.L.T.H. acronym and each of these criteria.

### The Road to Recovery

While it was difficult, we were able to rein in my neighbour's poor spending habits and gradually turned her finances around. Before long we'd managed to wipe out most of those nasty store credit cards, which charged massive rates of interest. Next on the hit list was her Visa card, which had a balance that had steadily risen over three years. Ultimately Jackie and I achieved success at which point she turned to me, smiled and said, "Right, now I'm back in control, tell me what I can do to start investing".

### Are You in Control?

Do you know the difference between your gross salary and what you receive as cash in your pocket? A simple test to determine whether or not you're on the right side of the lifestyle line is to calculate how much money you're saving (or using to repay old debts) and then dividing it by your base salary. A great rule of thumb is to put away 10% of your pre-tax pay to draw upon when you're ready to begin investing.

Are you in control, or are you sitting on a money-trouble time-bomb that is about to explode?

## 2: Equating the Joy of Spending with the Effort of Earning

The first component of effective money management is to take control over your spending. The second component is translating the cost of something you buy back into the hours of work it took to earn the money in the first place.

People underestimate the true cost of an item because they have to pay for it in after-tax dollars. For example, $100 worth of groceries to someone earning over $62,500 per annum is closer to $200 in pre-tax terms, which might then equate to a day's work.

Translating money into equivalent days or hours at work is often an excellent way to see the financial impact of your spending. For example, $70 per month for a gym membership is $840 per annum, which in pre-tax terms for someone paid $45,000 per annum is a little over $1,226. This equates to ten working days, so you'd work two weeks each year just to pay for your gym membership alone, which is another week spent working for someone else and less time and money available to start investing.

### Steve's Money Tip

It takes less effort to *spend* than it does to *earn*.

If you had $100 and you spent $10 then you'd have $90 left, which would equate to a 10% fall. Yet to turn $90 into $100 requires an 11.11% gain. Similarly, if you have a $100 and spend $50 then you'd lose 50% of your savings. Yet to turn $50 into $100 requires a 100% return[2]. This is why it's easier to spend but so much more difficult to earn money to replenish your savings.

### Self-Inflicted Investment Paralysis

I certainly learned this concept the hard way when buying my third car. My first car was, frankly speaking, a total embarrassment. It was a 1964 Ford Cortina that my dad bought for me for the grand sum of $1,000. While it was certainly no Mercedes, it was a perfect 'scratch and dent' car, except that every time I tried to start the engine, it gave out the most terrible, gut-wrenching noise as the starter motor turned over – it sounded like something akin to a drunk seal. Restarting the car after filling it with petrol at the service station was never a fun experience; I'd turn heads for all the wrong reasons and occasionally people would actually point

2 – Thanks to Paul Nojin (www.MarketMad.com) for this example.

and laugh! Worse still, sometimes it wouldn't start at all, in which case I had to crawl under the car and whack the starter motor with a wrench to free up an internal mechanism – not a fun thing to do in the wet!

Suffice to say that I was happy to trade it in, except that my second car was a poo-brown 1980 Holden Commodore that my friends affectionately called "Poob". I think you can now appreciate that by the time I scored my first decent paying job, fresh out of university, I was keen to buy a new car and escape the social embarrassment of 'Sporty-Corty' and 'Poob'. I didn't have the necessary cash so I entered into a hire-purchase agreement of 60 easy monthly repayments of $388. I thought I could comfortably make the payments as I was still living at home while earning an impressive graduate salary package of $35,000 per annum, or a little over $2,900 per month. But I underestimated the impact of having to make my repayments in after-tax dollars. After tax and superannuation were deducted my $35,000 shrank to $27,000, or around $2,250 per month. Now all of a sudden over 17% of my purchasing power went to the leasing company. Put another way, I would have to work the equivalent of two months a year just to pay off my car loan!

Then I had to pay board, petrol and a whole plethora of other expenses which meant that I was just managing to break even and I certainly had no money to start saving or investing. It made no difference whether or not I *wanted* to invest – I didn't have the money, or the time, which meant that I was stuck in a state of paralysis.

A great friend of mine is an internet guru. He's an awesome guy and his work is first class. Unfortunately though, ever since the internet industry took a tumble, he's found it difficult to gain enough work to make ends meet. His situation is not helped by the fact that he has a mortgage, multiple credit cards with balances outstanding, a large loan to his father and a significant debt to the tax department too.

Things started to go wrong when he had more business expenses than business income, and paid the shortfall with personal debt – first by redrawing his mortgage and later with credit cards. This story is not uncommon amongst struggling business owners. On top of this my friend also has to support his wife – who is a full-time mum – and their three young children. It was one of his wife's constant fears that she'd be paying at the supermarket checkout or service station counter, only to have her credit card rejected for lack of funds. You can put the groceries back on the shelf, but it's difficult to get petrol back out of a tank!

Just the other day his washing machine stopped functioning properly and now the clothes are coming out covered in fluff. His wife cut out an advertisement from a large retail outlet offering new washing machines for $600 on two years interest-free terms.

"How about it?" she asked. "We can pay it back before the interest kicks in."

Once upon a time my friend would have taken up the offer without thinking, but after spending time with me he's come to appreciate the importance of avoiding commitments today which will later need to be repaid from future earnings. Speaking to him on the phone, he was adamant that there was little that was free about the washing machine – $600 after-tax equated to about a week's work. Over a family meeting it was agreed that until the old debts were repaid, non-critical spending would have to be eliminated, and this meant that they had to make do with the washing machine they had for the time being.

## SUMMARY OF EFFECTIVE MONEY HABITS

The rat race is a trap for people who spend first and then have to work to pay for yesterday's extravagances with tomorrow's earnings. A car payment here, a gym membership there and the occasional emergency washing machine on interest-free terms will keep you needing to work. If you want freedom, then you must become a good steward of your money. It's not easy, but effective money habits demand that you master your finances by allocating a portion of your pre-tax earnings to investing, and then only spending what's left in your pocket.

## The Cost of Investing

If your money goal is financial independence then a key skill you'll need to acquire is the ability to delay gratification – the ability to forego today to set up a better opportunity tomorrow. If you don't want to delay gratification then you'll be left in the land of the get-rich-quick schemes that promise maximum return for minimum effort and we all know, in our heart of hearts, that sustainable wealth creation doesn't happen that way.

For me, the sacrifice needed to become financially free has been significant. In 1999 I made two deals. First, I promised my wife Julie that she could retire from the workforce forever in May 2004 provided:

➪ She continued to work until then to pay for our living expenses since every dollar Dave and I made in our business was allocated to investing; and

➪ We had to continue renting rather than owning our home because we needed to lend our investing company all our private savings to buy more real estate. However, when we could afford to buy a home from the positive cashflow profits then we'd get the home of her dreams.

Secondly, my business partner, Dave, and I agreed that he would need to continue working full-time as an accountant to earn the money to invest while I'd source investments that made a dollar from day one.

These were the first, and perhaps most important, win-win deals I ever negotiated. There were no losers in these negotiations since Julie and Dave both received immediate light at the end of the work tunnel, and I was finally able to sever the invisible handcuffs and move beyond working as an accountant.

### Steve's Investing Tip

For more discussion on renting vs owning, visit: www.PropertyInvesting.com/RentOrOwn.

## Solving Your Money Problem

If you have a money problem then there are three strategies you can implement to beat it:

*Option 1:* Rein in your lifestyle expenses to match your take-home income. This can be difficult, since no-one likes to take a cut in his or her standard of living.

*Option 2:* Work harder, earn more money and don't increase your lifestyle expenses. This is a challenge because the more you earn, the more you pay in tax and superannuation.

*Option 3:* Invest in something that makes money to fund the shortfall between your income and lifestyle expenses.

Of these choices, only Option 1 provides a solution to the core of the problem. Options 2 and 3 are band-aid solutions that will not work to permanently stop a severe financial haemorrhage.

### Steve's Investing Tip

In every case of financial hardship that I've ever seen, the problem has not been earning too little, but spending too much.

Earning more might provide temporary relief, but pain will persist and it's just a matter of time before you will find yourself short of money again. A favourite saying of mine is "For things to change, first things must change". You must be willing to give something up to create room for a new opportunity. I'm not suggesting that you need to give up work entirely, but if you think you can create a personal fortune doing what you're doing now, then you're probably kidding yourself.

One of the most amazing ironies I discovered was that to earn more later, I had to earn less now. Sure, less hours behind the calculator meant a significant drop in money coming through the door, both at home and at work, but such was the sacrifice I had to make to free up the time needed to begin looking for investment deals.

### Steve's Money Tip

You will always be a slave to money until you discover how to become its master.

## I've Never Been More Adamant!

It's no accident that this chapter appears at the start of the book! Adopting the information in the remaining chapters of this book will ensure you have excellent success in your property investing activities. However, whether or not you achieve financial independence depends on your ability to master money, delay self-gratification (by reinvesting rather than spending your profits) and by having faith that you're on the right road, albeit the road less travelled, during the many inevitable setbacks. The biggest contributor to my success in property investing has been developing effective money habits that have provided the mindset needed for success.

## Chapter 2 Insights

### Insight #1:

Abundant wealth comes from using money effectively.

### Insight #2:

People with money problems don't earn too little, they spend too much.

### Insight #3:

The rat race is a trap for people who spend first and then worry about paying later. When you get into debt you start to need your job more and it can become very difficult to ever leave.

### Insight #4:

I can show you how to use real estate to make a lot of money, but how much of it you will keep depends on how effective your money habits are before you begin.

### Insight #5:

The more you need money, the harder it will be for you to attract wealth. I don't know why, that's just the way things are!

# Finding Deals

On returning from the Sydney wealth creation seminar, Dave and I were pumped to immediately take action and begin looking for properties that delivered passive income returns. It seemed to us that the logical place to start looking for these properties was in the suburbs in and around where we lived. My wife and I leased a two-bedroom unit and paid $200 per week in rent. The property was worth about $200,000. On the back of an envelope I worked out that the annual rent ($10,400) would be less than the interest on the loan (assuming a loan of 80% of the purchase price at an interest rate of 8% per annum). It was a similar story where Dave lived too. If passive income properties did exist, then it wasn't anywhere close to where I lived!

A little less enthusiastic but still determined to keep looking, I started searching amongst houses that were for sale on the internet using a simple formula that took the likely weekly rent and worked backwards to calculate a maximum purchase price. Provided the property was within these price guidelines I could reasonably expect the target property to produce passive income.

## 'THE 11 SECOND SOLUTION'

A short time later Dave and I gave this formula a name – 'The 11 Second Solution'. It's very easy to calculate – just follow the four steps outlined in Figure 3.1 below.

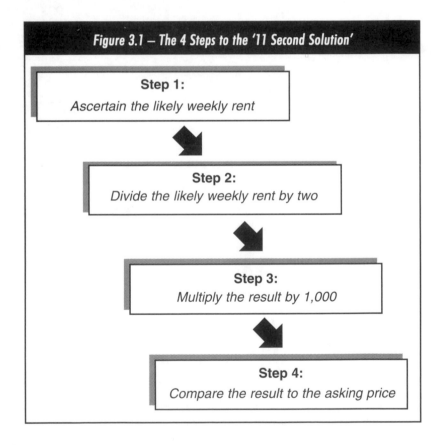

**Figure 3.1 – The 4 Steps to the '11 Second Solution'**

**Step 1:**
Ascertain the likely weekly rent

**Step 2:**
Divide the likely weekly rent by two

**Step 3:**
Multiply the result by 1,000

**Step 4:**
Compare the result to the asking price

Table 3.1, opposite, shows what 'The 11 Second Solution' would have told us about the unit where my wife and I lived.

| Table 3.1 – 'The 11 Second Solution' on the Unit Where We Lived | |
|---|---|
| **Step 1:**<br>What is the weekly rent? | $200 |
| **Step 2:**<br>Divide the weekly rent by 2 | *($200 ÷ 2)*<br>= $100 |
| **Step 3:**<br>Multiply Step 2 by 1,000 | *($100 x 1,000)*<br>= $100,000 |
| **Step 4:**<br>Is the property priced at<br>or below this figure? | No<br>*(The property was<br>worth $200,000)* |

Have a go at working out 'The 11 Second Solution' on the property where you're currently living in Table 3.2 below.

| Table 3.2 – 'The 11 Second Solution'<br>on the Property Where You Live | |
|---|---|
| **Step 1:**<br>What is the weekly rent? | $ |
| **Step 2:**<br>Divide the weekly rent by 2 | *(Step 1 ÷ 2)*<br>= $ |
| **Step 3:**<br>Multiply Step 2 by 1,000 | *(Step 2 x 1,000)*<br>= $ |
| **Step 4:**<br>Is the property priced at<br>or below this figure? | Yes / No |

If you answered 'Yes' at Step 4 then there's a good chance that the property where you are living would deliver a positive cashflow return to its owner if rented. If not, then it falls into the same category as over 90% of Australian residential properties, as it provides a negative cashflow outcome.

## How to Use 'The 11 Second Solution'

'The 11 Second Solution' will *always* provide a *gross* return on investment (ROI) of 10.4% per annum. Whether or not the *net* cashflow is positive depends on interest payments, management expenses and other relevant costs from owning a property. It's very important that you don't perceive 'The 11 Second Solution' as the be-all-and-end-all of property investing. Its *only* application is as a management tool that allows you to filter a whole range of potential deals into just a handful of opportunities that warrant further investigation.

Time is an investor's most important resource, so to have a tool that allows you to quickly test whether or not a property is likely to provide a positive cashflow result is a tremendous advantage. For example, say you want to quickly scan a list of 200 potential properties on a real estate agent's listing sheet. You can quickly do this using 'The 11 Second Solution' if all you know is the likely weekly rent. I don't know of any other tool that will allow you to leverage your time so effectively.

While a property might pass the '11 Second Solution' test, this does not mean that it will automatically provide a positive cashflow result. What it means is that you should allocate the time to further analyse and evaluate both the risk and return of the deal. It's also necessary to understand that the areas where you invest might have special conditions and associated costs that require you to earn more than a 10.4% return to expect a positive cashflow outcome. For example, in Tasmania the higher land tax and rental management charges mean that a property which just scrapes through the '11 Second Solution' test will, nevertheless, probably generate a negative cashflow return.

By the same token, if a property fails 'The 11 Second Solution' test, this shouldn't rule it out of consideration entirely. For example, most commercial properties require the tenant to pay for some or all of the outgoings, so a commercial property that marginally fails to meet 'The 11 Second Solution' criteria may still provide a positive cashflow outcome after all.

One final time – the best use for 'The 11 Second Solution' is as a filtering tool. If there are 100 properties that you want to scan, then you might use this resource to eliminate 80% of them immediately and then split the remainder into the 10% that meet 'The 11 Second Solution' requirements and the 10% that fall on the borderline. Then you'd allocate time to analysing the deals, from the highest yields down and, if time allowed, you could also include a few deals that were marginally outside the return requirement.

To this day, Dave and I continue to use and greatly value 'The 11 Second Solution' test.

## AN AUDITOR'S INSIGHT

While working as an auditor for a large international firm of accountants, I was very fortunate to gain access to confidential information about the inner workings of a wide range of businesses. One week I'd be watching cars whiz around an assembly line, the next week I'd be counting bottles of liquor at duty-free stores around Melbourne, and the week after I'd be working for gold mining clients with billion-dollar turnovers.

My job also required that I network with the movers and shakers at the top of global corporations – company directors and other successful people from around the world. All in all I've been very fortunate to be able to model my own approach to business and investing on the successful qualities that I've seen in others.

For example, I observed that a key difference between part-time and serious investors was the existence of predetermined rules. That's why in May 1999, as Dave and I were gearing up to buy our first property, we thought it important to create two fundamental rules about the properties we wanted to buy:

**Fundamental Rule #1:**

All our properties must pass 'The 11 Second Solution' test (that is, provide a minimum gross return of at least 10.4% per annum); and

**Fundamental Rule #2:**

The areas where we invested must have good potential for expansion.

## YOU'D BE CRAZY TO INVEST IN COUNTRY AREAS!

Ideally Dave and I planned to invest in the expanding metropolitan area where we could earn cashflow and capital gains returns. However, we found this was next to impossible for two significant reasons:

1.  We couldn't actually find any properties that would provide anything close to a gross 10.4% return in the greater Melbourne metropolitan area; and

2.  As our accounting practice had only been operating for a few months, Dave and I only had about $10,000 saved up in our business bank account that we could use as investment capital. With such a paltry sum we would have had trouble putting down a deposit on a single city car park space, let alone a house in Melbourne's metropolitan suburbs.

This left us with no choice but to look elsewhere, so we turned our attention to regional areas. Luckily, Australia is a country with large regional centres located within a few hours of all the major capital cities. In the case of Victoria, there are the smaller satellite or regional areas of Geelong, Ballarat and Bendigo that are all within easy travelling distance of Melbourne.

## A Lesson in Ignorance

One day in 1997, while I was working as an audit manager, one of my audit team members, Alina, approached me to ask my thoughts about investing in Ballarat. She had family members who lived in the area and knew that you could buy a good quality house for $60,000.

"Ballarat?" I inquired incredulously. "Why would you want to invest there? You'll never get capital growth in the country. Forget it."

A few years have now passed and, with the benefit of experience and hindsight, I can see that my comments came not from wisdom, but from ignorance. Having no knowledge about either investing in property or investing in Ballarat, all I could offer was a convincing yet ill informed opinion.

Today, having substantial regional investing experience, I'll tell just about anybody who'll listen that some of the best deals around are found in regional and country areas. Yes, it's true that regional and country properties may not appreciate in value as fast as city real estate, but I wasn't looking for capital growth... I was looking for passive income to fund my financial independence. My investing mantra was "cashflow, cashflow, cashflow", not "growth, growth, growth".

### Steve's Investing Tip

Invest in property to earn cashflow returns *first* and capital gains *second*.

I encounter a lot of people who say they have serious reservations about investing in rural areas. However, when pressed on the issue, these same people generally own no property and work very hard in a job that's making someone else rich. Their ignorance about the opportunities on offer is literally keeping them poor. Consider this – what difference does it make if your property achieves little or no capital growth if it, nevertheless, delivers enough reliable cashflow for you to never have to work again?

## Selecting the Right Area

Ballarat, the place where Alina had mentioned that cheap real estate existed a few years earlier, seemed as good a place as any to start looking for properties that met 'The 11 Second Solution'.

Located approximately one hour's drive from Melbourne, Ballarat became famous after gold was discovered there in the early 1850s. In fact there was no shortage of places rich in historical significance, but all I wanted to know was whether or not it was the sort of place where I could earn passive income.

Seated in the comfort of my home-office, I began to search the internet to see what sort of free economic data I could hunt down on the Ballarat region. Opening up my browser, I went to a search engine and typed in: "Ballarat" along with "economic profile". To my surprise, I hit a home run straight off the bat when the top search engine result was a report prepared by the Ballarat city council titled 'Ballarat Economic Profile'. I could hardly believe my eyes when the preface to the report noted it had been written for "…the potential investor who wants information about the existing economic structure." Things were looking especially promising when the report mentioned that "…housing is very affordable…"

OK, house prices seemed affordable in Ballarat, but could it also be seen as an area with good growth prospects? After a few more hours of researching various other websites, I selected five key factors that would determine whether Ballarat (or any other city for that matter) was likely to expand or contract in the near future. Those five critical factors were:

### Factor #1 – Population

More people moving into an area will create a demand for housing, both as rental properties and as homes. Similarly, an area with a diminishing population increases the risk of properties falling in value, together with the possibility of long-term rental vacancies, as the supply of properties will exceed demand. Ballarat's population in 1998–99 was 81,065. It was forecast to increase marginally at a steady rate.

### Factor #2 – Transport Infrastructure

Ballarat is situated on the Western Highway – the major road that runs between Melbourne and Adelaide. As the speed limit is mostly 110 kilometres per hour, it is easy travelling distance from Melbourne. In fact, some people commute daily to work from Ballarat to Melbourne, either by car or by train. Ballarat is also a major transport hub, with roads linking it to Adelaide, Geelong, Portland, Bendigo and Mildura. It certainly seemed like a good link between the country and the city.

### Factor #3 – Unemployment Levels

Perhaps one of Ballarat's biggest downfalls was its unemployment which was symptomatic of most regional areas that were recovering from the recession and drought. In June 1998 I discovered that Ballarat's unemployment rate was 13.8%, compared to 8.1% in Victoria generally. Despite this, I had a feeling that the bush had been ignored for too long. The state government was starting to allocate funds to building new infrastructure and creating local jobs, so I sensed this was an area on the improve. Some astute companies were also setting up business in the area, such as establishing call centres, as labour was cheaper than in Melbourne.

### *Factor # 4 – Average Household Incomes*

Household incomes are important because they reveal how much the average person can afford to pay in rent or house repayments. The 1996 census figure for the average Ballarat household was just $27,530, well short of the $33,580 for the average Victorian household. This could be attributed to the large body of transient students who reside in Ballarat, as well as the region's substantial unemployment problem. However, low household incomes presented a two-fold opportunity:

1.  The low pay had placed a ceiling on how high property prices could rise given that the average worker earned relatively poor wages compared to his or her city counterpart; and

2.  After living expenses were deducted, a large percentage of workers could only afford to rent since saving the money for a deposit was difficult for those on low wages.

### *Factor #5 – Nature of Housing Occupancy*

One of the most encouraging statistics I discovered was that a large percentage of the Ballarat population rented – 25% in fact. Another important lesson I'd learned from my auditing days was that it's much easier finding a market than trying to create one. If 81,065 people live in Ballarat, then 20,266 of them rented. This was a huge potential supply of tenant clients that were already accustomed to renting.

If you're thinking about investing in property and have found an area but are unsure whether or not it's a good place to invest, start by asking:

▷ *How far away is it from where I live?*

Ideally you'd find a property to invest in that was within a few hours drive from where you live so that if anything went majorly wrong then you could personally arrange to have it fixed. However, finding a great area that's a long way from home is *not* necessarily a valid reason to avoid investing.

The way to jump over that hurdle is to build a team of reliable advisers in their relevant area of expertise and pay them out of your profits.

▷ *Is there an established transport hub with rail and road access?*

Good tenants exist everywhere, but investing in a town that's on the way back from economic decline will maximise the potential of your investment. Towns that stand to recover the quickest are those that sit on major road or rail hubs.

You can determine where the government plans to complete major infrastructure projects (roads, hospitals, etc.) by looking at budget papers and reading the local news.

▷ *Do people want to live there?*

If you're investing in an area that has contracting housing demand then you may be at risk of having a property lie vacant for long periods of time.

Your vacancy risk can often be mitigated, so I'd still invest in a town with, say, 10,000 people provided I could somehow reduce my risk using landlord's insurance or, where suitable, by investing under a wrap strategy (see Chapter 13).

Ideally the areas where you invest would be forecast to have gradual increases in population, and a market where a substantial percentage of households rent.

## A TIME TO ACT

After completing hours and hours of research on the internet, Ballarat seemed more and more like a suitable place to start hunting for investment properties. But enough of the research and theories! I wanted to buy a bargain – it was time to get busy and physically start the ball rolling.

I approached Dave and suggested that we take a day out of our busy accounting schedules and drive to Ballarat to have a look around. Dave was enthusiastic, although he freely admits he was also a little hesitant because a day out of the office meant no accounting income would be coming through the door.

Early one morning a few days later, he picked me up and we headed off to Ballarat. Little did we know that a special welcome awaits people from out of town, especially the much-prized, but somewhat illusive, investor from Melbourne.

## Chapter 3 Insights

### Insight #1:

Just because you can't find positive cashflow properties in the area where you live doesn't meant they don't exist.

### Insight #2:

Time is your most valuable asset, so look for ways to leverage it wherever possible. There are just so many properties for sale that you need to establish ground rules to enable you to distinguish a good deal from a bad deal.

### Insight #3:

'The 11 Second Solution' is a useful filtering tool, rather than the answer to all your property investing prayers.

### Insight #4:

Find an area where you'd like to invest and then take the time to visit. There is no substitute for getting to know an area personally.

### Insight #5:

A great place to start investing is in an area that's on the way back from economic decline. Don't be afraid of regional areas – good tenants live everywhere.

### Insight #6:

You can research as much as you like, but sooner or later you'll need to take action. Your greatest opportunity for personal development comes when you move beyond an established comfort zone.

# Professional Investors from Melbourne

The day of our great Ballarat property expedition had finally arrived. Feeling that it was important to look the part, we wore our finest business suits and packed clipboards and business cards to show the world that we were professional investors from Melbourne. The drive lasted a little over an hour and a half. I spent the travel time studying a map of the Ballarat area and discussing the results of the economic profile with Dave.

It was still early when we arrived at the city limits, so we decided to stop for a hot chocolate and to formalise our plan of attack. As we cruised up Sturt Street, Ballarat's major thoroughfare, it was still dark and quite cold outside. Not many shops were open, and few looked even close to opening, which provided a sleepy atmosphere. I had to check with Dave to make sure that it was, in fact, a weekday and not a Sunday morning.

Eventually though, we came across a cafe which seemed to be open judging by the fact the lights were on inside. Dave didn't have any trouble finding a park as there wasn't another car parked within 100 metres anywhere on the street. I held the cafe door open as we entered and escaped the biting chill of the wind. The only person in the cafe was a waiter – a young guy who was genuinely surprised to see customers so early.

"Ah... I've only just opened", he said. "The grill's not warmed up yet so all I can do is toast."

"No problem", I replied. "We'll have some toast and two hot chocolates then."

Sitting down at a table near the service counter, I unfolded the map and tried to gain a feeling for the layout of Ballarat, including the major streets and landmarks. Dave picked up the local paper and began to flick through the property section. A few minutes later the waiter brought over our hot chocolates. Offering thanks, I thought I'd try and start up a conversation to glean some local knowledge of the area.

"We're new in town", I said, at which the waiter looked us up and down and shot a glance that said "No kidding!"

"Where's a good place to live?" I inquired.

Leaning over the map the waiter said "Here" – pointing to a spot on the map we now know as Alfredton. "Oh, and anything central too", he added waving his finger in a wide circle around the Sturt Street area. "And if you're rich then you live by the lake".

Dave and I exchanged shrugs and smiles. "OK, and where wouldn't you want to live?" I asked.

The waiter considered his response and then pointed to the map and said emphatically "Here" as he pointed out the area of West Wendouree.

"Why not?" I asked.

"Oh, it's a rough area with lots of housing commission houses", the waiter replied before hurrying off to investigate a noise coming from the kitchen area. He returned a few minutes later with a plate of hot toast.

"So, who are you guys?" he asked.

Dave replied, "We're professional investors from Melbourne".

### Steve's Investing Tip

Often the best way to discover information about an area is to ask a local.

## The Agent Who Should Have Been in School

When we emerged from the cafe it was around 8:30 am. I wouldn't say that the streets were crowded, but there was certainly more activity with people going about their early morning tasks. Dave and I were keen to begin looking for houses as soon as possible. We decided that talking with several local real estate agents would be a good place to start. While this seemed like a good idea, none were open as yet, so instead we just drove around for about half an hour to see what the houses in Ballarat looked like.

I'm not sure what I expected, but I was certainly pleasantly surprised with the majority of houses – mostly old weatherboard period homes. Occasionally there would be a more modern dwelling or maybe a home made of brick but, all in all, the houses seemed pretty normal and what you would expect in some suburbs of Melbourne.

One thing we did notice though was the large number of properties that had 'For Sale' signs out the front. It seemed the property boom that had hit the Melbourne market hadn't quite made it all the way to Ballarat.

Having no idea what the houses were worth, Dave and I began to write down the addresses and pencil in what we thought their asking price might be. Later, once we had a better understanding of the market, we'd discover that we weren't too far wrong with our initial guesses. After driving around for nearly half an hour, we headed back to Sturt Street and finally found a real estate agent that was open.

As I opened the door, a bell rang announcing our arrival. The interior was modern and well kept, giving a professional ambience to the office. There was only one person on duty and he was a young guy who, by the look of him, should have been in a Year 10 science class rather than acting as the front person for a real estate agency. The name tag on his shirt read "Hi, I'm Tom".

"Can I help you?" he asked.

"Yes", I replied. "We're from Melbourne and are interested in buying some investment property."

Now, Tom's boss had promised that a day like this one might eventually occur, when a couple of chumps, as green as green could be, would walk in off the street and want to buy something without any idea of what they were really doing.

"Oh", Tom said thoughtfully. "Investors from Melbourne. Hmmm, right", he repeated with the hint of a smile. "Well then, what exactly are you looking for?"

My initial thought was "Come on! Money trees, show me the money trees! How hard can it be?" But to be honest, I hadn't thought this far ahead. I didn't think to work out a budget, or to use our available deposit to work backwards to a possible purchase price. I didn't even think to start with properties that were for sale and came with tenants (which would have allowed me to use 'The 11 Second Solution' in a practical context for the first time).

A little lost for words, but not wanting to sound cheap or look like a fool, I asked if he had any blocks of units for sale. After all, that's the sort of thing an investor from Melbourne would say, right? Tom switched the phones over to answering machine mode and ushered us into one of the several client meeting rooms, following us in and closing the door behind him. He pulled out a large, bound, blue book that contained all the properties they had listed for sale and flicked to a tab that said 'Units'. Scanning through his list he asked, "How much do you want to spend?"

Dave answered "We have an open budget, provided we like the property."

Tom scribbled down a few details on a pad, closed the book, looked up, clasped his hands and then told us that he only had one property that he thought might be suitable. It was a block of eight units in a brick complex just a few blocks from the middle of town. He invited us to immediately inspect the property, since he could show us through a few of the units that were currently vacant, as well as one that was occupied as he was on good terms with one of the tenants who was home nearly all the time.

Since we didn't know the way, Tom suggested that he drive us. Dave and I happily accepted and we headed out of the office backdoor to a carpark. The only car in the lot was Tom's – an early model Ford Falcon that had quite a few dents and scratches.

Accepting a ride from Tom was one of the bigger mistakes I've made in my investing career. He drove fast – 90 kilometres per hour through the back streets. He overtook a truck turning right on the inside lane of a roundabout, and all the while loud thump-thump music belted out from two huge rear sub-woofer speakers.

## OUR FIRST PROPERTY INSPECTION

The only saving grace of the car ride was that it lasted just five minutes. We parked out the front of the property and walked down the side driveway. The complex was built with four units on the ground level and four units on the first level. It was a brick structure and you didn't have to be a builder to see that the exterior needed some urgent cosmetic repair. Tom warned us that the interior wasn't exactly Buckingham Palace either. But no amount of preparation could have helped me to mentally prepare for what was about to happen.

The first unit Tom showed us through was the one rented to his friendly tenant who didn't mind showing us through at a moment's notice. It was still quite early, about 9:30 am, so when

Tom knocked on the door it took a few minutes before it was opened by a sleepy looking middle-aged woman. Tom inquired as to whether it was OK to come through. The tenant agreed and opened the door allowing us to walk inside. Well, I was totally speechless.

The entire unit was covered in wall-to-wall crochet. Truly, it was like someone had placed a thick rug, like the one your grandma might have knitted, on just about everything – the walls, ceiling, floor, over the furniture, over the light stand, over the toilet seat... everywhere. The only other object of any note was a suspicious looking incense burner on the coffee table with two strange cylindrical openings... but that's another story.

Apart from inspecting a few properties as a tenant when Julie and I were looking for a place to live, I'd had precious little education about what to look for when walking through a potential investment. Undaunted by my lack of experience, I left the crocheted lounge-room, stepping over the crocheted rug and ventured into the hallway to inspect the remainder of the apartment. The few visible fixtures that weren't covered by crochet were quite basic, and the interior was of very late 1970s design – right down to the brown kitchen tiles and orange kitchen bench.

In what was about to become known as our 'good cop, bad cop routine', Dave took Tom aside to ask questions about the sale terms, while I returned to the lounge room and spoke to the tenant, Connie, who was already smoking her second 'herbal' cigarette, since we'd arrived.

"Connie", I asked "Do you like living here?"

I'll never forget her response, because it taught me a critical investing lesson. Connie was thoughtful for a few seconds and then replied "Yeah. I love being here. I love hearing the sound of the traffic all night long, it helps me to go to sleep."

Personally I doubted if Connie needed anything to help her sleep since she seemed pretty calm as it was. I don't know about you, but I've lived on a main road before and I vowed never to do it again. The sound of the cars and trucks didn't put me to sleep –

it kept me wide awake all night! Connie didn't just tolerate the noise, she enjoyed it. The lesson learned was to buy houses for *other people* – not yourself – to live in.

### Steve's Investing Tip

Remember that you buy houses for *other people* to live in.

I didn't know what else to ask Connie, partly because I was totally speechless. However after composing myself, I did manage to ascertain that she had lived in the property for a number of years, there wasn't a major problem with crime or hard drugs in the area, although a few of the tenants had been evicted recently for disruptive behaviour. When Tom and Dave reappeared, they indicated that it was time to move on to the next unit. I thanked Connie for allowing us to look through her home and bid her a good day.

The next unit we inspected was one that Tom hadn't been through before since this was the unit that the rowdy tenants had been evicted from a week or so earlier. He warned us that tenants sometimes leave surprises, but what was in store for us was something completely out of the ordinary.

Taking a key from his trouser pocket, Tom inserted it into the lock and pushed firmly on the door. With a little pressure it gave way to reveal a very sparse unit – no sign of crochet here, quite the opposite; there was no carpet, no curtains, no stove, no light globes and no smell. We walked through a small hallway into a combined lounge and kitchen area. The floorboards were bare timber, revealing that the carpet had been recently ripped up.

And there it was, in the middle of the lounge room – a homicide-style chalk outline of a life-sized body that had been spray-painted on the floor. This was the previous tenant's idea of a parting joke and, I must confess, Dave and I thought it was pretty funny. Even Tom had a chuckle.

We had a brief look through the rest of the unit and aside from the spray-painted homicide body, there wasn't much else to see or note so we moved on to inspecting the exterior of the property. The carport area where the tenants parked their cars needed repair, and the grounds were generally overgrown with long grass and weeds.

Was this a good deal? Was it a diamond in the rough that we could polish up and turn into positive cashflow? Even though Dave and I didn't have enough money to pay for a deposit, we nevertheless submitted an offer for about $100,000 less than the asking price. We justified this by saying that we'd have to spend about this amount of money bringing the property back to its former glory. This offer was submitted to the vendor but it was rejected because the seller needed full price to settle other debts.

A few weeks later we learned that the property did sell, to another investor (from Melbourne) who paid full price sight-unseen on the basis that it provided an excellent negatively geared return.

## Not Making the Same Mistake

Tom dropped us back at his office and, sensing that we were serious, (perhaps because we submitted an offer on the spot) he made a more determined effort to sell us something else. He reopened his blue book of property listings and wrote down several more addresses – this time mainly single family homes.

He explained that he could only show us through one of the properties as the others were tenanted and would require 24 hours notice to arrange inspections. Tom offered to drive us out to look at the property we could inspect, but we didn't want to risk our lives a second time, so we politely declined. I suggested that we follow him instead.

It was one of the funniest experiences of my life sitting in the passenger seat as Dave tried to follow Tom to the property. Instead of driving sedately and making it easy for us to stay on his tail, Tom seemed to go out of his way to lose us. He'd accelerate through orange lights, make hard right turns without indicating and he drove at excessive speeds. Dave did his best and tried to keep up, but to no avail. It was a good thing that I'd kept the piece of paper Tom had written down the address on, as well as my trusty map, otherwise there's no way we could have found our way. By the time we arrived at the property Tom gave the impression that he'd been waiting around for hours.

We didn't end up buying any properties through Tom. In fact, a few weeks later we called into his office only to discover that he'd moved on to another job in a different field of expertise. Perhaps it was for the best.

## THE LESSON WE LEARNED

Dave and I spent the rest of the day with various other real estate agents looking through 14 other properties located all over Ballarat. While it was time consuming and we didn't really know what we were doing, talking face to face with agents and inspecting properties pushed us well beyond our comfort zones and provided the practical context for us to learn and grow as investors. This experience was more valuable than any seminar or any book, as there's simply no substitute for taking action.

We decided to call it a day at about 4 pm and drove back to Melbourne. Although Dave and I returned from our first trip without signing any contracts, we had discovered a valuable property investing lesson; that there was one price for locals and another higher price for investors from out of town.

By dressing in suits and trying to give a professional image, we were, in fact, providing the real estate agents with a sign that said 'These guys are from out of town'. This meant that the asking price was often inflated since we seemed to have money and didn't know the market or the value of what we were buying.

**Steve's Investing Tip**

When you look like you're from out of town, then you get treated like you're from out of town too.

This point was best demonstrated a few months later when Dave and I were sitting in a real estate agent's office negotiating to buy three houses from the one vendor. The first question the seller asked the agent was "Are they wearing suits? People in suits will pay more".

Luckily we'd learned the lesson and switched our attire to mainly tracksuit pants. Occasionally, if it was going to be really cold, I'd also wear a beanie.

When buying an investment property I recommend splitting the process into three phases:

1. Researching the market;

2. Inspecting properties; and

3. Submitting offers.

Ideally you should know the area that you're investing in like a local, or else you may find your ignorance is exploited.

By the time we arrived home, Dave and I were exhausted. Yet we were also encouraged by our experience and we agreed to return to Ballarat the following week to keep looking. Just one week later, we'd find our first positive cashflow investment – a house that delivered the passive income return we so earnestly sought. But that's a story for the next chapter.

## Chapter 4 Insights

### Insight #1:

If you want to be treated like a local, look like a local.

### Insight #2:

Dave and I have successfully used the 'good cop, bad cop' routine many times. Dave takes the agent to another area while I start asking the tenant or vendor questions.

We use our routine to seek answers to the same kind of questions; "Why are you selling?", "Has there been much interest?", "How much are you after?" etc. There can sometimes be a difference in the answers that the tenant, vendor and agent provide, and one extra piece of information can allow you to create a win-win deal where otherwise your offer would be rejected.

### Insight #3:

A large part of learning the property investing ropes occurs without necessarily having to buy anything. The process of dealing with agents and looking through properties cannot be taught at seminars or learned by reading books. It requires action.

### Insight #4:

Never get into a car with someone called Tom who was working as a real estate agent in Ballarat in May 1999. There are bad drivers, really bad drivers, and then there's Tom.

# Wheelin' and Dealin'

After being mentally prepared and firmly expecting to buy our first property, returning to Melbourne empty handed was certainly a disappointment. But I'm not one to dwell on negatives – I live by the motto "Look backwards to yesterday and forwards to tomorrow."

Over the next few days I shared my Ballarat experience, including our lucky escape from Tom the real estate madman, with a few family members and friends. To my surprise, instead of being enthusiastic, the people I confided in were far more concerned about my plans for buying property in the country than they were about Tom's poor driving!

"But Steve", they'd say with concerned looks on their faces, "you'll never get capital growth investing in the sticks".

For some reason I felt that it was important to win their approval, so I tried in vain to help them understand why I was more interested in cashflow returns (since that's what is needed to become financially independent) rather than potential capital gains. Sadly, my attempts to sway the opinions of my family and friends largely failed. This certainly wasn't the positive affirmation I was expecting and I immediately began to question the wisdom of my investing strategies.

"Could they be right?" I wondered. "Perhaps I'm better off sticking with what I know best – accounting – because maybe country areas aren't good places to invest after all."

These nagging self-doubts weren't at all helpful, and I had to repeat over and over again that in order to achieve financial independence I had to do something *differently*. At the very least I owed it to myself to try, because I could always go back to working as an accountant if my property investing endeavours proved unsuccessful. You should expect negative reactions when you try to explain your investing intentions to your friends and relatives too.

### Steve's Investing Tip

Don't underestimate the detrimental impact on your confidence when the feedback you receive from the people you respect is just raised eyebrows and disapproving looks.

Today I'm in a position where I never have to work again while the same family and friends who'd initially cautioned me to avoid country properties remain bound to their jobs like 21st century slaves. Instead of seeking to replicate what I've done, they now shrug their shoulders and say things like "Steve – you were lucky you bought in the right place at the right time."

This was, and still is, quite insulting. Dave and I found the opportunities and made them work – no luck involved. These same opportunities exist for you today too – provided you don't let anyone talk you out of at least trying something different. You can always go back to what you're doing now, so what's there to lose other than the possibility of financial independence?

# OUR SECOND EFFORT

The week leading up to our next scheduled visit to Ballarat flew by. Determined to be better prepared the second time around, Dave and I allocated our spare moments in between accounting clients to search for potential deals in the local Ballarat paper and on the internet. We even created a profile of our 'ideal' investment, since a lot of agents needed a specific description of the sort of property we wanted – apparently our initial answer "Anything that's positive cashflow", was too vague. The profile we created was of a three (or more) bedroom home, in a neat and tidy condition, priced at up to $60,000 that could be expected to rent for about $120 per week.

## Building Business Relationships

On the morning of our scheduled second trip to Ballarat, Dave again dropped by to collect me at a reasonably early hour so as to avoid the Melbourne peak-hour traffic. This time I met him in more informal attire – old jeans and a casual t-shirt. Dave wore his 'house buying pants' – track suit pants that were well worn after many years of use. We spent our time in the car on the way to Ballarat happily chatting about many aspects of life. We were both recently married and were going through the same sorts of experiences.

While good friends, Dave and I also bring different skills to our business, which is an important element of our success. All too often I see friends try to join forces in an investing partnership, only to fail because they have competing rather than complementary skills. Not too long ago Dave held a meeting with two of his accounting clients, Stuart and Ruth – a husband and wife investing team. Stuart was a painter and Ruth was a full-time mum. Earlier they'd decided that Ruth would do the investing and Stuart would earn the money to invest by working as a contract painter. However, six months had passed by and the investing results they'd achieved were ordinary at best. The meeting was a good opportunity to take a breath and look back at what had gone wrong. Over coffee it became evident that both Ruth and Stuart were out looking for deals while no-one was bringing in the money.

Instead of identifying their place in the team, Stuart and Ruth both wanted to be the deal makers and, as a result, instead of lifting each other up they were, in fact, holding each other back. Without being disrespectful to Dave, in our business relationship, I'm the one with the ambitious ideas and Dave vetoes them, since he's the one who has to make them work. Dave brings in the money, and I invest it.

### Steve's Investing Tip

Don't just go into business with someone you like. Find someone who has a different skill set but who, nevertheless, shares the same goals and work ethic as you.

What Dave and I have been able to do as partners would not have been possible for us as individuals. Some of the best advice I can offer is, when deciding on a potential investing partner, don't just go into business with someone you like. Find a partner who has different skills but who, nevertheless, shares a common goal.

## The Difference Two Lanes of Asphalt Can Make

It was once again quite early by the time we turned off the Western Highway and onto the road that led into Ballarat. Unlike our previous visit, on this occasion we had made an effort to book ahead with several agents and to schedule appointments at different intervals throughout the day in order to maximise our time.

As expected, there wasn't a lot open in Ballarat when we arrived, so we drove around for a while and continued to familiarise ourselves with the layout of the town. Have you ever seen a movie where the properties on one side of the railway line are a good place to live, while houses on the other side are regarded as a place for the 'down-and-outers' to reside? Well, in Ballarat it isn't a railway line, it's a street – Gillies Street – which differentiates Wendouree from West Wendouree (or 'The West' as the locals call it). The difference in houses is remarkable. On the good side are established brick properties with attractive gardens. On the bad side are housing commission weatherboard homes build in the late 1940s or early 1950s, with sparse yards and overgrown trees. Houses on the 'right' side of Gillies Street were selling for $80,000. Houses on the 'wrong' side sold for $45,000. All that separated them was two lanes of asphalt.

Dave and I also noted the gradual improvement in the quality of houses as we travelled closer and closer to the middle of town, and then the deterioration as we headed through town and out again on the other side.

By the time of our first appointment, Dave and I were starting to feel like we knew the Ballarat area reasonably well – and certainly much, much better than we had on our first visit just one week earlier. The lesson for you in all of this is that if you plan to invest in an area that you don't live in then you'll find it next to impossible to pick up a feel for properties unless you spend time 'on the ground' there yourself.

## A Word on Due Diligence

By the time of our last appointment, Dave and I must have spoken to a dozen or so agents and looked through a further 20 properties. While a number of houses showed promise, there was nothing we saw that really stood out as a blatant good deal.

However, with each dwelling that we looked through, Dave and I learned more about property and especially about the way houses are built. We also refined our 'good cop, bad cop' routine – our charade where Dave would distract the agent while I'd grill the tenant for any information that was relevant to the property, the vendor, or our purchase.

Another task I assigned myself was to complete a due diligence over every property we inspected. Due diligence is a fancy accounting term for the process of trying to uncover information that isn't obvious at first glance. After looking through so many properties on our first visit, I knew that unless I implemented a standard way of inspecting properties then there was a huge risk that I'd forget something important. When you look through multiple properties in an afternoon, unless you have a photographic memory then they all start to blur into one.

To jolt my memory I created a series of 'tick the box' templates that ensured every property I inspected was given the same thorough once-over. It wasn't a substitute for a proper builder's report, but it was an excellent first glance over a property that forced me to pay closer attention to details that I might otherwise have glossed over or missed entirely.

Later I'd come to know that real estate agents are experts at showing you the things they want you to see, while subtly deflecting your attention away from potential problem areas. Using a 'tick the box' style template ensured I completed a thorough preliminary property inspection, and allowed me to unearth the sorts of things that might cost thousands to fix if there was a problem.

For example, one property I inspected featured a central heating service that was turned off on the day of my inspection. When I asked for it to be switched on it sounded like an aeroplane taking off down a runway. When I looked over the unit it was clearly old and would probably have been difficult to find parts for. This meant that it was more of a potential problem than a benefit.

Other issues I watch out for include:

⤷ Old-style wiring (easy to tell by whether or not the fuse box has been rewired)

⤷ The condition of the floor boards under the carpet (pull up a corner of the carpet)

⤷ Illegal sheds out the back (if they don't have downpipes then they're probably illegal); and

⤷ The age of the hot water service (see the compliance plate on the unit).

Whereas the tools of an accountant are a pen and a calculator, the tools a property investor needs are a spirit level and due diligence templates. While using the template allowed me to identify potential issues, of equal value was the agent's perception that I was a serious investor because I used a form and looked organised with my clipboard and pencil. Apparently, next to no-one else bothered, so I stood out as a professional when in truth I was just a beginner.

This inflated perception was very valuable at negotiation time. On more than one occasion I've overheard the agent tell the vendor (on the phone) that there was no point trying to eke out a few thousand dollars extra since the interested buyer was a professional investor.

### Steve's Investing Tip

If you want to find out more about the due diligence templates I use (which can potentially save you thousands of dollars) then please visit:

www.PropertyInvesting.com/BuyerBeware

## Meet Michael Golding

The last agent who Dave and I were scheduled to meet was Michael Golding, or Micky G. as we later affectionately called him. Micky G. is a great guy – a real character and a true country lad. I'm not being patronising – I regard Michael as a friend, although since property prices in Ballarat have risen lately, I don't have as much cause to be in contact with him as I did in the early days.

I recall with great fondness the afternoon that Dave and I had some time out from inspecting Ballarat property and played cricket in the nets for an hour or so (Dave carries his cricket gear in the car with him). Mick happened to call and when he heard that we were having a hit he immediately came down and bowled a few overs wearing his business suit.

Michael is a smart agent. I'm not sure whether he'd ever admit it, but I'm certain he used a trick right out of the agent's 'How To Sell Property' manual the first time he met us. The trick is simple; show the purchaser through a few houses which you know are not suitable and then, like magic, present the most appealing house as the final property on the inspection list.

It was late afternoon when Mick drove us across Gillies Street and into West Wendouree – the area where the waiter of the cafe that we'd eaten breakfast in on our first trip had warned us to stay away from. "It's a rough suburb", he'd said, and judging by the look of some of the houses and a few of the people walking the streets, that was no exaggeration!

There were several upcoming auctions of Ministry of Housing properties to be held by Michael's agency and he had the keys to show us through many of the houses. We began by looking through some properties in Violet Grove, a particularly rough part of West Wendouree that was apparently dubbed 'Violent Grove' – perhaps a fair title judging by the disaster of a first house we inspected.

Micky G. simply opened the door and said "I'll let you boys wander through this one by yourself – just watch out for holes in the floorboards."

Most ex-commission properties have a similar layout. Built after the end of World War II, they are constructed offsite and trucked in as two rectangular halves and then joined together. There's not a lot of architectural finesse, but they're solid homes that are built to last.

Anyway, the ex-commission house that we looked through made the unit with the spray painted homicide body on the floor look like a palace. There was thick black graffiti on the walls, the entire kitchen was burnt out and where the stove once stood there were blackened walls and small clumps of charcoal – evidence of a small fire close to where the gas pipe came up to service the stove. As Dave and I walked around the house we noted that many floorboards were missing and any chattels of worth had been either vandalised or ripped out. Most of the walls had several holes where someone had punched into them and there was a constant smell of stale urine emanating from the half-intact carpet.

In all respects, this house was a disgrace but Micky G. was optimistically cheerful winking at me while he told Dave that the property was "a renovator's delight if ever he'd seen one."

## OUR FIRST DEAL

Things were looking grim as the sun started to set on another day in Ballarat. We had been through three more houses and there was only one more property that Michael had us down to inspect – another ex-commission house in The West. Our prospects weren't looking good if the hovels we'd inspected were any indication of what was to come.

As we drove to our final inspection Mick said "This one's different to the others we've just been through. It's been privately owned for several years and is in good condition."

Whereas other properties in the street had their house numbers spray painted on the chimneys, this dwelling had its own letterbox and was painted a unique blue colour – evidence for all to see that this was, in fact, a privately owned house. Even the yard at the front was tidy.

In fading light, Micky G., Dave and I walked up and knocked on the front door. Despite the generally positive appearance, I left my clipboard and evaluation form in the car, having long since abandoned the idea of buying a property in this area.

If the exterior of the property was well kept, then the interior was immaculate with a real homely feel about it. While I raced back to the car to get my clipboard, Dave started to quiz Mick about the house.

It turned out the owners, who were watching television as we completed our inspection, were a retired couple who needed to sell due to poor health. Interestingly, the property had been previously sold twice before (for $54,000 and $52,000) however both times the sale had fallen over because the purchasers couldn't secure finance. With the owners now becoming more determined to sell, they had dropped the asking price to "offers above $50,000".

As I completed my due diligence template it was clear that the property didn't need any money spent on it to make it appealing to a future tenant. Dave asked Michael to estimate how much it would rent for, and he replied "at least $110 per week."

Applying 'The 11 Second Solution' formula (dividing the weekly rent by two and then multiplying the result by 1,000), Dave and I would expect to pay around $55,000, so the asking amount was certainly in our price range. I exchanged glances with Dave and we both knew that, finally, we'd found the sort of property we were looking for. We thanked the owners for allowing us to trounce through their home before walking out the door and through the front gate with Micky G. in step behind us.

"Well boys", Mick said, "What do you think? Is this the sort of thing you're after?"

As the last rays of afternoon sun touched the nature strip, Dave and I requested a few minutes to talk it over in private. We both quickly agreed that this property was exactly the sort of property we wanted, but how much should we offer? Without any science or method, we just pulled a number out of the air. Returning to Mick, who had walked a dozen or so paces further down the naturestrip, I said "We'd like to submit an offer of $40,000."

Michael smiled as he replied that he'd submit the offer immediately, although he wasn't sure whether or not it would be accepted since it was a little on the low side. My heart was thump-thump-thumping as Dave and I waited by the car while Micky G. disappeared inside to put our offer to the owners.

Dave and I used the time while Mick was inside to chat about what we'd do if our offer was rejected. We concluded that we were happy to go a few thousand higher, but we agreed to wait and see what the agent came back with before upping our offer.

Micky G. returned a few minutes later. "They won't go below $48k guys" he countered with a concerned look on his face. We were now at the final stages of negotiating. Dave and I again moved away for a few moments to confirm our next step. When we rejoined Mick on the nature strip, this time Dave (bad cop) spoke. "All right. Last offer. We'll meet you half way at $44,000."

Although this was less than the figure that Mick had said was the minimum the vendor's would accept, he went back inside with a hopeful look upon his face. After what seemed an eternity but was in fact about five minutes, Mick came back outside and said, "It's a deal".

With an exchange of handshakes, the Bradley McKnight property investing empire had begun. Figure 5.1, overleaf, shows what our first investment looked like.

## The Numbers

The vendors wanted to sell as quickly as possible so we agreed to a 30-day settlement period. However, it turned out that they needed a few extra months to organise their personal and financial affairs, so we agreed to rent the property back to them on a short-term lease at $120 per week. Not only had we bought our first property, but we'd also managed to secure our first tenants too.

Figure 5.1 – Our First Property Investment

When Dave and I purchased this property we had absolutely no clue about closing costs, nor how the final numbers would pan out. Unless you're an experienced investor you might be in the same boat, so I've reproduced our settlement statement in Table 5.1, opposite, and provided an analysis of our budgeted initial cash-on-cash return in Table 5.2, on page 68. This might provide an insight on how to analyse the numbers.

Additional costs (not shown in Table 5.1) paid directly by us included $713.80 in mortgage application, legal and registration costs. Our cash-on-cash return is shown in Table 5.2.

## The Car Ride Home

Eureka! We'd finally bought our first investment property – Dave and I enjoyed an amazing sense of satisfaction on our return drive to Melbourne. Had you met us that afternoon you might have mistaken us for investors who had just negotiated a 44-million-dollar deal, rather than a $44,000 property in the backblocks of Ballarat. There was no shortage of high fives and talk about how easy it was to find good opportunities. Sure, we'd spent two full days looking for the property, but now we'd found one, others were sure to follow.

| Table 5.1 Summary of Settlement Adjustments | | |
|---|---|---|
| **PURCHASER'S SETTLEMENT STATEMENT** | | |
| To: Purchase Price | | $44,000.00 |
| To: Purchaser's Solicitor Costs & Disbursements (Current Bill) | | $375.55 |
| To: Purchaser's Solicitor Costs & Disbursements (Prior Bill) | | $200.00 |
| To: Bank Cheque Fees | | $18.00 |
| To: Rate Adjustment | | $14.46 |
| To: Stamp Duty Fee — Transfer | | $856.00 |
| To: Titles Office Fee — Transfer | | $204.00 |
| To: Misc. Transaction Charges | | $36.77 |
| By: Total Deposit Paid | $8,800.00 | |
| By: Balance Required To Settle | $36,904.78 | |
| Total | $45,704.78 | $45,704.78 |

| Table 5.2 – Cash on Cash Return for our First Property | |
|---|---|
| **Purchase Price:** | **$44,000** |
| **INITIAL CASH SPENT TO ACQUIRE THE DEAL** | |
| Deposit (20%): | $8,800 |
| Closing costs: | $1,705 |
| Loan establishment: | $714 |
| **Initial Cash Needed:** | **$11,219** |
| **OUR LOAN** | |
| Principal: | $35,200 |
| Type: | Principal and interest |
| Term: | 25 years |
| Initial interest rate: | 8.05% |
| **Weekly Repayment:** | **$62.82** |
| **ANNUAL CASHFLOW RECEIVED** | |
| Rent per week: | $120 |
| **Total Cashflow Received:** | **$6,240** |
| **ANNUAL CASHFLOW OUT** | |
| Loan repayment: | $3,267 |
| Management costs: | $840 |
| Rates: | $690 |
| Insurance: | $200 |
| Repairs budget: | $200 |
| **Total Cashflow Out:** | **$5,197** |

| Table 5.2 – Cash on Cash Return for our First Property (cont'd) | |
|---|---|
| **ANNUAL CASHFLOW POSITION** | |
| Total cashflow received: | $6,240 |
| Total cashflow out: | $5,197 |
| **Annual Net Cashflow:** | **$1,043** |
| **CASH ON CASH RETURN** | |
| Annual net cashflow: | $1,043 |
| ÷ Initial cash needed: | $11,219 |
| **Cash on Cash Return:** | **9.30%** |

We were right in thinking that others would follow, but it would be a further two months before Dave and I would acquire our second property – a house that would turn out to be our worst deal ever. I'll save that story for Chapter 15. Meanwhile, let's turn our attention to some of the home truths of property investing in the next chapter, as we sharpen our focus.

## Chapter 5 Insights

### Insight #1:

Recently I completed a personality profile that revealed I was a 'feeler', as opposed to a 'thinker'.

If you're the same then you may believe it's necessary to win the support of your family and friends before you begin investing. That's OK, but don't allow any negativity you experience to stop you from at least trying something new.

If I hadn't started investing in property then I'd still either be an auditor, a nervous wreck or both.

### Insight #2:

Creating a profile of your ideal property will be a useful tool to help real estate agents find an appropriate investment.

### Insight #3:

Don't just go into business with people that you like. It's much more sensible to join forces with someone who will keep you accountable and also deliver a complementary skill set. Most important of all though – you must share a common goal.

### Insight #4:

You can certainly buy a property sight-unseen, but unless you know the area well then there's an increased risk that you'll buy a dud.

Ideally you'd be able to familiarise yourself with your target area by looking through properties and by face-to-face networking with real estate agents.

You can only buy like a local when you feel like a local.

## Chapter 5 Insights *(cont'd)*

### Insight #5:

If you're planning to get serious about your property investing then using templates will save you time and help ensure you don't make an expensive oversight. To find out more about the templates that I created and regularly use in my investing activities visit:

www.PropertyInvesting.com/BuyerBeware

### Insight #6:

Occasionally you'll meet an agent who you'd be proud to call a friend. Learn from them, be honest with them and empower them to work as your representative.

Look at ways to create a win-win outcome where your property empire can expand while the agent earns a healthy commission. A good deal generates enough money to be spread around several times over.

### Insight #7:

The world of property investing is full of surprises. Enjoy the experience.

### Insight #8:

You'll only ever do your first deal once. From then, as your experience broadens, you'll become more and more confident in dealing with agents, inspecting property and making offers. It's nowhere near as scary the second time around.

# PART II:

# Property Investing Home Truths

Avoid properties that suck your cashflow...

...buy properties that make money from day one.

# INTRODUCTION TO PART II

Part I of this book provided a glimpse into my background prior to investing and also several of our experiences as Dave and I kick-started our real estate empire. While I'm sure you've enjoyed the tales, I'm conscious that I also want to provide you with a substantial amount of information to equip you with a detailed understanding of both the nature of property, and how you can use it to invest profitably.

Some of the information in Part II may be a little dry – especially if you're not a numbers person. Please persevere, as many of the concepts discussed later in the book build on issues discussed in Chapters 6 to 11.

If you feel your mind drifting then take a moment and regain your focus as knowledge is the difference between success and failure. Let's start our discussion of real estate by looking at the ways and means that you can profit from property.

# The Ways and Means of Profiting from Property

I've met thousands of investors who have bought real estate with various motives in mind, however only a tiny minority have ever had a formalised plan detailing their expectations of how to make money, what their required minimum return is and which factors might trigger a sign to sell.

I wonder, why is it that you've become interested in real estate investing? Are you about to jump right in the deep end and buy something that might cost hundreds of thousands of dollars under the assumption that you can't help but profit from property? This could be a huge mistake.

As you read through this chapter it would be helpful to keep this question in the back of your mind – what comes first, the property or the profit? While there are many reasons why someone might choose to invest in property, they all ultimately boil down to a choice of three alternatives.

# THREE PROPERTY INVESTING ALTERNATIVES

## Reason #1 – To Make Money

It might not buy happiness or love, but money can certainly be used to buy back the time you'd otherwise spend working in a job. There are two types of real estate profits:

1. *Capital gains* – where your property appreciates in value above the price that you paid for it (this topic is expanded upon in Chapter 7); and

2. *Recurring positive cashflow returns* – where you receive more money in cash receipts than you pay in cash payments (this will be explained further in Chapter 8).

## Reason #2 – To Save (Income) Tax

One of the most popular methods of minimising tax is a property investing strategy called 'negative gearing'. Negative gearing allows investors to access an immediate tax deduction whilst also potentially building wealth via long-term capital appreciation.

Australian tax law allows investors to claim a deduction for expenses associated with owning an investment property. If these expenses are more than your property's income, the result is a loss that can be used to offset other taxable income that you might have, such as your salary or wage. For negative gearing to build wealth, your capital appreciation must be greater than your after-tax loss. When this occurs, such as during the property boom that's lasted between 1999 and the time of writing, then the concept certainly achieves its objective.

Yet there are some serious limitations to negative gearing, which are rarely discussed. Outlining the pros and cons of negative gearing is a book all by itself, so my discussion (which is by no means brief) of the technique will be limited to Chapter 10 (page 129) and Appendix B (page 347).

## Reason #3 – Out of a Love of Landlording

I'm yet to meet anybody who seriously falls into this category in its own right. Instead, most landlords feel they're doing tenants a favour by letting them stay in their property.

Treating a tenant like a potential menace rather than a valued client is a limiting attitude that impedes the development of a good tenant-landlord relationship. I've managed to avoid many of the 'tenant from hell' stories you hear and read about by implementing simple reward strategies, rather than ranting and raving with threats about nasty consequences unless my needs are promptly fulfilled.

Being a landlord can be a rewarding experience provided you create win-win outcomes where the needs of the tenant become intermeshed with your own. I outline strategies that reveal how you can do this in Chapter 12 (page 185).

# DECISION TIME

Once I'd isolated these three possible alternatives, my next step was to make a decision about which outcome I wanted to focus my attention on achieving.

### Steve's Investing Tip

Your choice of desired profit outcome, and therefore the class of property you seek to acquire, stems from the reason you're investing in the first place.

## Saving Tax?

With respect to saving tax, my accountant brain told me that the only way to reduce my tax bill was to create a situation where I had more expenses than income, which in layman's terms meant making a loss.

If you could only choose two of the four outcomes identified in Table 6.1 below, which would they be?

| Table 6.1 – Property Investment Outcomes | | | |
|---|---|---|---|
| | ✓ | OUTCOME | TAX IMPACT |
| Either | | Positive cashflow | Make money, pay tax |
| | | Negative cashflow | Lose money, 'save' tax |
| Either | | Capital gains | Make money, pay tax when you sell |
| | | Capital losses | Lose money, 'save' tax when you sell |

As I was trying to *make* money, as opposed to *lose* money, I quickly eliminated the goal of saving tax from my reasons for investing in property.

## A Love of Landlording?

Being a good landlord is certainly a noble idea, but this motivation for property investing was quickly eliminated too. It was secondary to my aim of creating a better lifestyle for myself.

### The Mr A Case Study

One of Dave's accounting clients, we'll call him Mr A, had just sold his business for a tidy profit and was looking to maximise his return by earning some quick capital gains. He attended a seminar and, without consulting Dave, went on to purchase an 'off-the-plan' apartment in the Melbourne Docklands precinct for $680,000.

## The Mr A Case Study *(cont'd)*

Mr A's strategy was to sell the property and cash in on his capital gains around the time of completion, which would be about 18 months after the date he signed the contract.

While the building was being constructed, Mr A received regular reports from both the developer and sales agent to say that the project was going to plan and because the real estate market was booming, his property was rapidly rising in value.

The property was considered complete in March 2002. Mr A made an appointment to see his real estate agent to discuss selling but was told "not to bother" because a glut of similar property had hit the market and, with supply now more than demand, Mr A's apartment was, at that time, worth less than what he'd paid for it.

Dave's accounting client had no option but to settle and take possession of the apartment. With no surplus money available, Mr A had to redraw funds from his home mortgage which resulted in him financing 100% of his purchase price at an average interest rate of 6.5% per annum (interest-only loan).

For the next six months the apartment sat hopelessly vacant. It was a victim of an over supply of properties and a lack of tenants.

Mr A's wallet was the real casualty as it was being sucked dry by a massive cashflow shortfall as shown in Table 6.2, overleaf.

The first Dave heard of this predicament was when Mr A came in to have his annual income tax return prepared.

## The Mr A Case Study *(cont'd)*

While lamenting his real estate losses, Mr A was at least consoled that his $27,851 loss would offset his other taxable income to reduce his overall tax bill.

Dave rightly pointed out that if Mr A's goal was to save tax then he was doing an exceptional job, but the crippling side-effect was that saving tax was also sending him broke.

| Table 6.2 – Mr A's Cashflow (First Six Months) | |
| --- | --- |
| **CASHFLOW RECEIVED** | |
| Rent per week: | $0 |
| **Annual Cashflow Received:** | $0 |
| **CASHFLOW OUT:** | |
| Loan repayment: | $22,100 |
| Advertising costs: | $209 |
| Body corporate fees: | $5,182 |
| Rates: | $360 |
| **Total Cashflow Out:** | **$27,851** |
| **Net Six Month Cashflow:** | **($27,851)** |

## Making Money?

The only alternative that I could see which would allow me to achieve my goal of no longer having to work as an accountant was to invest in property and make enough passive income to replace the salary I derived from billing my clients. If I could do this then I'd be well on my way to my ultimate goal of achieving financial freedom.

Working through the three investing alternatives helped me to create a 'never-break' golden rule of property investing – to only invest in real estate that made money from day one.

### Steve's Investing Tip

If all your investments earned a profit, then you'd have no option but to make money!

If you're currently investing (in property, shares or anything else) and you're not making money, then you're breaking this golden rule and need to reconsider your approach. What you are doing is not sustainable and has little chance of long-term success.

Now it's your turn to make a decision. Go back and read over the three alternatives that can eventuate from investing in property and once you are familiar with them, complete the pledge in the multiple choice questionaire in Table 6.3, overleaf.

If you answered 'D' then there's not a lot of benefit that you'll receive from this book as what you put in will be what you take out. Please, at least have a go.

## THERE ARE MANY TYPES OF PROPERTY

A short while ago I was presenting my revolutionary ideas about making money in property investing to an audience of about 300 Queensland investors. During the half-time break, a middle-aged lady approached me to seek my affirmation that the way she was investing was consistent with my methodology. She'd come across an unusual property – a caravan park in a small regional area that was priced for a quick sale at $120,000. Many of the 16 caravans were rented to permanent residents at $70 per week, which included power and also water, since most tenants used the public amenities to shower and do their washing.

| Table 6.3 – Multiple Choice (Circle Your Answer) | |
|---|---|
| **Today's Date:** | |
| **Instructions:** Grab a pen and circle *one* of the multiple choice answers from the selection below that *best* summarises the reason why you plan to invest in property. | |
| *The Outcome I Desire from My Property Investing is...* | |
| **A** | To make money that I can reinvest into my financial future. |
| **B** | To save tax – I see money paid in tax as dead money and I'd rather lose a dollar than have to pay it in tax. |
| **C** | I love the idea of dealing with tenants irrespective of whether or not I'm making a profit. |
| **D** | I don't know... I don't want to be challenged, I just want to keep reading. |

Quickly grabbing my trusty financial calculator, it was soon apparent that the deal on offer wasn't just a good opportunity, it was an exceptional one. Table 6.4, opposite, shows why.

Don't worry for now if you don't understand how I've evaluated the numbers – this is explained in Chapter 8. For the time being just note that the annual return was 65.21%, which is substantially more than what the balance in your cheque account is earning!

Now, I'm certainly *not* suggesting that we should all run out and buy a caravan park, but this example provides valuable proof that there are many ways to make money in real estate, at various price ranges, above and beyond buying residential real estate.

| Table 6.4 – Return on Caravan Park Example | | |
|---|---|---|
| **ITEM** | **AMOUNT** | **NOTES** |
| Purchase price: | $120,000 | |
| Closing costs (stamp duty etc.): | $6,000 | Allow 5% for closing costs. |
| Deposit: | $36,000 | Most commercial loans are a maximum lend of 70%. |
| Cash needed: | $42,000 | |
| Rent: | $49,280 | Based on reasonable estimates that each caravan is vacant for eight weeks per annum. |
| Annual loan payments: | ($7,109) | Loan of $84,000, 25-year term, weekly repayments, 7% interest. |
| Budgeted admin. costs: | ($14,784) | Assume 30% of rent |
| Positive cashflow: | $27,387 | |
| **Cash on Cash Return:** | **65.21%** | **And that's before any capital gains!** |

I've made a list of some of the many options you can use to make money from real estate below.

## Residential Property

This is by far and away the most popular class of real estate investment. It involves buying a dwelling that another person will live in as his or her principal place of residence.

Examples of residential property include:

⇒ Single family houses (on a separate parcel of land)

⇒ Duplexes (two houses on separate titles that share a common wall)

⇒ Flats (usually clusters of ground floor dwellings that are not detached)

⇒ Units (usually clusters of ground floor dwellings that are detached); and

⇒ Apartments (usually multi-storey dwellings within a large complex).

## Commercial Property

Commercial property is real estate leased to a business. It's an all encompassing term that includes:

⇒ Offices

⇒ Retail sites (where goods are offered for sale to the general public)

⇒ Industrial sites (typically where goods are manufactured or assembled, such as a factory)

⇒ Hotel and motel accommodation including bed and breakfasts; and

⇒ Caravan parks.

## Miscellaneous

Other classes of real estate include:

⇒ Self-storage facilities

⇒ Rural and farm land

▷ Vacant land

▷ Retirement accommodation

▷ Holiday accommodation; and

▷ Public housing (dwellings owned privately and leased back to government organisations which then provide them for people in need).

The reason why I've provided this list is to open your eyes to the huge opportunities outside of simply buying single family houses. Sure, each class of property carries with it different risks and rewards, but there's certainly no secret handshake or special prerequisite that precludes you from purchasing commercial or other property types rather than just residential real estate.

## Steve's Investing Tip

In the world of real estate, a dollar earned from residential property buys the same as a dollar earned from commercial property.

I wish someone had told me that there was no reason why I couldn't start with commercial property because some of my more profitable deals have come in the form of business premises.

For example, one weekend I was interstate visiting a friend. We had some time on our hands and we decided to go for a walk through town and go window shopping for real estate – one of my favourite pastimes. You can do this by pounding the pavements and looking in the windows of real estate agent's offices to see what properties they have available for sale.

It turned out that I was going to have a lucky day when I noticed the following ad in an agent's window:

---

**Industrial property comprising 8,594 sq. metre land area with newer 600 sq. metre warehouse/workshop building all fully leased to a secure tenant**

Six-year lease plus a further five-year option

Current rent $20,800, rising to $22,100 after the next rent adjustment due in two months

Council rates and Land Tax paid by the tenant

**For Sale at $160,000**

**13.8% Return Warehouse Investment**

---

Bingo! This was just the sort of property I was looking for because I could tell the return was high enough, and the price low enough, to guarantee I'd make money from day one. I made an offer of $155,000, which was accepted and I became the new owner of a warehouse. Table 6.5, opposite, shows a summary of the preliminary numbers.

A cash on cash return of 24.7% is more modest than the caravan park example, but it's still very attractive, plus I also benefit from any capital appreciation! (If you're wondering why my numbers don't include rates or land tax, it's because these costs are usually paid by the tenant in a commercial lease.)

## SUMMARY

An essential question that you need to consider is: "What comes first, the property or the profit?" Before you answer, it's wise to identify the reason why you're investing in real estate, since your choice will provide the framework for selecting the type of property you decide to buy. For example, if you want to save tax then there are many opportunities to buy real estate that delivers tax breaks today and the promise of a profit tomorrow. On the other hand, if you want to make money from day one then you'll need to find a specific type of property that fits within the strategy you will need to achieve your goal.

| ITEM | AMOUNT | NOTES |
|---|---|---|
| *Table 6.5 – Return on Commercial Warehouse Example* | | |
| Purchase price: | $155,000 | |
| Closing costs (stamp duty etc.): | $7,750 | Allow 5% for closing costs. |
| Deposit: | $46,500 | Most commercial loans are a maximum lend of 70% of the purchase price |
| Cash needed: | $54,250 | Deposit of $46,500 plus closing costs of $7,750 |
| Rent: | $22,100 | |
| Annual loan payments: | ($7,595) | Loan of $108,500, 10-year interest-only term, weekly repayments, 7% interest |
| Repairs budget: | ($1,105) | Assume 5% of rent |
| Positive cashflow: | $13,400 | |
| **Income (Cash on Cash) Returns:** | **24.7%** | **And that's before any capital gains!** |

There's more skill required to maximise your property profits than simply buying any type of real estate under the assumption that everything will make a profit if you give it enough time. If it were that easy then everyone would be making millions and this certainly isn't the case.

Once I'd made the decision to invest in property to make money, the next question to ask myself was "What *type* of profit did I want to attract?" I'll look at this in the next chapter.

### Chapter 6 Insights

#### Insight #1:

There are only three reasons to invest in property – to make money, to save tax or because you love being a landlord. It's important to decide why you're investing in real estate, as your decision will determine the types of property you look to acquire and the investing strategy you will implement.

#### Insight #2:

While most investors choose to buy residential property, there's no reason why you need to make this your niche too. In fact, there are many ways to invest in commercial and other property that will see you earn a return far in excess of what's possible by investing in single family homes.

#### Insight #3:

If all your investments made cash returns of 24.7% per annum (i.e. the return on my commercial property) then your success would not be a matter of *if*, just a question of *when*.

# Capital Gains...
# Can they be Banked on?

Capital gains are a form of investing profit that occur when your property increases in value or, to put it more bluntly, when you can sell your asset for more than it cost you to acquire and hold it. Capital appreciation is by far and away the most popular reason why investors buy property.

Looking at Table 7.1, overleaf, you can see that the expectation of your property increasing in value is realistic if you look at the movement in median house prices over the ten years from December 1992 to December 2002. Table 7.1 is also presented graphically in Figure 7.1 on page 91.

During this ten-year time period the market was coming out of a recession and home loan interest rates were falling from their peak of 17% (March 1990) back to 10% (December 1992), 6.7% (December 1997) and 6.55% (in December 2002).

## Table 7.1 — Movement in Median House Prices 1992 to 2002

| City | DECEMBER 1992 Median House Price | DECEMBER 1992 to DECEMBER 1997 Median House Price | % Change | DECEMBER 1992 to DECEMBER 2002 Median House Price | % Change |
|---|---|---|---|---|---|
| Adelaide | $110,400 | $116,500 | 5.53% | $190,500 | 72.55% |
| Brisbane | $118,000 | $142,000 | 20.34% | $256,000 | 116.95% |
| Canberra | $161,000 | $162,000 | 0.62% | $246,000 | 52.80% |
| Darwin | $132,000 | $180,000 | 36.36% | $208,000 | 57.58% |
| Hobart | $102,300 | $111,000 | 8.50% | $147,300 | 43.99% |
| Melbourne | $144,000 | $192,000 | 33.33% | $335,000 | 132.64% |
| Perth | $100,000 | $136,600 | 36.60% | $194,400 | 94.40% |
| Sydney | $185,000 | $245,000 | 32.43% | $450,000 | 143.24% |

**Source:** Real Estate Institute of Australia (REIA)

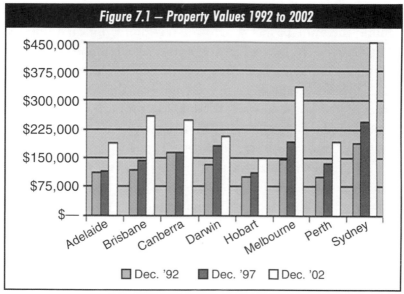

Figure 7.1 – Property Values 1992 to 2002

**Source:** REIA data

If you had purchased a property in one of Australia's eight capital cities back in December 1992, and still owned it today, then you should be sitting on a handsome capital gain.

# THE THREE WAYS TO EARN CAPITAL GAINS

## 1. Buying Below Value

You'll be well poised to earn capital gains if you can **buy below value**. The cheapest house Dave and I have purchased, at the time of writing, was bought in June 2000 for the meagre sum of $29,500. While certainly no mansion, it was a neat and tidy two-bedroom home on a quarter acre block in a regional town about two hour's drive from Melbourne. When flicking through the sale contract, I noticed in the Vendor's Statement that the local council had valued the property at $36,000 for rates purposes. "Hang on... the council have valued the property for $36,000", I thought "and we are going to pay just $29,500?" This was beginning to smell like a bargain.

Another major plus was that you couldn't possibly hope to rebuild the same property with today's money for anything less than $70,000. In fact, when we tried to secure home insurance, the minimum value our insurer would accept was $100,000. What made this deal really attractive though was that you could have removed the house altogether from the property, and the land value alone would have been worth what we paid. To put it another way, we essentially got the building for free!

The property was also rented at $90 per week, which meant it would provide an immediate positive cashflow return and thus it satisfied my requirement that it make money from day one.

Even though we weren't investing specifically for capital gains, Dave and I are still interested in maximising our investment return and we felt that buying a property such as this one meant we stood to outperform the market if prices rose. The basis for this belief was that a property valued at below council valuation would have some room to appreciate up to market value and then beyond market value should demand increase. That is, if the market moved and the next cheapest house on the market was $40,000, then our property that was cheap to begin with would provide a better return than a similar property in a similar area that sold for, say, $35,000.

This proved to be the case. Just over a year later we decided to sell and plough our profits into another property with a higher return. On top of our positive cashflow, we made a further 27.08% net capital gain. A purchase price below replacement or council assigned value is an indication that your property is primed to achieve good capital growth.

## 2. Adding Value

Another strategy to achieve capital gains is to add value by commissioning structural and/or cosmetic improvements to the property. Provided you add more value than the cost of the improvements then you'll achieve capital gains. This strategy is covered in more detail in Chapter 15.

## 3. Demand Exceeds Supply

My only lingering memory, other than severe boredom, from years of studying economics was that prices rise when demand is greater than supply. This is certainly true in property. This is an important concept so let's look at it in more detail.

### Location, Location, Location!

Have you heard it said that the secret to success in property is "Location, location, location"? While this is correct in respect to capital gains returns, the reason why location is so important is rarely explained.

The logic behind investing for location is that there will be fewer properties in sought after areas than investors and residents who want to own them. With demand greater than supply, house prices must rise. A great example is beachfront properties. There's not a lot of new beach being created and, this being the case, the number of beachfront properties is generally limited. Yet the demand for beachfront properties means that buyers must pay a premium above what the property is intrinsically worth to secure a limited resource.

Whether prices rise or fall, a property with a sought after feature should achieve a higher price than other properties in the same area. Other than beach access, sought after location related features that can drive a price up include city views, access to amenities such as schools and hospitals, proximity to major arterial roads (to cut commuting time) and the size of property lots.

### Intended Use

If a property has a unique intended use that cannot be easily replicated then it will also be well poised for capital growth. One of the biggest deals we've bought to date was a large residential block of units in regional Victoria for $510,000. It was an old motel site of 27 one-bedroom dwellings. One block had 16 units and the other had 12 units. The 12th unit in the second block was transformed into a communal laundry. The units were built in the 1970s and were subject to the planning code of the day. Today, however, such high-density living would not be allowed as planning regulations have changed. A lot with 27 dwellings that could not be rebuilt today gave the property a unique appeal for investors.

Other examples that illustrate the point include older-style high-rise apartments, purpose-built self-storage complexes and areas that have limited council zoning that can't be easily expanded. A property will be primed to earn good capital growth if it appeals to people as somewhere they would want to live (residential), work (commercial) or invest.

It's fair to say that what makes a property valuable has very little to do with its structure (bricks and sticks) and a lot to do with its aesthetic/architectural qualities, scarcity and intended use.

## WHAT'S A REASONABLE EXPECTATION FOR CAPITAL APPRECIATION?

Presenters at many of the free seminars I've attended have explained that it's reasonable to expect property to double in value every seven to ten years. These claims are easy to make, but until they can be supported by statistics I remain a sceptic. In the absence of any presenters providing meaningful data, I did my own research.

Using median house price data from the Real Estate Institute of Australia (using figures since data has been recorded until December 2002) Table 7.2, opposite, tracks how long it has taken for prices to double (and then not fall back below) their previous base figure.

### What Does Table 7.2 Reveal?

Apart from Darwin and Hobart, the first price double occurred within the ten-year expected timeframe. However, as property became more expensive, it generally took longer for prices to double for the second and third time, although, to be fair, there's been a considerable improvement in the trend after the 2001 and 2002 boom.

| Table 7.2 – The Doubling of Property Prices | | | | |
|---|---|---|---|---|
| **MELBOURNE** | | | | |
| | **Beginning** | **1st Double** | **2nd Double** | **3rd Double** |
| Date | March 1980 | March 1986 | June 1997 | June 2002 |
| Base value | $40,800 | $81,600 | $163,200 | $326,400 |
| Time | | 6 years | 11.25 years | 5 years |
| **BRISBANE** | | | | |
| | **Beginning** | **1st Double** | **2nd Double** | **3rd Double** |
| Date | March 1980 | June 1988 | June 1997 | ——— |
| Base value | $34,500 | $69,000 | $138,000 | ——— |
| Time | | 8.25 years | 9 years | ——— |
| **SYDNEY** | | | | |
| | **Beginning** | **1st Double** | **2nd Double** | **3rd Double** |
| Date | March 1980 | Dec. 1987 | Dec. 1998 | ——— |
| Base value | $64,800 | $129,600 | $259,200 | ——— |
| Time | | 7.75 years | 11 years | ——— |

*Cont'd...*

## Table 7.2 – The Doubling of Property Prices (cont'd)

### PERTH

|  | Beginning | 1st Double | 2nd Double |
|---|---|---|---|
| Date | March 1980 | Sep. 1988 | Sep. 2001 |
| Base value | $41,500 | $84,000 | $168,000 |
| Time |  | 8.5 years | 13 years |

### CANBERRA

|  | Beginning | 1st Double | 2nd Double |
|---|---|---|---|
| Date | March 1980 | June 1984 | Dec. 1999 |
| Base value | $39,700 | $79,400 | $158,800 |
| Time |  | 4.25 years | 15.5 years |

### ADELAIDE

|  | Beginning | 1st Double | 2nd Double |
|---|---|---|---|
| Date | March 1980 | Dec. 1984 | June 2001 |
| Base value | $36,300 | $72,600 | $145,200 |
| Time |  | 4.75 years | 16.5 years |

### DARWIN

|  | Beginning | 1st Double | 2nd Double |
|---|---|---|---|
| Date | Dec. 1986 | June 1999 | ——— |
| Base value | $87,500 | $175,000 | ——— |
| Time |  | 12.5 years | ——— |

### HOBART

|  | Beginning | 1st Double | 2nd Double |
|---|---|---|---|
| Date | March 1991 | ——— | ——— |
| Base value | $88,800 | ——— | ——— |
| Time |  | ——— | ——— |

**Source:** Based on median house price data from the REIA.

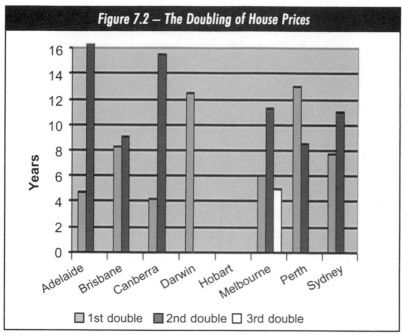

**Figure 7.2 – The Doubling of House Prices**

**Source:** Based on median house price data from the REIA.

A good post on this topic was made by 'APIM' on the forum at www.PropertyInvesting.com.

---

I thought this might be interesting to some of you. We often hear that property values double about every seven to ten years. But what does that correspond to in interest rate terms? OK, here is the breakdown: A property will double in value every ten years if the compounded yearly interest rate is equal to 7%.

10 years --> 7% (Approx.)

9 years --> 8% (Approx.)

8 years --> 9% (Approx.)

7 years --> 10% (Approx.)

---

A reply to APIM's post was made by 'Young Gun', who wrote:

---

Another way to work out how often your property will double (roughly) is to divide the yearly growth percentage into 72.

If a property grows at 8% per year then...

72 ÷ 8 = 9 years to double.

---

'Young Gun' has actually outlined a financial principle known as the 'Rule of 72', which says that to find the number of years required to double your money, you simply divide 72 by the applicable interest rate.

### How Long Can You Really Expect it to Take for Properties to Double in Value?

Unless you have your own personal crystal ball, the best data you can use to determine what's likely to happen to future property values is long-term (to smooth out any abnormal variances) historical data.

If the 20-year average growth in medium house prices is a good indicator of likely future performance, then Table 7.3, opposite, shows you how long it will take for property prices to double.

If this table is indicative of what you can expect for future house price growth, then the claim that property prices double every seven to ten years appears largely valid, however:

1.  As prices increase it's generally taking longer for property values to double; and

2.  Today property prices in major cities are doubling at a rate much closer to ten (or more) years rather than seven.

Be sure that your capital gains projections allow for these trends.

| | Average 20-year Annual Growth | Expect Property to Double Every (Approx.): |
|---|---|---|
| | **Table 7.3 – Time Taken for Prices to Double** | |
| Adelaide | 7.44% | 9.68 years |
| Brisbane | 8.26% | 8.72 years |
| Canberra | 7.77% | 9.27 years |
| Darwin | 5.89%* | 12.22 years* |
| Hobart | 4.84%* | 14.89 years* |
| Melbourne | 9.92% | 7.26 years |
| Perth | 7.54% | 9.55 years |
| Sydney | 10.33% | 6.98 years |

**Source:** REIA and Reserve Bank of Australia. Data based on 20-year average, Dec. 1982 to Dec. 2002, except for Hobart and Darwin.

(*) indicates for data available – Darwin: Dec. 1986 to Dec. 2002, Hobart: Dec. 1991 to Dec. 2002

# THE IMPACT OF INFLATION ON CAPITAL GAINS

Inflation represents the erosion of money's buying power as a result of increasing prices. The most recognised measure of inflation in Australia is the Consumer Price Index (CPI). A good example of inflation is the price of hot chips. When I was a boy (now I sound like my Dad) I can remember that a 'minimum chips' at my local fish and chip shop cost 30 cents. Today, minimum chips cost about $2.00! Same potatoes (hopefully not the same oil!) but the cost has gone up 567%.

A figure that's been adjusted for inflation is also known as a *real value* figure.

## Inflation and Capital Gains

The impact of inflation on capital gains is largely overlooked and to illustrate the point I'll use one of my father's stories as an example.

My Dad acquired a property in Collingwood (an inner suburb of Melbourne) in 1984 for $64,000. He sold it for $295,000 in 2001. On the surface of it (before purchase, sale and closing costs), Dad made a substantial gain of $231,000 ($295,000 – $64,000)

However, his $231,000 needs to be adjusted (or discounted) back to 1984 dollars in order to calculate his *real* or after-inflation capital gain. Using the average inflation rate between 1984 and 2001 of 4.28%,[1] Dad's *real* sale price falls from $295,000 to $144,550 and his inflation-adjusted profit falls to $80,550 ($144,550 – $64,000).

Annualising $80,550 over the 17 years Dad owned the property, his after-inflation gross return on investment (ROI) was a little over $4,700 or 7.4% per annum. Don't get me wrong; this is quite a good result, and it's important to remember that as he borrowed a large portion of the purchase price he was able to achieve a higher net return.

However, my point here is that when you adjust for the impact of inflation – which is necessary to provide a real gauge of how his investment has performed – Dad's real capital gain was eroded by 65.13%! And Dad's lucky! He doesn't have to pay any capital gains tax as his house was purchased before the regime was introduced. If he had to pay capital gains tax on his profits then his return would be even less.

Let's redo Table 7.3 to reveal the *real*, or inflation-adjusted, returns that property has delivered. Taking Adelaide, for example, Table 7.4, opposite, indicates that if you bought the median house price today, then you could expect that it would take 23.68 years for your property to double in *real*, after-inflation value, provided both inflation and median house prices followed the 20-year trend.

1 – **Source:** Reserve Bank of Australia.

| Table 7.4 – Time Taken For Prices To Double Using Inflation-Adjusted 20-Year Average (Dec. '82 – Dec. '02) | | | | |
|---|---|---|---|---|
| | Average 20-Year Annual Growth | 20-Year Average Annual Inflation | 20-Year Average Real Annual Growth | Time Taken for Property Prices to Double |
| Adelaide | 7.44% | 4.59% | 3.04% | 23.68 yrs |
| Brisbane | 8.26% | 4.59% | 3.37% | 21.36 yrs |
| Canberra | 7.77% | 4.59% | 3.17% | 22.71 yrs |
| Darwin | 5.89%* | 3.86%* | 2.76% | 26.09 yrs |
| Hobart | 4.84%* | 2.38%* | 3.02% | 23.84 yrs |
| Melbourne | 9.92% | 4.59% | 4.05% | 17.78 yrs |
| Perth | 7.54% | 4.59% | 3.08% | 23.38 yrs |
| Sydney | 10.33% | 4.59% | 4.21% | 17.10 yrs |

**Source:** Data from the REIA and Reserve Bank of Australia.

Median House Price Movements. (*) indicates for data available Darwin: Dec. '86 to Dec. '02, Hobart: Dec. '91 to Dec. '02.

## What Does All this Mean?

Confused? I understand... there are a lot of numbers here! What I'm trying to do is establish a long-term figure that you could use as a reasonable guide as to the budgeted precentage rate at which your property might rise in value.

As I have mentioned, many of the free seminars I have been to, and much of the property investment literature that I've read quotes seven to ten years as the timeframe in which property values can be expected to double. My own independent research tends to agree with that claim – with two important provisos.

First, as prices rise across the country it's generally taking longer for values to double. This means that if you bought a 'median priced property' in Adelaide today, then applying the 20-year average, it's more likely that it will take 9.68 years, or maybe even longer, before it will have doubled in price.

Second, you need to realise that your capital gain will buy less in 9.68 years because of inflation. This means that your gain might seem impressive on paper, but your *real* purchasing power is eroded because your profit buys less. That same Adelaide property could be expected to take 23.68 years to double in real (after inflation) value – and that's before your gain is eroded by capital gains tax.

The bottom line here is that the claim that property prices double every seven to ten years is a partial truth only.

# CAN YOU BANK ON CAPITAL GAINS?

Despite what people might tell you, property does not always rise in value. If you study the movement in median house prices then you'll notice that most of the time property prices do not appreciate rapidly, rather they increase at a slow and steady rate. There are even periods when prices fall.

The important point to note is that investing in property for capital gains is a little like jumping on an escalator and enjoying the ride. However, there are times when the escalator may seem more like a rollercoaster, as we have seen at the time of writing with near vertical growth rates.

## Funding Your Retirement with Capital Gains

If your goal is to use capital gains to finance your retirement then you're going to face three major problems:

### Problem #1: Once You Spend Your Capital Gain then Your Money Stops Working for You

If you're living off your investment capital, as opposed to your investment income, then one day you'll find you've spent or borrowed against all your profits. How will you fund your retirement then?

### Problem #2: Capital Gains are Uncertain and Take Time to Accumulate

Capital gains are never guaranteed and when the market is flat, it can take several years for your property to increase in value. In times when your property is not appreciating you'll need to find other sources of income to fund your financial independence.

### Problem #3: Tax Deductibility of Interest

Expenses of a private nature are not tax deductible. If you borrow against your capital gains and use the money to fund your lifestyle then the interest on that borrowing will not be tax deductible and must be repaid using after-tax dollars. I've outlined a numerical example to illustrate this point in Chapter 18 (see page 293).

Without substantial sources of income, the only way to fund the non-deductible interest on your loan repayments will be to:

A.   Borrow/redraw more money which, unfortunately, will not qualify as a tax deduction. The result will be that your retirement equity will begin to diminish in ever increasing circles; or

B.   Sell the property, which may mean that you have to pay capital gains tax.

Many wealth creators advocate using equity and capital gains to fund lifestyle expenses, but this is very, very dangerous as you don't want to have compounding negative wealth at a stage in your life where you have a diminished earning capacity.

I write this as a dire warning for people looking to use capital gains to fund their financial freedom. Be very careful about seeing equity as your retirement saviour.

## THE FINAL WORD ON CAPITAL GAINS

If you can buy and hold for the long-term you can make substantial capital gains from investing in property. There will be times when growth is good, and there will be times when your property's price stagnates. The worst thing you can do though is to invest with the expectation that gains, like those that occurred between 1999 and 2002, are either representative of the long-term trend, or can be sustained into the foreseeable future.

Personally, because I didn't want to work in a job while I waited for capital gains to accumulate, I needed to adopt a different strategy that would see me receive an immediate profit which I could use to replace my salary. As outlined in the next chapter, I managed to do this by investing in recurring positive cashflow returns.

## Chapter 7 Insights

### Insight #1:

Capital gains occur when your property increases in value above and beyond the price that you paid to acquire it plus the cost of holding it.

### Insight #2:

There are three ways you can earn capital gains: buying below value, adding value or creating a situation where demand exceeds supply.

### Insight #3:

In the long term, it's reasonable to expect that property prices will generally increase. However, the claim that real estate prices double every seven to ten years is becoming less of a reality.

### Insight #4:

Inflation erodes the real value of your capital gain because a dollar tomorrow buys less than it will today.

### Insight #5:

I don't invest for a long-term capital gain – I can't use it to pay for my day-to-day needs and, as my objective is financial independence, it's not the profit outcome that will turn my dreams into reality. Regular cashflow income is what I require.

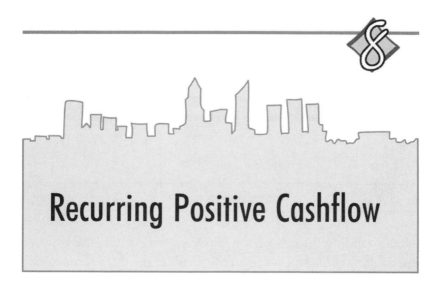

# Recurring Positive Cashflow

If the only way to make a profit in property was to invest for capital gains returns, I'd be a much stronger advocate for buying in a good location, and using real estate as a legal way to minimise tax. But capital appreciation is not the only way to make a profit in real estate. An alternative – and, in my opinion, a better option – is to invest for recurring positive cashflow returns. This delivers an instant profit that you can immediately use as a substitute for your wages.

## NET CASHFLOW RETURNS

The formula to calculate your net cashflow return is illustrated in Table 8.1, oveleaf. Be very careful not to confuse cashflow received and cashflow paid with the accounting terms 'income' and 'expense'. For example, if you were to use 'expenses' rather than 'cashflow paid', non-cash depreciation charges would be included, while the principal component on your loan repayments would be omitted. A lot of companies have gone broke making a paper profit, so good cashflow is seen as a cornerstone of success in a well-run business.

| Table 8.1 – Formula to Calculate Your Cashflow Return | | |
|---|---|---|
| | Cashflow received | $ |
| Less | Cashflow paid | $ |
| Equals | **Net cashflow** | $ |

Understanding the distinction between profit and cashflow was a particularly difficult transition for me to make. As an accountant I had been trained to believe that *profitability* was an excellent measure of performance. Yet as an investor, my focus is *cashflow* since it directly relates to dollars in the bank; my philosophy is if I have more money at the end of the day than I did at the start, then it's been a good day. Table 8.2, opposite, shows this difference in philosophy.

### Steve's Investing Tip

If you have more money at the end of the day than you did at the beginning, then it's been a good day.

You can also measure your cashflow return in percentage terms, which is especially helpful when comparing projects. The way I do this is by calculating the cash on cash return, which is done by dividing your annual net cashflow return by the amount of cash spent buying the property.

| Table 8.2 – Who Measures What | |
|---|---|
| **WHAT *ACCOUNTANTS* MEASURE** | **WHAT *INVESTORS* MEASURE** |
| Income | Cashflow received |
| *Less* expenses | *Less* cashflow paid |
| *Equals* **Net Profit** | *Equals* **Net Cashflow** |

## Calculating the Cash on Cash Return

I like to keep things as simple as possible, which is why I like the cash on cash return. It's simply a matter of working out my net annual cashflow, and then dividing it by the cash I paid to acquire the property. Table 8.3, below, shows the difference between a return on investment and a cash on cash return.

| Table 8.3 – The Difference Between ROI and CoCR | |
|---|---|
| **Return On Investment (ROI)** | **Cash on Cash Return (CoCR)** |
| (Net profit ÷ Asset value) | (Net cashflow ÷ Cash outlay) |

Table 8.4, overleaf, is an example of one of the first positive cashflow properties that Dave and I bought. We heard about it when the agent rang us up and said the vendor wanted a no-fuss, quick sale and was willing to sell at a 'fire-sale' price. Similar units in the area were selling for between $40,000 and $45,000, yet the asking amount on this property was just $33,000. The rent was $90 per week.

With an annual cash on cash return of just 8.34%, I'd have to say that this was one of the lowest cashflow yields we have ever achieved. So why did we go ahead?

| Table 8.4 – Return on Unit Example | |
|---|---|
| **Purchase Price:** | **$33,000** |
| **INITIAL CASH SPENT TO ACQUIRE THE DEAL** | |
| Deposit (20%): | $6,600 |
| Closing costs: | $1,369 |
| Loan establishment | $2,004 |
| **Initial Cash Needed:** | **$9,973** |
| **OUR LOAN** | |
| Amount: | $26,400 |
| Type: | Principal and interest |
| Term: | 25 years |
| Initial interest rate: | 7.65% |
| **Weekly Repayment:** | **$45.51** |
| **ANNUAL CASHFLOW RECEIVED** | |
| Rent per week[1]: | $90 |
| **Annual Cashflow Received:** | **$4,680** |
| **ANNUAL CASHFLOW OUT** | |
| Loan repayment: | $2,367 |
| Management costs: | $234 |
| Rates: | $444 |
| Insurance: | $499 |
| Repairs budget: | $300 |
| Total cashflow out: | $3,844 |
| **Annual Net Cashflow:** | **$836** |

| Table 8.4 — Return on Unit Example *(cont'd)* | |
|---|---|
| **CASH ON CASH RETURN** | |
| Annual net cashflow: | $836 |
| ÷ Initial cash needed: | ÷ $9,973 |
| **Cash on Cash Return[2]:** | **8.38%** |

**Notes:**

1. When we purchased this property it came with a secure tenant on a long-term lease. As such we did not allow for any vacancies.

2. If we were measuring the profit rather than the cashflow on this deal then we would need to include the principal portion of the loan repayments. The interest component on our loan repayment was $2,007 making the principal component $360. As such the profit for tax and accounting purposes would be $1,196 ($836 + $360). As you can see, this would overstate the actual cashflow outcome.

There were two reasons:

1. We could acquire the property and make an instant capital gain. The epilogue to this deal was that we sold it 18 months later for $48,250. When you add the net capital gains and the positive cashflow, our annualised return was 150% per annum.

2. While the cash on cash return was on the low side, at least it was cashflow positive and earning a net return in excess of what we could achieve by having our money invested in the bank.

# THE FOUR VARIETIES OF CASHFLOW RETURNS

It doesn't matter whether you invest for passive income or capital gains, every property you buy will generate one of the following four varieties of cashflow returns.

## Type A: Positive Cashflow (Income) Returns

As you'd expect, a positive cashflow return occurs when your total cashflow received is more than your total cashflow spent. With this kind of outcome, it's very likely that you'll have to pay income tax because you're making money.

### A Quick Recap of 'The 11 Second Solution'

A great 'rule of thumb', which indicates whether or not a property is likely to be positive cashflow is 'The 11 Second Solution' (as outlined on page 30). By way of a quick reminder, the formula for 'The 11 Second Solution' is:

## Steve's 11 Second Solution

(Weekly rent ÷ 2)   x   1,000

The best way to become familiar with how 'The 11 Second solution' works is to have a go at it yourself using the template in Table 8.5, below.

| Table 8.5 – 'The 11 Second Solution' Matrix | | | |
|---|---|---|---|
| | **EXAMPLE OF:** | | |
| | **Caravan Park (p. 83)** | **Commercial Property (p. 87)** | **Unit (p. 110)** |
| 1: What is the weekly rent? | $1,120 | $425 | $90 |
| 2: Divide the weekly rent by 2 | _____ | _____ | _____ |
| 3: Multiply the result by $1,000 | _____ | _____ | _____ |
| 4: Is the property priced at, or below, this figure? | _____ | _____ | _____ |

The answers can be found at:

> www.PropertyInvesting.com/11SecondSolution

## Type B: Negative Cashflow Returns

A negative cashflow return occurs when your cashflow paid is more than your cashflow received. In other words, unlike positive cashflow where you're making money, a negative cashflow outcome means you're losing money. Negative cashflow properties are typically advertised with "Own an investment property from just $9.37 (or some other nominal figure) per week."

## Type C: Positive Cashflow/Income Negative

This investment category can be a little complicated to understand, but the following factors are usually present:

▷ Looking at the investment alone, the cashflow received is less than the cashflow paid (i.e. it is negative cashflow).

▷ Non-cash tax deductible expenses, such as depreciation and building write-offs can provide perceived tax benefits.

▷ After adjusting for the tax losses, which are offset against other taxable income, the initial negative cashflow becomes an overall positive cashflow (as the tax benefits are greater than the cashflow loss).

Confused? Don't feel alone. This concept is further explained in Chapter 9.

## Type D: Cashflow Neutral

A cashflow neutral outcome exists when your cashflow received equals your cashflow paid.

### Which is Better... Capital Gains or Cashflow Returns?

One of the most common questions I'm asked is "Should I invest for capital gains or cashflow returns?" There has been a lot of debate about this issue lately and the property experts seem divided. Some swear that capital appreciation is the way to go, whereas others strongly advocate positive cashflow returns.

The truth is that there's no absolute right answer. In other words, the best anyone can say is "It depends". Depends on what? Well, the reason why you want to make a profit in the first place. You need to clarify your investing purpose so that you can decide what type of property you should buy to obtain an outcome that's consistent with your investing objective. This is an essential statement so I'm going to write it again.

### Steve's Investing Tip

The type of return you should aim for depends on what you're trying to achieve by investing.

## FINANCIAL INDEPENDENCE AND PASSIVE INCOME

Some investors perceive a flash car in the driveway and a boat harboured at the marina as the hallmarks of success, but if having an extravagant lifestyle compels you to keep working then it's your freedom that's the real casualty.

A focus on financial freedom is seeing more and more investors turning to a concept called financial independence. It's not necessarily sexy, nor does it involve a jet-setting lifestyle, but financial independence provides freedom and a release from the *need* to work. It can occur in varying degrees, from partial independence where you get to take a few hours off work a week, to complete financial freedom where you no longer need to work at all.

The way to secure financial independence is by acquiring recurring and sustainable sources of passive income (also known as residual income). Passive income is largely independent of how hard you work in your normal nine to five job.

I need to point out that a common mistake people make is to confuse passive income for getting paid to do nothing. I've found that there's no such thing as completely passive income, because every dollar of residual income is first created from some kind of work or effort. For example, while rental income might seem to be residual income, the task of finding and investing in property, together with managing the tenant, filling in tax returns, etc. is anything but passive!

A good example of passive income is royalty payments paid to musicians. They write a song once and are potentially paid a royalty each time the song is played. The initial act of writing and recording the song wasn't passive, but the ongoing payments when it is included on music CDs (sometimes many years later) is. Just think of The Beatles!

The word 'passive' really means not being paid by the hour. Instead you seek to work today to create a future cashflow stream, which is a form of time leverage.

Applying the concept to property, if you invest to achieve a positive cashflow outcome then you hope that the work involved in finding and acquiring the property will create ongoing passive income until you decide to sell. Put another way – it's one day's work now for a lifetime of returns later. If you're astute then you'll perceive this as a form of delayed gratification.

## Time and Money

To understand financial independence you need to value time more than money. As we age we begin to perceive that time is quickly running out. Sooner or later we even realise that time is actually more valuable than money. For example, if you knew the exact moment that you were going to pass away, what price would you put on your last hour alive? Time is finite – money isn't.

**Steve's Investing Tip**

The key to achieving financial independence is to value time more than money.

In our jobs, we sell our time in exchange for a salary. Financial independence is the reverse – trading money for time as we buy back the precious seconds and minutes that we'd otherwise have to spend working to fund our lifestyles.

Now, for some people, freedom from having to work means little because they love their jobs to begin with. That's fine... but wouldn't it be better if *you* had the power to decide whether or not you work? I'm sure that most of us have other things that we'd rather be doing than working. Simple things like giving more time to the kids, exploring spiritual matters, making the world a better place or maybe even playing more golf.

All this would be possible, if only we didn't have to work in the first place! After all, electricity isn't free and neither are the groceries. If you want to work less but don't want to take a cut in your lifestyle then you're going to need to focus on finding sources of passive income.

It's your choice whether you spend your time in such a way as to get paid once, or if you allocate it to sourcing and harvesting opportunities that will pay you into perpetuity.

## PASSIVE INCOME AND PROPERTY INVESTING

Let's do a quick review of the discussion so far in respect to financial freedom. There are two ways to make money in real estate.

1. Your property can increase in value; and/or

2. You can earn recurring positive cashflow, provided your annual cashflow received is higher than your cashflow paid out.

Both are valuable and can occur independently of each other. That is, you can have:

A.  Capital gains and negative or no cashflow returns (a negative cashflow position); or

B.  A positive cashflow return and no or negative capital appreciation (a positive cashflow position); or

C.  No capital appreciation and no positive cashflow (a cashflow neutral position).

Table 8.6, below, compares capital gains and cashflow returns.

| Table 8.6 – Funding Financial Independence | | |
|---|---|---|
| | **Capital Gains** | **Recurring Cashflow Returns** |
| *Sourced by:* | Ongoing capital appreciation | Annual cashflow received being higher than annual cashflow paid out |
| *Accessed by:* | Refinancing, loan drawdowns or selling | The annual positive cashflow surplus |
| *Dependent on:* | Increased market demand and the ability to refinance | Annual cashflow received remaining higher than annual cashflow paid out |
| *Once Spent on Lifestyle:* | Must wait for further capital gains | Wait until the next positive cashflow payment period (week/fortnight/month) |
| *Pay Tax:* | When you sell | As you go |
| *Likely Outcome:* | Need to remain in a job while earning capital gains | Can gradually scale back working as passive income rises |

## Which is Better, Capital Gains or Positive Cashflow Returns?

If you're looking to retire from your job without necessarily taking a lifestyle or pay cut, then it's critical to source regular and reliable passive income to replace the wages you'll forego when you cut back at work.

As shown in the 'Recurring Cashflow' column in Table 8.6 (previous page), one way you can achieve this outcome is by drawing down your capital appreciation. However, once you spend your capital gains on lifestyle expenses the money is gone forever. Your financial independence becomes dependent on further capital appreciation, which is by no means certain. While property prices generally trend up over the long term, they also experience periods of flat and even negative growth. You don't want to be caught short of cash and need to go back to the workforce.

On the other hand, positive cashflow returns regenerate, which means they continue indefinitely. Each week, fortnight or month you will receive a cash injection into your bank account that you can use to fund your lifestyle. When you run dry, you just have to wait another month! Sure, tenants will come and go and there may be times when your property will be vacant, but this risk can be mitigated with sensible landlording.

Positive cashflow returns occur independently of what is happening to property prices and, as such, are a more secure and reliable source of passive income. You can't use a capital appreciation Eftpos card to fund your weekly grocery bill, but you can pay for it out of a property's positive cashflow surplus. As such, if your investing purpose in buying real estate is financial independence, it makes sense to focus on positive cashflow returns first and capital appreciation second.

It's fair to say that different classes and types of property offer the potential for varying types and degrees of returns. Some properties are better suited to capital appreciation as they focus on location irrespective of cashflow returns (such as properties within a ten-kilometre radius of a capital city's central business district). At the other end of the spectrum, there are investments that offer high cashflow yields but little or no prospect of capital gains (such as regional or country properties).

Only *you* can determine which property is right for you. And this can only be done once you've clarified the investment outcome you're working towards. It's time for you to make another decision. Grab a pen and circle the multiple-choice answer from the selection in Table 8.7 below, that best summarises your investing purpose (only one answer is allowed).

| Table 8.7 – Multiple Choice Time (Circle Your Answer) | |
|---|---|
| **TODAY'S DATE:** | |
| *My End Purpose for Investing in Real Estate is...* | |
| A | Financial freedom within the next eight years or sooner. |
| B | Financial freedom, but I'm happy working in my job for the next decade or so. |
| C | So that when I reach retirement age I have a safe and secure nest egg of capital appreciation that I can draw on to live off for the rest of my life. |
| D | I don't know... I just want to read the next chapter! |

I'm well on the way to achieving option A and plan to be at my financial independence goal on or before 9 May 2004. I've done this by focusing solely on positive cashflow returns. Which of the options in Table 8.8, below, would you rather choose?

| Table 8.8 – Certain and Uncertain Property Outcomes | | |
|---|---|---|
| | ✓ | OUTCOME |
| *Either:* | | Buy a property that **will** make money from day one |
| | | Buy a property that **might** return a profit at some time in the future |

## Chapter 8 Insights

### Insight #1:

My favourite way to profit from property is via recurring positive cashflow returns (also known as passive income).

### Insight #2:

You can use the passive income you earn as a substitute for your wages, which will enable you to gradually divorce yourself from the need to work.

### Insight #3:

Leave the profit calculations to the accountants. Instead focus on cash-on-cash returns, which you can measure by dividing your net cashflow by the cash you needed to acquire the asset.

### Insight #4:

If you have more cash at the end of the month than you did at the beginning, then you're heading in the right direction.

### Insight #5:

Remember it's a journey! Two of my friends, Alina and Reiner, have a picture of a flying moneybox pig with a caption underneath that reads "Everyday we are growing more financially prosperous".

# Why 92% of Investors Only Own 1 or 2 Properties

Not long ago I was pedalling hard on the exercise bike at my local gym when Scott, an old friend from Primary School whom I hadn't seen for 18 years, approached me out of the blue. We eagerly began catching up and swapping life stories about our achievements since the glory days of late childhood.

Scott was interested to learn that I was investing in property and mentioned that another person we both knew from our early school days, Dean, had not long ago purchased an off-the-plan, inner city apartment and was considering buying another. Sensing that I might be able to provide some useful advice, Scott asked if it would be OK for Dean to contact me. I agreed and gave Scott my phone number. A few days later Dean rang and I invited both him and his girlfriend, Kim, over for dinner. After swapping our life stories since primary school, we launched right into the topic of property.

It turned out that a friend had given Dean and Kim a compact disc (the kind that have recently been infiltrating fish and chip shops by the thousands) outlining how property investing builds wealth. This CD was produced and published by a marketing company that makes a profit by sourcing buyers for developers; it was an electronic version of the 'all-hype, no-substance' seminar that my wife and I attended a few years earlier.

Convinced that owning property would improve their financial prosperity, Dean and Kim made a wealth assessment booking with a consultant from the marketing company. At the meeting they were shown the benefits of buying an off-the-plan, inner city apartment, including how doing so would save large amounts of stamp duty while also reducing their total annual income tax bill. They were also told that, being close to the city, their investment was primed to earn impressive capital gains.

An essential component of the free wealth assessment was the preparation of a tailored property summary pinpointing, in dollars and cents detail, how buying a property like those which the marketing company had available for sale was going to help make them rich.

Signing on the dotted line, Dean and Kim purchased an apartment on St Kilda Road in Melbourne. It was one in a complex of 192 dwellings. The contract price was $275,000 and, as this apartment building was being built from scratch, the scheduled completion date was 18 months after construction began.

Following on from their adviser's recommendation, Dean and Kim borrowed 100% of the purchase price by using equity in their home. Talking about their experience, Dean said "At the time we were sold on the idea, but later we realised everything we heard and saw was based on a best-case scenario.

"Only later did we begin to realise that the property was a huge obligation", Dean said. "When it came time to settle we had to come up with $27,500 for the deposit and we were also worried about the large number of other inner city properties which were about to come onto the market and how they might blow the capital gains potential of our investment out of the water."

"You have to understand, Steve, that the sales pitch was very slick", Kim said. "Having never purchased an investment property before, we were largely guided by the advice of the company we bought off and we were confident that the example we saw stacked up."

"Yes", Dean agreed "it all looked good on paper."

The apartment complex was finished two months after our dinner catch-up. Dean and Kim considered renting it out at $270 per week, but instead decided to sell their home and move into the apartment. Talking to Dean about their revised plans he said, "We thought that the time was right to cash-in on our home equity and reduce our debt. Besides, trying to rent the property with such a large mortgage meant that our cashflow would have broken-even at best."

I asked Dean whether or not he would consider buying another property off-the-plan. "No," he replied. "We wouldn't have been able to afford it. Having to make more mortgage repayments would max us out."

So, how is Dean and Kim's investment going? "The good news" Dean recently advised, "is we had a real estate agent complete a market appraisal on the apartment recently and it came in at $330,000. That's great because other people we know who also bought property off the plan in another part of town have done their dough. After allowing for sale costs (if we sold), loan interest and property costs – we have now broken even. At the end of the day though, we bought the property in the hope of having to work less, but we both seemed to end up working harder than ever."

Dean and Kim's experience is quite common. Each year, thousands of investors buy property in the hope that it will further their wealth creation plans, only to later discover that the assumptions on which they bought, such as expected capital gains and rental potential, were based on a best-case scenario – which is rarely achieved. Instead of getting out of the rat race, such investors often find themselves working harder than ever just to make ends meet.

### Steve's Investing Tip

When you buy off someone who stands to make a commission by closing the sale, you're paying a retail price for something that you might purchase for less if you bypassed the middleman.

## SURPRISING STATISTICS

In 1997 the Australian Bureau of Statistics (ABS) conducted a survey[1] of property investors with the following surprising results:

▷ 76% of investors owned **one** rental property

▷ 16% of investors owned **two** rental properties; and

▷ 8% of investors owned **three** or more rental properties.

These results are illustrated in Figure 9.1, opposite.

A 1990 New South Wales Department of Housing research paper[2] found a similar trend, reporting that only 3.6% of all NSW landlords own five or more properties. A question that must be asked is: *If owning real estate builds wealth, then why do so many investors own so few properties?* I would have thought that if becoming rich was just a matter of owning property then you wouldn't just stop at one or two – you'd want to acquire as many as possible.

---

1 – *Household Investors in Rental Dwellings, Australia, 1997* (Cat. No. 8711.0)

2 – *Rental for Investment – A Study of Landlords in NSW*, Research and Policy Paper No. 3, 1990.

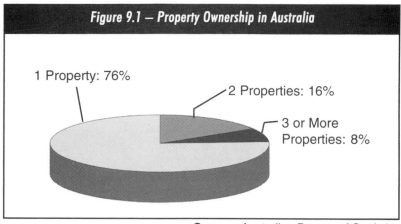

Figure 9.1 – Property Ownership in Australia

1 Property: 76%

2 Properties: 16%

3 or More Properties: 8%

**Source:** Australian Bureau of Statistics

One possible answer is the impact of land tax. Land tax is levied on the unimproved value of the land and is cumulative, meaning that the more land you own, the more land tax you have to pay. This might act to dissuade investors from owning multiple properties, but I don't think so since the amount of land tax payable on most residential investments is negligible and can be compensated via a minor increase in rent.

The reason I feel that investors are prevented from owning more properties is, just like in Dean and Kim's case, they simply cannot afford to own any more houses because they're not making enough money to pay for further acquisitions. The majority of property investors seems to adopt a 'wait and see' approach which, in practical terms, means continuing to work in a job and paying off their mortgage while waiting for prices to rise. Yet what the ABS data reveals is that this approach does not work particularly well, since only 8% of investors manage to find a way to afford three or more properties.

However, this is not to say that the capital gains focus does not work. As I've outlined in Chapter 7, if you allow enough time, prices will eventually increase, if for no other reason than to keep pace with inflation.

These statistics shocked me into realising that my success was dependent on doing something different, for if I followed the model that other investors were using, then I could expect the same results. My goal was to work less, not more!

## Steve's Investing Tip

If you follow the approach adopted by the majority of property investors then it stands to reason that you'll achieve similar results: You will only own one or two investment properties and will need to keep working in your job. Is that what you're trying to achieve?

OK. I knew I had to do something differently, but what? Where do you find someone who'll personally mentor you as you try to build a real estate portfolio that will put you in the top 1% of all property investors? I looked hard and apart from the occasional speaker from the United States doing the seminar circuit, I couldn't find one Australian real estate investment guru offering anything other than the usual negative gearing spiel. Taking the initiative, I began to think in revolutionary terms by challenging every accepted property idea I'd ever heard.

Starting from scratch, it wasn't long before I began building my own revolutionary investing system that most of my family and friends thought was little more than scary new age thinking. Dave, my business partner, also committed to the goal of financial freedom. When he outlined our plans to his father he was rebuked with "Stop playing games and get a real job for the sake of your family".

My re-education was, and continues to be, a journey rather than an outcome. Sometimes I'd succeed and source a property that met my selection criteria. On other occasions I'd experience setbacks, like the time I was angrily abused by a real estate agent for successfully selling a property the week after I'd bought it through them for an additional $25,000. He incredulously suggested I should pay the original vendor a further $5,000, in which case I wouldn't be such a bad person after all. I was speechless.

Each new experience enabled me to tweak my investing system until the results weren't so much due to luck, but the execution of a structured plan providing an expected outcome.

## SUMMARY

Let me be blunt. The reason why 92% of investors only own one or two properties is because they can't afford to own any more. Even worse – the houses they do own require them to stay in their jobs to be able to make the repayments. This doesn't sound like a wealth building outcome to me.

## Chapter 9 Insights

### Insight #1:

If owning real estate builds wealth then it makes sense that you would want to own as much of it as possible. Why is it then, that 92% of investors only manage to acquire one or two rental properties?

The reason why so many investors own so few properties is simply that they cannot afford to own more. Instead of building wealth, their approach to property investment keeps them needing to work, so if your goal is to regain control over your time, a different strategy is needed.

### Insight #2:

If you want the same result as 92% of property investors then follow their lead and invest in the 'normal' way, which is negative gearing. If not, then you're going to have to do something different in order to achieve a different outcome.

# 10

# The Truth Behind the Hype of Negative Gearing

Let's briefly fast forward in time to mid-2001. At this point Dave and I had purchased around 40 properties that provided roughly $100,000 per annum in passive income. In particular, there is one August day I want to focus on. It was a beautiful morning – sunny, yet quite cold – typical for Melbourne as winter draws to an end and the promise of spring is in the air. I'd risen out of bed early and caught the train into town where I'd arranged to meet Tim, our 20-year-old office manager. I'd given him the day off and we were both attending a free wealth creation seminar being staged by a group of Americans as part of a national speaking circuit.

It began at 9 am sharp with the first presenter outlining the way he'd made a fortune from buying blocks of units (in Alaska I think) and then subdividing them and selling them off individually. The idea was that the receipts from the sale of the individual units would be far more than the lump sum paid for the entire block.

For example, if you bought a block of ten units for one million dollars and then sold them individually for $125,000 each, then your profit (before costs and tax) would be $250,000 ([$125,000 x 10] – $1,000,000).

There wasn't a lot by way of specific detail provided, but one important overhead that caught my attention was a photocopy of a six-figure cheque. Conveniently though, there was a thin black line through the date so we couldn't tell how long ago this amazing opportunity occurred, but by the look of the bank stationery, it was quite old – possibly early 1980s.

"It's really that easy to make money!" the presenter enthusiastically said. "Here, let me show you again..." Once again the presenter provided some general numbers before making claims that he'd managed to secure 100% financing and that the deal provided positive cashflow. The end result was that he'd converted just $10 into $1,000,000 – with no risk and very little effort.

I was stunned... this guy had captivated the audience with the flimsiest of details. All he had done was pull a financial white rabbit out of his magical wealth creation hat to gasps of awe and rounds of applause. Surely people aren't that naive, I thought. Personally, without having seen any substance or reliable numbers my internal 'BS meter' was showing a reading off the scale.

Mentally leaving the presentation for a while, I used the pen, paper and calculator that I'd brought with me to conjure up all manner of financial models, but no matter how hard I tried, there was simply no way I could make his numbers add up. By the time I rejoined the presentation, the presenter had added an extra zero and turned one million into ten million. The majority of the audience still seemed to be lapping it all up, numbed by the prospect of massive riches.

Nudging Tim I asked incredulously, "How did he do that?"

Tim began to reply "Well... he..."

"Don't worry," I interjected.

Returning my attention to my trusty pen and paper, I began to draft up graphical representations to illustrate the two ways of investing in real estate – negative and positive gearing. By the time I'd finished my initial sketches, the presenter was making his sales pitch – a "never to be repeated" discount only available for the next half an hour. He invited people interested in buying to join him at the back of the room and immediately there was a rush to exchange credit cards for plastic bags filled with tapes, folders and the presenter's personal business card with his home phone number on it.

Did his strategy work for Australian conditions? Who knows – and as far as the presenter was concerned, once the sales were made, who could care? Shaking my head in disbelief, I made a silent pledge that I was going to work hard to help ordinary investors bust through the hype and see that the fundamentals of investing are quite basic.

Tim saw some benefit in staying to hear all the speakers but I couldn't stomach any more of the hype so I returned to the office to continue to finetune my initial designs. The following day Tim told me that the remainder of the event was more of the same hard sell and little of anything that was of real benefit.

## THE NEGATIVE GEARING MODEL

The challenge before me, while sitting at that free seminar, was to somehow draw up a diagram that cut through all the hype of negative gearing to explain how the concept worked in a way that was easy to understand. Here's what I came up with.

### Step 1 in the Negative Gearing Model:
### Equity and Lifestyle

The negative gearing model begins with you working in your job, from which you earn money that can be invested, less your living

expenses, income tax instalments and superannuation payments. Any surplus is collected in your savings account. Alternatively, you might already have equity in your home or other assets that you can use to fund the acquisition of investment properties.

## Step 2 in the Negative Gearing Model:
## Choosing to Invest

The diagram on the right illustrates Step 2 in the Negative Gearing model. Once you've accumulated equity or savings, you can use your cash and/ or equity to pay for the deposit and closing costs on properties you purchase. The black arrow pointing towards your property represents the redistribution of wealth from your equity or savings into your real estate portfolio.

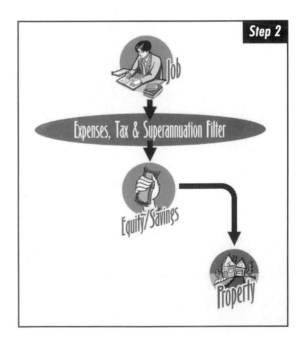

## Step 3 in the Negative Gearing Model: Cash Outflow

When you acquire a negatively geared property, not only is there a once-off payment (for the deposit and closing costs), there's an ongoing cash outflow too, which arises because your property's cash outflows are higher than your property's cash inflows. This cash shortfall is illustrated by the arrow from equity/savings, through the cashflow circle and into the property icon.

If you buy a negatively geared property then you do so knowing that your dwelling is certain to create a cashflow shortfall that must be funded by either:

1. Your after-tax salary – which ties you to your job; and/or

2. Equity in other assets you own – which will increase your level of debt.

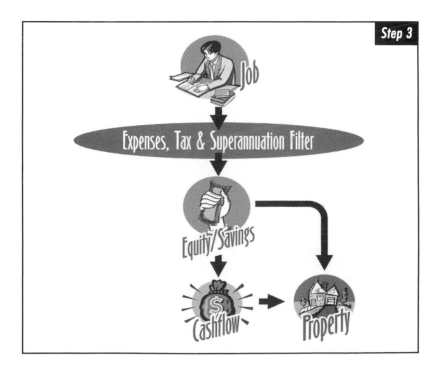

## Step 4 in the Negative Gearing Model: Capital Gains

The only two ways you can profit from a negatively geared property are:

1.  When your property rises in value at a rate in excess of the after tax loss plus inflation – otherwise you're simply recycling your money at a low, no, or negative return; and/or

2.  If your cashflow increases and/or the expenses decrease so that it becomes positively geared.

Capital gains are shown in the diagram below via the dotted line.

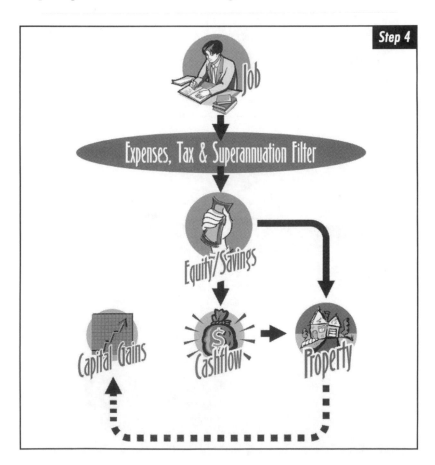

I've used a dotted line for two reasons – first, capital gains are not certain and second, capital gains usually come in fits and starts rather than steady and reliable long-term increases.

## Step 5 in the Negative Gearing Model: Reinvestment

Our final diagram, below, reveals the last stage of the negative gearing model. Once you've earned capital gains then you can access these profits (see Chapter 18) and use the proceeds to either fund your lifestyle or to acquire more assets.

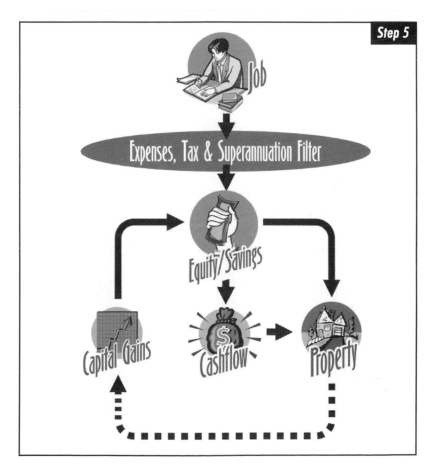

An important point to note is that in the absence of further savings, the only way you can continue to afford additional properties is by accessing the equity you earn from capital gains. Since capital gains generally take a number of years to accrue, expanding your property portfolio can take a long time, which is more evidence to account for the fact that 92% of investors only own one or two properties.

## THE TRUTH BEHIND THE HYPE

When you negatively gear your investment there are only two possible cashflow outcomes (as explained on pages 111–114):

1.   Negative cashflow – *Type B cashflow return*; and

2.   Positive Cashflow/Income Negative – *Type C cashflow return*.

Understanding the difference can be a little confusing, so let's use two numerical examples to try to explain.

Imagine you buy a brand new property for $190,000. It's completed six months later and your budgeted first year's cashflow is shown in Table 10.1, below.

| Table 10.1 – Type B and Type C Cashflow Property Investments | |
|---|---|
| **PROPERTY 1**<br>*Genuine Negative Cashflow*<br>*(Type B Cashflow Outcome)* | **PROPERTY 2**<br>*Income Negative/Cashflow Positive*<br>*(Type C Cashflow Outcome)* |
| **Property Summary** | **Property Summary** |
| Property value[1]            $190,000 | Property value            $190,000 |
| Deposit and closing costs[2]        $0 | Deposit and closing costs[3]        $47,500 |
| Loan amount[4]            $190,000 | Loan amount[4]            $152,000 |

*Cont'd...*

| Table 10.1 – Type B and Type C Cashflow Property Investments (cont'd) | |
| --- | --- |
| **PROPERTY 1** *Genuine Negative Cashflow* *(Type B Cashflow Outcome)* | **PROPERTY 2** *Income Negative/ Cashflow Positive* *(Type C Cashflow Outcome)* |
| **Cashflow Summary** | **Cashflow Summary** |
| *INCOME* | *INCOME* |
| Rent[5]     $10,400 | Rent[5]     $10,400 |
| *EXPENSES* | *EXPENSES* |
| Rates     ($1,500) | Rates     ($1,500) |
| Insurance[6]     ($1,150) | Insurance     ($550) |
| Loan interest[4]     ($14,250) | Loan interest[4]     ($11,400) |
| Rental agent fees[7]     ($1,000) | Rental agent fees[7]     ($1,000) |
| Total expenses     ($17,900) | Total expenses     ($14,450) |
| Cashflow loss     ($7,500) | Cashflow loss     ($4,050) |
| **Other Allowable Tax Deductions** | **Other Allowable Tax Deductions** |
| Building write down[8]     ($2,750) | Building write down[8]     ($2,750) |
| Chattel depreciation[9]     ($3,600) | Chattel depreciation[9]     ($3,600) |
| Acquisition costs[10]     ($1,320) | Acquisition costs[10]     ($1,320) |
| Total non-cash amounts     ($7,670) | Total non-cash amounts     ($7,670) |
| Cashflow loss     ($7,500) | Cashflow loss     ($4,050) |
|     ($15,170) |     ($11,720) |
| Tax saving[11]     $6,599 | Tax saving[11]     $5,098 |

*Cont'd...*

| Table 10.1 – Type B and Type C Cashflow Property Investments (cont'd) | |
| --- | --- |
| **PROPERTY 1**<br>*Genuine Negative Cashflow*<br>*(Type B Cashflow Outcome)* | **PROPERTY 2**<br>*Income Negative/ Cashflow Positive*<br>*(Type C Cashflow Outcome)* |
| **After-Tax Investment Position** | **After Tax Investment Position** |
| Gross cashflow ($7,500) | Gross cashflow ($4,050) |
| Tax saving $6,599 | Tax saving $5,098 |
| Owner's contribution ($901) | After-tax cashflow $1,048 |
| – Per day[4] ($2.47) | – Per day[4] $2.87 |

**Notes:**

1. The figure of $190,000 includes the purchase price and all acquisition/closing costs too.

2. Assuming that you have equity in other property, you can use this collateral and take out a deposit bond instead of having to use your savings. The cost will be about $600.

3. Buying the same property but paying a 20% deposit and closing costs of $9,500 shows how a property can turn from negative cashflow to positive cashflow (after tax).

4. The loan attracts interest at 7.5% p.a. (interest-only). The cost per day is the total divided by 365.

5. Rent is charged at $200 per week and because there's a rental guarantee for three years, we'll assume that there are no vacancies.

6. Insurance includes the deposit bond of $600.

7. Rental fees at 7% ($728) plus letting and advertising costs ($272).

8. Building value is $110,000 and is written down at 2.5%.

9. The property comes with chattels worth $30,000 that can be depreciated at 12%.

10. We can claim a tax deduction for a portion of the acquisition ($3,960) costs over three years.

11. Applying a personal tax rate of 43.5%, the amount of the loss can be used to offset other taxable income and reduce the overall amount of income tax payable.

## Analysis

At a pre-tax level, it doesn't matter whether you buy Property 1 or Property 2 because they both provide a negative cashflow outcome – put more bluntly, they both lose money, as shown in Table 10.2 below.

| Table 10.2 – Summary: Pre-Tax Cashflow Outflow | | |
|---|---|---|
| | **Property 1** | **Property 2** |
| Pre-tax cash outflow | ($7,500) | ($4,050) |

However, Table 10.3 shows that, after tax, Property 1 loses money whereas Property 2 makes money.

| Table 10.3 – Summary: After-Tax Cashflow | | |
|---|---|---|
| **After-Tax Cashflow** | **Property 1** | **Property 2** |
| Gain/loss | ($901) | $1,048 |

The reason why Property 2 now makes an after-tax cashflow gain is twofold. First, Property 1 is 100% financed, meaning that the interest payments are a lot higher than Property 2, which only has a loan for 80% of the purchase price. The additional gearing means higher interest costs that ultimately result in Property 1 having a bigger cashflow loss.

Secondly, as Tables 10.4 and 10.5 (overleaf) reveal, the non-cash tax deductible expenses act to transform the negative cashflow into a positive cashflow. If you owned Property 2 and, assuming you paid income tax at 43.5%, then the total tax loss of $11,720 would translate into an income tax offset of $5,098 ($11,110 x 43.5%). As the amount of your tax deduction ($5,098) is more than your cashflow loss ($4,050), it stands to reason that you'll actually make an after-tax cashflow gain.

| Table 10.4 – The Tax Impact of Non-Cash Expenses | | | |
|---|---|---|---|
| PROPERTY 2 | | | |
| | Gross Amount | Tax Deduction at 43.5% | Unrecouped Loss |
| Pre-tax cashflow loss | ($4,050) | $1,762 | ($2,288) |
| Total non-cash tax deductions: | | | |
| – Building depr. | ($2,750) | $1,196 | ($1,554) |
| – Chattel depr. | ($3,600) | $1,566 | ($2,034) |
| – Acquisition costs | ($1,320) | $574 | ($746) |
| | ($7,670) | $3,336 | ($4,334) |
| **Total Tax Loss** | **($11,720)** | **$5,098** | **($6,622)** |

| Table 10.5 – Turning a Negative into a Positive | |
|---|---|
| Cashflow loss | ($4,050) |
| Tax deduction | $5,098 |
| **After-Tax Positive Cashflow** | **$1,048** |

Given that we're now earning positive cashflow, should we be happy with this result? No, I don't think so. I regard the use of non-cash tax deductions to turn negative into positive cashflow as dangerous. While I've gone into a detailed analysis in Appendix A, I'd also like to raise four quick points here too.

### Issue #1 – You're Still Losing Money

Never lose sight of the fact that, in order to qualify for a tax deduction, you must actually incur a loss or outgoing which can only ever be recouped to the extent of your marginal tax rate (i.e. to a maximum of 48.5%).

For example, in Table 10.4, our taxable loss of $11,720 gave rise to a tax offset of $5,098. The remainder of $6,622 ($11,720 – $5,098) must be paid for out of your savings and will hopefully be recouped over time as a capital gain.

### Steve's Investing Tip

Sometimes making a loss is said to be a good way of reducing your tax. This is a very limiting belief, because the more tax you save, the more money you'll lose.

### Issue #2 – There's a Limit to the Number of Properties You Can Afford to Own

Once you've wiped out your tax bill then all the depreciation benefits in the world won't help you to plug the nasty cashflow hole in your hip pocket. For more information on this point see Appendix A.

### Issue #3 – Tax Deferral, Not Tax Savings

Claiming depreciation allows tax deferral, not tax savings. Eventually you'll either need to spend money replacing or repairing the asset, or alternatively all the depreciation claims will be recouped in the form of capital gains when you sell. As such, no one is saving tax by claiming a deduction for property losses – all they're doing is deferring the payment of tax until a later date. This might seem like a minor point, but when it comes time to sell, the value of your property for tax purposes might be a lot less than what you paid for the property, this could leave you with a taxable capital gain a lot higher than your cashflow profit.

For example, let's imagine that you've owned Property 2 for five years (assuming all the variables stay the same as in year one) and then you decide to sell it for $240,000 (net of sale costs). Table 10.6, below, summarises your taxable gain.

| Table 10.6 – The Difference Between a Paper Profit and a Taxable Capital Gain | | |
|---|---|---|
| | **CASHFLOW GAIN** | **TAXABLE GAIN** |
| Purchase price | $190,000 | $190,000 |
| Non-cash tax deductions | | |
| Year 1 | | ($7,670) |
| Year 2 | | ($7,670) |
| Year 3 | | ($7,670) |
| Year 4 | | ($7,670) |
| Year 5 | | ($7,670) |
| | | ($38,350) |
| Written down value | $190,000 | $151,650 |
| Sale price | $240,000 | $240,000 |
| **Paper Profit:** | **$50,000** | |
| **Taxable Gain:** | | **$88,350** |

If you think that you're making a gain of $50,000, you might get a nasty surprise to discover that you'll have to pay tax on $88,350!

### *Issue # 4 – The Fatal Flaw is the Silent Assumption*

In order to pay enough tax to soak up your property depreciation benefits you'll have to earn a substantial salary. To earn a substantial salary you'll have to work hard. If you don't want to continue to work for the medium to long-term, or you don't earn enough money to soak up the tax deductions then, unfortunately, negative gearing might look good on paper, but it fails the true wealth creation litmus test in real life.

## Crackers

It's time to tell you about Crackers – another real estate agent in Ballarat. While he's gone on to achieve some pretty impressive things, when I first met him he was the kid fresh out of high school, employed to drive around putting up and taking down 'For Sale' signs, as well as running general errands.

One day I wanted to complete a property inspection and the only person available to show me through the house was Crackers. Normally he wouldn't be given such responsibility, but his supervisor knew we'd met before and that I wasn't looking to be dazzled by an impressive sales display.

After about five minutes of walking through the house, it was clear it wasn't what I was looking for as it was in a shabby condition and a touch overpriced. On the way back to the car Crackers and I struck up a conversation about investment property and the difference between making and losing money.

Crackers was intrigued that Dave and I seemed to be buying a lot of properties whereas other investors stopped after about one or two acquisitions. I began explaining the difference between positive and negative gearing, and sensing an eager young mind, I went into quite a bit of depth. Perhaps I went into a little too much detail, because when I'd finished, Crackers simply replied "Steve, where I come from a positive is always better than a negative!"

Feeling like I'd been shown an easy way to solve a complicated problem, I was temporarily speechless before being totally impressed by the ability of this young kid to grasp a concept that many adults can't.

## WHEN TO USE NEGATIVE GEARING

Negative gearing is like a knife – used at the right time, it has tremendous benefits. However, when used incorrectly it has the potential to cause great harm. Generally, I believe negative gearing is a poor long-term strategy for wealth creation because:

1. Your gains are savagely eroded by inflation.

2. When you decide to sell you'll pay capital gains tax on your lump-sum profits. If this is at retirement then a significant percentage of your gain will flow into the hands of the taxman.

3. It keeps you bound to your job, either to fund the negative cashflow or to make use of the depreciation deductions.

4. It only builds wealth when property prices are increasing.

5. The more properties you own the poorer you become (see Appendix A).

Although it might seem at odds with what I've written, I am not totally against the idea of negative gearing. All I'm against is the hard-sell or hype that dupes many investors into buying property for the wrong reasons.

So, can negative gearing ever be a good investment? Yes. Negative gearing is an excellent strategy, but only if your timing is right. Provided you get in and out at the right time, then you stand to make a lot of money. For example, take a look at Figure 10.1, opposite, which tracks quarterly median Melbourne house prices since March 1980.

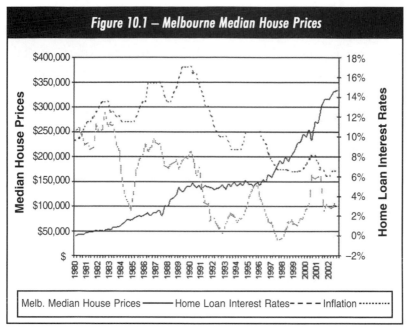

**Figure 10.1 – Melbourne Median House Prices**

**Source:** Data from the REIA and Reserve Bank of Australia

With the benefit of hindsight you could say that there have been two prime time periods for capital gains:

> **Period 1:** March 1988 until June 1990, when median property prices rose from $100,000 to $147,000. At this time interest rates had briefly fallen before hitting all time highs. Inflation was around the 8% mark.

> **Period 2:** March 1997 until March 2002, when property prices rose from $158,000 to $316,500.

It's interesting to speculate about what's caused the sustained and dramatic price rise since March 1997. Certainly falling interest rates have helped make home loan repayments more affordable. Inflation was also falling to its lowest level in 20 years. This, together with the pent up demand over the previous flat seven or so years may have triggered the initial spike in property.

145

But in mid-2000, just as the market seemed to be pausing for breath and prices dipped, a new wave of demand carried property prices even higher. Then in mid-2001 a further wave struck again and prices rose further after the First Home Owner Grant was introduced and even more demand hit the market.

What will happen next? It could take off again or alternatively we may have seen the top and might now expect a period of time when prices will, again, be flat or, given the nature of the rapid increase, slightly decline.

What's important to note though is that our analysis of the Melbourne median house price market over the 22 years between March 1980 and March 2002 has revealed:

▷ We've had historic high-low extremes in interest and inflation rates.

▷ There have only been two instances of substantial growth totalling six and a half years (approximately 30% of the time).

▷ For the remaining 16 years (70% of the time), the market has generally trended slightly up or churned sideways.

If buying property for capital gains only works 30% of the time, then it seems to me that it's a pretty ineffectual long-term wealth creation strategy. As such, negative gearing would be appropriate only when the market is experiencing rapid growth.

## What to Look for to Time Your Entry and Exit in the Market

It's very easy to look back with hindsight and say that a great time to buy was in March 1997. In practice though, it's a lot more difficult. At the time the smart money seemed to be in shares, which were at the beginning of the tech boom. There was also a lot of fear about home loan interest rates with many people remembering the highs of 17% only a few years earlier. Now, however, we can identify the favourable (and conversely unfavourable) market conditions to watch out for next time in order to try to time our entry and exit in the property market. Factors such as:

## *1. Interest Rates*

Without doubt, interest rates have the biggest influence on property prices since they directly affect the affordability of property. Looking back at Figure 10.1 on page 145, it was not until interest rates fell to, and remained below, approximately 8% that property prices really started to boom.

The 30-year average bank home loan interest rate (between December 1972 and December 2002) is 10.58%. This suggests that we are currently in a period of wholesale interest rates.

Home loan interest rates will eventually rise, and when they do, I belieive there will be a shift in the psychology of investors, particularly as rates approach the 8% mark.

## *2. Concessional Tax Treatment*

If the government were to abolish tax deductions for the loss components of negatively geared transactions (like they did in the United States), then there would be a substantial price correction as many investors would be forced to sell their properties, which would no longer be affordable. Even less severe changes in government policy, such as a removal of the First Home Owner Grant or the 50% capital gains tax discount would impact on the psychology of investors and perhaps produce a shift in the momentum of prices.

## *3. Unemployment and Economic Decline*

The good times won't last forever. Every economy moves through periods of growth and recession. Increases in unemployment, especially amongst white-collar professionals, will impact on the demand for housing.

### 4. General Supply and Demand

This point is aimed fairly and squarely at the inner city apartment market. A glut of supply without rises in demand must see prices stagnate or fall.

### 5. Key Real Estate Statistics

*Auction Clearance Rates*

The number of properties sold and passed in at weekend auctions is usually reported in the major daily papers. Looking at the trend in terms of percentage of properties sold (called the auction clearance rate) provides a good indication of the strength of the property market.

*Rental Vacancies*

If rental vacancies are high then it might be that a lot of people are competing in the home buying market. As rental vacancies decrease it could be an indication that house prices have reached a ceiling in terms of affordability.

## SUMMARY

Don't expect a major headline to appear in the daily paper telling you when the time is right to buy or sell property. Instead you need to be alert to the signals which may trigger or indicate a shift in the psychology of the market.

If you're investing for capital gains then remember that your goal is not necessarily to buy lowest and sell highest. The aim is to buy low and sell high, or maybe even buy high and sell higher.

## The Bottom Line on Negative Gearing

My aim has *not* been to pour freezing cold water on the idea of negative gearing. Rather my objective has been to present an independent perspective outlining that all is not as rosy as the free seminar presenters would have you believe. When you allow for holding costs, tax and inflation, negative gearing does not seem like a great long-term wealth creation strategy. Indeed, when prices are flat or going backwards then negative gearing builds no wealth at all.

### Steve's Investing Tip

For negative gearing to be effective you need the loss that you're **certain** to make today to be lower than the profit you **might** make tomorrow.

Since I didn't want my wealth creation plans and financial independence to be a matter of chance, it became apparent that negative gearing was not an investing tactic that would bring me closer to my ultimate goal of financial independence inside five years.

### Steve's Investing Tip

Is your success a matter of choice or a matter of chance?

The only way I've been able to acquire 130 properties in such a short amount of time has been to throw the approach to traditional real estate investing straight into the bin and to adopt an altogether different methodology.

## The Negative Gearing Model

When I taught at RMIT I was given the responsibility of lecturing one of the most technically difficult subjects on the curriculum – Advanced Financial Accounting. In fact, I'd studied this subject a few years earlier as a student and only managed to grasp about 50% of the content. This wasn't RMIT's fault – it was more to do with my attitude to study and the complex nature of the subject matter. However, as the teacher I needed to know the topics like an expert or else risk being made to look like a fool.

What I found was that when I could explain the concept, sometimes in three or four different ways, and also answer questions too, then my own understanding grew tremendously.

### Your Homework

Your homework is to explain how negative gearing works to a friend or family member using Figure 10.2, opposite. Remember to encourage questions, since answering them will determine how well you understand the concept.

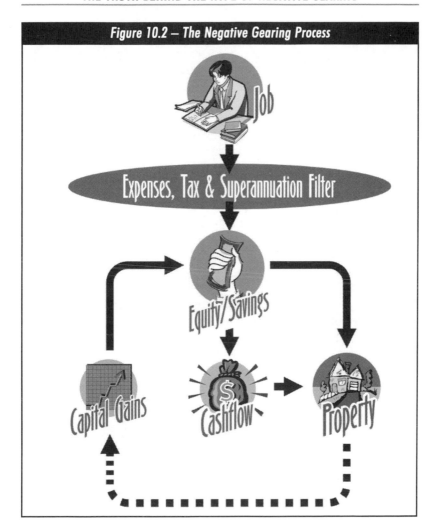

Figure 10.2 – The Negative Gearing Process

## Chapter 10 Insights

### Insight #1:

Negative gearing is a strategy designed to make a loss. Since when did making a loss sound like a good idea?

### Insight #2:

You can't save tax, only defer it.

### Insight #3:

For negative gearing to be effective the capital gains must be higher than your holding costs, tax and inflation.

### Insight #4:

The diagram below represents the impact on your cashflow as you acquire multiple negatively geared properties. Wealth creation is about expanding your empire, not watching it diminish in ever decreasing circles.

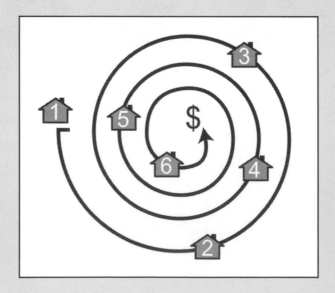

### Chapter 10 Insights *(cont'd)*

#### Insight #5:

Negative gearing can work, provided you time your entry into and out of the market. As such, it's a useful short-term strategy while prevailing market conditions are favourable.

#### Insight #6:

Negative gearing will keep you in a job. If you want to be free from the need to work then it's not a strategy you would want to adopt in the long-term.

#### Insight #7:

Why lose money when you can invest in property and make money from day one?

# The Positive Cashflow Model for Property Success

Although this is a long chapter, it contains some of the most important insights in this book about how I've been able to buy so much property in such a short period of time. So, grab yourself a coffee and let's knuckle down.

## MONEY NOW OR MONEY LATER?

**Steve's Investing Tip**

Losing money is *never* a good idea.

If the only way to invest in property was via negatively geared real estate then perhaps I'd understand why so many intelligent investors become convinced that losing money today for the sake of making money tomorrow is a good idea.

The key to understanding my approach to property investing is to answer the question in Table 11.1 below.

| Table 11.1 – Multiple Choice Time (Circle Your Answer) | |
| --- | --- |
| **TODAY'S DATE:** | |
| *Which Would You Rather Have?* | |
| A | A dollar now; or |
| B | A dollar in a year's time. |

Ideally you'd want both, but at least take the dollar now so you can invest it and earn interest. Besides, a dollar in a year's time will buy less because of the impact of inflation.

## THE POSITIVE GEARING MODEL

Remember the seminar that Dave and I attended which changed our lives forever? The revelation we walked away with was that there was a way to invest in real estate (called *positive cashflow* or *positively geared* invest-

ing) that allowed us to make money, in the form of a cashflow return, from day one.

### Step 1 in the Positive Gearing Model: Equity and Lifestyle

Step 1 in the positive gearing model is exactly the same as the first step in the negative gearing model outlined on page 131. You work in your job to earn income from which expenses, tax and superannuation must be deducted. Any surplus accumulates as savings, which can be used to pay the deposit and closing costs on investment property. Alternatively, if you can access equity, then you may be able to borrow against it to buy property irrespective of how much money you've saved.

## Step 2 in the Positive Gearing Model:
## Choosing to Invest

The second step in the positive gearing model is again conceptually the same as the negative gearing model in that you use your equity and/or savings to fund the deposit and clos- ing costs on your property investment.

The redistribution of wealth from savings into property is shown in the chart opposite by the solid arrow out of the equity/savings circle and into the property circle.

## Step 3 in the Positive Cashflow Model:
## Positive Cashflow

OK. Here's where it starts to get interesting. Do you remember that in the negative gearing model the cashflow icon was under the savings circle, representing a net cashflow loss? Well, in the positive cashflow model, the cashflow icon flows on from the property circle, indicating that your positively geared property makes money from day one – irrespective of whether or not you're experiencing any capital appreciation. Your net positive cashflow return is created by the surplus of your cash inflows over your cash outflows.

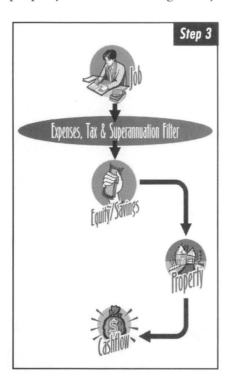

### What's a Good Cashflow Return?

Making a dollar is certainly better than losing a dollar, but it's important to try to match the return on offer with the risk of your investment. Which of the investments in Table 11.2 would you be comfortable with?

| Table 11.2 – Multiple Choice Time (Circle Your Answer) | | |
|---|---|---|
| **TODAY'S DATE:** | | |
| *Would You Enter into These Investments?* | | |
| **Investment 1** | $5,000 down to make a profit of $1,000 but with a 95% chance you could lose the lot. | Yes |
| | | No |
| **Investment 2** | $5,000 down with a 1% chance you would lose the lot to make a profit of $100. | Yes |
| | | No |

**Steve's Investing Tip**

A general rule of investing is: the higher the return, the higher the risk.

The sorts of cash-on-cash returns I earn from my investments range between 20% and 100% plus. Applying the general rule above, you'd expect the risk to be high, yet my knowledge about real estate allows me to dramatically reduce the chances of something going wrong.

**Steve's Investing Tip**

You can never totally eliminate your investment risk, but you can limit it as much as possible.

While there's no maximum return you should aim for, there's certainly a minimum return you need to earn in order for the investment to be worth your while.

### Deal Evaluation

This is where the economic concept called **opportunity cost** becomes relevant. Opportunity cost is the value of the benefit foregone. Here's how it works. Let's imagine that you find a property for sale for $100,000. Your financier is willing to lend you 80% of the purchase price, so all you need to contribute is $20,000 ($100,000 – $80,0000) plus say another $5,000 for the closing costs. The opportunity cost of investing the $25,000 ($20,000 + $5,000) is what you *could* have earned by placing the money elsewhere, say in a term deposit earning around 4% per annum.

So, when it comes time to weigh up your return, you'd want to be achieving a positive cashflow of at least $1,000 per annum ($25,000 x 4%), or else you'd be better off leaving your money in the bank where there's next to no risk.

When analysing the merits of potential property deals, it's wise to pay a lot of attention to the **Cash on Cash Return** (CoCR). You might recall (from page 109) that the CoCR is calculated by dividing your net annual positive cashflow by the amount of cash that you originally needed to acquire the property.

| Table 11.3 – Multiple Choice Time (Circle Your Answer) | | | |
|:---|:---:|:---:|:---:|
| **TODAY'S DATE:** | | | |
| *You Paid a Deposit of $40,000, Plus a Further $10,000 in Closing Costs to Acquire a Property Earning a Net Cash on Cash Return of 25% Per Annum. What is Your Annual Net Positive Cashflow?* | | | |
| A | $10,000 | C | $15,200 |
| B | $12,500 | D | $20,000 |

(check your answer at: www.PropertyInvesting.com/CoCR)

The only two hard and fast rules I apply to my property investments are that they:

1. Must make money from day one; and

2. That my CoCR must be higher than simply leaving my money in the bank.

On top of this I also apply two CoCR benchmarks. I expect a CoCR return of over 15% per annum for residential real estate and 20% per annum for commercial property.

A deal that came across my desk recently was the freehold title to a country pub priced at $295,000. The rent was $33,600 per annum and it was already rented on a five-year lease, with a further three five-year options (total 20 year lease). What's your initial gut feeling telling you about this investment?

After some quick negotiation (called asking what the vendor is really looking for) the agent revealed that the seller wanted at least $250,000. Spend a few minutes now trying to work out how the preliminary figures stack up based on the information in Table 11.4 below.

| Table 11.4 – CoCR Using the Country Pub Example | |
|---|---|
| **INITIAL CASH DOWN** | |
| Deposit (30%)[1] | $_____ |
| Closing costs[2] | $_____ |
| **Total Cash Needed** | $_____ |
| **CASH INFLOWS** | |
| Rent | $_____ |
| **CASH OUTFLOWS** | |
| Outgoings[3] | $_____ |
| Repairs[4] | $_____ |
| Interest[5] | $_____ |
| **Total Cash Outflows** | $_____ |
| **CASH ON CASH RETURN** | |
| Cash inflows | $_____ |
| Cash outflows | $_____ |
| Net cashflow | $_____ |
| Initial cash down | $_____ |
| **Cash on Cash Return** | _____% |

**IMPORTANT:** Please make an attempt at the numbers before continuing. You can check your answers at:

www.PropertyInvesting.com/CoCR

**Notes:**

1. You are required to put down a 30% deposit.

2. Closing costs are 5% of the purchase price.

3. All outgoings are paid by the tenant.

4. Allow 5% of the rental for repairs.

5. Interest on your interest-only loan is fixed at 8% per annum.

You should have arrived at a CoCR of 20.48%. If I was your mentor then I'd suggest that the return on this deal was nothing special given the risk involved.

However, before you accept or reject this opportunity, we need to consider ways of negotiating different terms that will increase or maximise our CoCR. You can do this by increasing the net annual cashflow and/or decreasing your initial cash outlay.

One suggestion is to request that the vendor carry back a five-year second mortgage of $50,000 on interest-only terms of 10% per annum. If this could be negotiated then the numbers on your new deal would look like those in Table 11.5 opposite.

Negotiating this deal would be particularly beneficial if you could use the $50,000 in cash you saved by seeking a second mortgage and apply it to another investment providing an after-tax return in excess of the 10% annual interest rate. The trick is to remember that you'll need to repay the second mortgage in five years time!

When evaluating a CoCR, don't just dismiss deals that fall on the borderline. Look at creative ways to massage the opportunity to access even better returns. You never know what will be accepted until you ask.

| Table 11.5 – CoCR Using the Country Pub Example with a Second Mortgage | |
|---|---|
| **INITIAL CASH DOWN** | |
| Deposit (10%)[1] | $25,000 |
| Closing costs[2] | $12,500 |
| **Total Cash Needed** | **$37,500** |
| **CASH INFLOWS** | |
| Rent | $33,600 |
| **CASH OUTFLOWS** | |
| Outgoings[3] | Nil |
| Repairs[4] | ($1,680) |
| Interest – Bank[5] | ($14,000) |
| Interest – 2nd Mortgage[6] | ($5,000) |
| **Total Cash Outflows** | **($20,680)** |
| **CASH ON CASH RETURN** | |
| Cash inflows | $33,600 |
| Cash outflows | ($20,680) |
| Net cashflow | $12,920 |
| Initial cash down | $37,500 |
| **Cash on Cash Return** | **34.45%** |

**Notes:**

1. Deposit needed is 30% less the second mortgage.
2. Allow 5% for closing costs.
3. The tenant pays all outgoings in most commercial leases.
4. Allow 5% of the rent for repairs.
5. Interest at 8% on a ten-year interest-only loan.
6. Interest at 10% on a five-year, interest-only second mortgage.

### Steve's Investing Tip

Always assess the risk in the investment and compare it to the likely return. No investment is ever foolproof, so avoid being a fool.

## Step 4 in the Positive Gearing Model:
## Reinvest Your Returns

Once you've earned your cashflow return, you must then decide what you plan to do with it. You can save it, or else either spend it on acquiring more investments or on funding your lifestyle.

I explained in Chapter 2 that by spending your money you lose the benefit of it multiplying or compounding for your benefit. Instead it goes to work for someone else.

You might choose to save your positive cashflow return, but at the low-interest returns that deposits currently earn, you'd be lucky just to keep pace with inflation. Finally you could choose to reinvest your cashflow surplus and buy other assets. So long as you invest and make money, your personal wealth empire will continue to grow. The model that I use, as shown in the chart opposite, is a combination of all three. In fact, I conceptually break my total cashflow into thirds and allocate the money as follows:

## The First Positive Cashflow Third

The first third of my cashflow surplus is immediately reinvested back into the property that created the cash in the first place. I do this by:

### 1. Repaying Debt

A great way to increase your cashflow is to reduce your debt, since less debt means lower interest payments, and lower interest payments means more cash in your pocket. Paying off just a few extra dollars a week will dramatically reduce your interest bill and shave years of your mortgage.

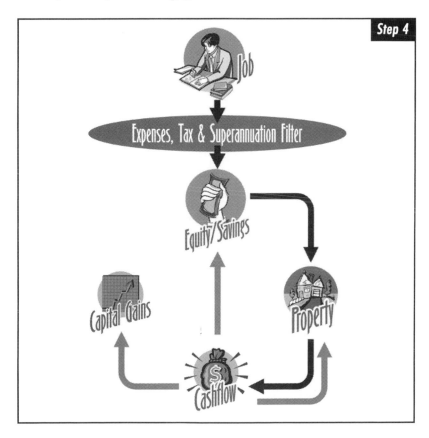

For example, assuming you owned a property that earned $50 per week in net positive cashflow and you reinvested just one third ($16.67) of it to repaying the debt, then you'd save a massive $27,066 in interest over the life of the loan. Furthermore, as shown in Figure 11.1 overleaf, you would also repay your mortgage over five years earlier. The standard loan reduces to nil at the end of 25-five years, yet the loan with extra repayments expires towards the end of year 19.

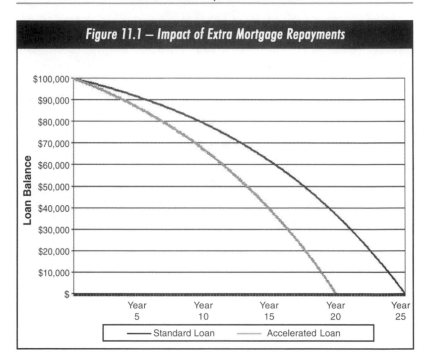

*Figure 11.1 – Impact of Extra Mortgage Repayments*

Making additional payments does not necessarily cause your money to be locked away forever. Today, most lenders encourage borrowers to redraw since it keeps the interest dollars rolling in. Accessing your advance repayments can be as simple as filling in a form.

In practice, Dave and I use a **mortgage offset account**, which allows us to park our surplus money in a 24-hour, at-call facility. While it pays no interest, this allows us a 100% offset against our loans. Here's how it works.

Let's imagine that you owe $500,000 and have a surplus $50,000 in your cheque account. You could either leave it earning about 1% interest, or alternatively add it to your mortgage offset account which, while it doesn't earn interest, will nevertheless reduce the interest you have to pay on your loan as shown in Table 11.6, opposite.

| Table 11.6 – Difference Between Interest Earned and Saved | |
|---|---|
| **CHEQUE ACCOUNT** | |
| Savings | $50,000 |
| Interest on cheque account | 1% |
| **Annual Interest Paid To You** | **$500** |
| **MORTGAGE OFFSET** | |
| Loan | $500,000 |
| Mortgage offset | $50,000 |
| Interest based on | $450,000 |
| Interest paid on loan | 7% |
| Interest payable | $31,500 |
| Interest on $500,000 | $35,000 |
| **Annual Interest Saved By You** | **$3,500** |

Reducing the amount of money you owe also mitigates your **credit risk**, which is the impact on your investing activities should there be a sudden increase in interest rates. My grandfather, considered by many to be quite astute with his money, had a favourite saying; "No-one went broke because they owed too little."

## 2. Tenant Incentives

Were you or anyone you know ever put on detention in high school? Did it really ever stop the bad behaviour? The same is true when it comes to tenants in that it makes no sense to penalise them. In fact, given that most state tenancy laws grant renters up to 14 days grace before a landlord can instigate eviction proceedings, only conscientious tenants will make their rent payments on time and it's almost unheard of to hear about a tenant paying the rent early.

Ranting and raving may make you feel better, but it won't do much to get the tenant to pay the rent that's due or put you higher up the pecking order when dealing with overworked rental managers. On the contrary, if you want to get what you want then you need to start rewarding tenants for doing the right thing, rather than penalising them when they don't. The attitude I adopt is that my tenants fund my financial independence, so I need to respect them and look for ways to keep them pleasantly surprised.

One of the incentives I've used in the past has been to provide a nursery voucher when new tenants move in. I believe that having a tenant plant something in the garden makes them feel like the property is more of a home.

Tenants who pay the rent on time and look after the property receive free movie tickets and minor property improvements of their choice to increase the quality of their tenancy, and the value of the house.

A good friend of mine, Peter, has done a deal with the local video store where he supplies his tenants with a free movie voucher (it costs Pete $2.50 per voucher) provided his tenants pay the rent on time.

This is a win-win-win outcome as the tenants get a bonus for doing what they are obliged to under the lease, Peter gets his rent paid on time and the video store has the chance to upsell to the tenants once they have entered the store.

### Steve's Investing Tip

The best way to get the outcome you desire is to provide an incentive.

### 3. Minor Property Improvements

A great way to increase rents as well as building equity is via low-cost capital improvements. Heat lamps in the bathroom are a great example. Unless substantial rewiring is necessary, most electricians can install a base model for a total cost of about $350.

You could go to your tenant and say "Mr Tenant. You're doing a great job and thanks for paying the rent on time. I know that the bathroom can be a little cold from time to time, so how about I pay for a heat lamp to be installed? All I'd have to do is increase the rent by $1 per day. How do you feel about that?"

The rental increase will not only see you cover the cost in year one, but you'll also make an additional $365 per annum in years ahead too. Even better, a rise of $7 per week in rent equates to $3,500 in added value when you apply 'The 11 Second Solution' formula! And all this is paid for out of your profits to begin with!

## The Second Positive Cashflow Third

The second third of my positive cashflow return is redirected back to my equity/savings account and is used to either:

### 1. Replace My Salary

Contrary to what many of the 'get-rich-quick' seminar presenters want you to believe, financial independence is not achieved overnight. It's a gradual process that can take years while you grow your passive income to the extent needed to phase out your need to work. Still, every dollar of passive income you acquire will weaken the bonds that tie you to your job.

A great idea is to break up your financial independence into the amount of weekly passive income you need to take a day off work. This is shown in Table 11.7 overleaf.

For example, if you earned $50,000 per annum (excluding superannuation) and you wanted to work one less day per week without suffering a lifestyle cut, then you'd need passive income of $193 per week. Complete financial independence would occur when you had passive income of $965 per week.

| Table 11.7 – Passive Income Matrix | | | | |
|---|---|---|---|---|
| Passive Income Needed To Take: | Annual Salary Excluding Superannuation | | | |
| | $40,000 | $50,000 | $60,000 | $70,000 | $80,000 |
| 1 day off | $154 | $192 | $231 | $269 | $308 |
| 2 days off | $308 | $385 | $462 | $538 | $616 |
| 3 days off | $462 | $577 | $692 | $808 | $924 |
| 4 days off | $615 | $769 | $923 | $1,077 | $1,232 |
| 5 days off | $769 | $962 | $1,154 | $1,346 | $1,538 |

Achieving financial independence is no fluke. It starts by determining the amount of passive income you need and then acquiring assets that will bring you closer to your goal.

### 2. Reinvest to Grow Your Empire

You can also take the third of your net positive cashflow allocated to your savings/equity and use it to acquire other positive cashflow property, which is also known as 'pyramiding your profits'. When you do this you create a new positive cashflow model and begin compounding your returns.

## Final Positive Cashflow Third

The final third of my positive cashflow is allocated to purchasing assets that are specifically designed to earn capital gains (rather than cashflow) returns. The two most popular classes of asset for capital growth are:

▷ *Shares:*

One of the most attractive features of shares is that it's possible to make money in a stock market that is both trending up (going long) and also trending down (going short). The stock market is my preferred method for earning capital gains.

&#x262A;  *Property:*

As discussed in Chapter 7, property can also be used to earn capital growth, provided the prevailing market conditions are right.

In fact, if you were absolutely convinced that negative gearing was a strategy you wanted to pursue, then you could use this third of your positive cashflow to fund the cashflow shortfall rather than having to rely on your salary.

## A Summary and Example

The positive gearing model will allow you to earn an immediate cashflow return as your cash inflows will exceed your cash outflows. Once you earn a profit, you can upscale your wealth building by taking advantage of a three-way compounding return.

First, you compound the return of your existing property by channelling one third of your cashflow surplus into repaying debt or making improvements to increase the value. Second, take a third of your cashflow surplus and use it to buy more positive cashflow property.

Finally, use the remainder of your cashflow to buy assets that have a low income but high capital gain return. Adopting this approach means that irrespective of what happens to the value of your (positive) cashflow property, you'll still be primed to earn capital gains.

Assuming that you can earn a weekly net passive income of $50 per property, Table 11.8, overleaf, reveals the future value after 25 years of investing one third of your positive cashflow at various capital growth percentages. Remember, these figures are based on just one third of your positive cashflow being invested for the long-term. The other two thirds of your cashflow can be reinvested back into your property, allocated to your savings account, or simply spent.

| No. of Prop. | Wkly $ | One Third | VALUE IN 25 YEARS TIME AT RATE OF CAPITAL GROWTH P.A. | | | |
|---|---|---|---|---|---|---|
| | | | 5% | 10% | 15% | 20% |
| 1 | $50 | $16.67 | $43,138 | $96,682 | $238,625 | $632,779 |
| 2 | $100 | $33.33 | $86,251 | $193,305 | $477,107 | $1,265,178 |
| 3 | $150 | $50.00 | $129,389 | $289,986 | $715,731 | $1,897,956 |
| 4 | $200 | $66.67 | $172,528 | $386,667 | $954,356 | $2,530,734 |
| 5 | $250 | $83.33 | $215,640 | $483,290 | $1,192,837 | $3,163,133 |
| 6 | $300 | $100.00 | $258,778 | $579,971 | $1,431,462 | $3,795,911 |
| 7 | $350 | $116.67 | $301,916 | $676,652 | $1,670,087 | $4,428,689 |
| 8 | $400 | $133.33 | $345,029 | $773,275 | $1,908,568 | $5,061,088 |
| 9 | $450 | $150.00 | $388,167 | $869,956 | $2,147,193 | $5,693,866 |
| 10 | $500 | $166.67 | $431,305 | $966,638 | $2,385,817 | $6,326,645 |
| 130 | $6,500 | $2,166.67 | $5,606,860 | $12,566,051 | $31,015,048 | $82,244,857 |

Table 11.8 – The Power of Compounding Returns

**Note:** To be fair, these compounding return figures will be eroded by inflation.

Table 11.8 reveals the power of multiple property income steams, compounding at various interest rates, and invested for the long-term. Not only does this look good on paper, I can tell you that from personal experience it works even better in reality!

## Step 5 in the Positive Gearing Model: Capital Gains

In addition to the capital gains generated by investing the final third of your positive cashflow in growth focused assets, you'll also benefit from any capital appreciation in the value of your underlying property too. This increase is illustrated in the Step 5 flow chart by the dotted line between the property and capital gains images.

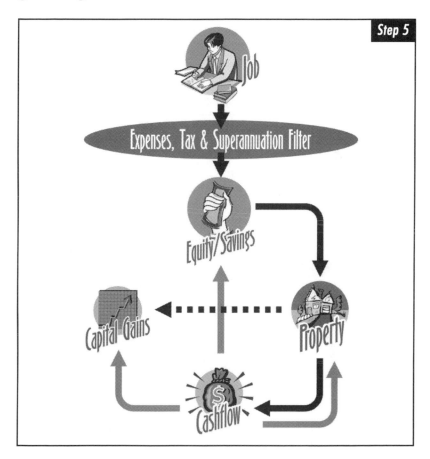

## Step 6 in the Positive Gearing Model:
## Reinvestment of Capital Gains

The final step in the positive gearing model is when you access your capital gains, either by:

1.  Selling the property and turning the gain into cash. (However, before you sell, it's important to weigh up the tax consequences.)

2. Borrowing against the asset, which will allow you to turn a portion of your gain into cash. Be careful to properly weigh up the risk versus reward of doing this, remembering that you will pay more interest and have higher levels of debt.

You can then use the cash to invest in more cashflow positive property.

## EXPANDING YOUR EMPIRE

The hurdle I find most difficult to jump when it comes to negative gearing is the way your cashflow position deteriorates as you own more and more property. Put another way, there's no way I could ever afford to own over 130 negatively geared properties. The only way I can afford to own over 130 positive cashflow properties is if they all make money, which they do – on average about $50 each per week in passive income.

### Key Questions:

How many properties that *lose* money can you afford to own?

How many properties that *make* money can you afford to own?

Now, I'll admit that $50 per week might not sound like a lot of money and won't buy a lot of financial independence. But when you acquire multiple properties that provide $50 per week returns, then all of a sudden things start to get interesting. For example, 130 properties at $50 net per week over fifty-two weeks totals $338,000 per annum in passive income, and that certainly does make for financial freedom!

Figure 11.2, overleaf, reveals the wealth building effect of positively geared property in that each time you acquire another dwelling you increase your cashflow. It's the perfect solution to my golden rule of investing; so long as each property you buy makes money, then you'll have no option but to make money!

Will you have to pay more tax? Yes, because you can't make money and save tax at the same time. Will you be able to gradually work less and less in your job? Yes, because you can use your new found passive income to replace the salary from your job.

How long will it take you to become financially free? That depends on how much time it takes before you can get this model

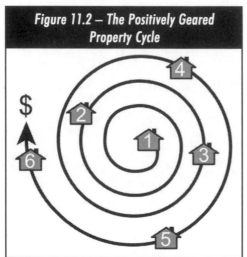

**Figure 11.2 – The Positively Geared Property Cycle**

to start working for you. I find it encouraging that many people from diverse backgrounds have already used the positive cashflow model to build a lifetime of passive income. In fact I've included three personal testimonies in Chapter 20.

You don't need to be a real estate agent, an accountant, economist or rocket scientist. All that's required is common sense, which is sometimes a big problem because investments that make sense are anything but common.

## Summary of the Positive Gearing Model

Hopefully you've already received the insight that much of what's preached about successful property investing won't immediately help you to become financially free. If your goal is to work less then you must acquire enough passive income so that when you stop earning a salary you can still maintain the lifestyle you're accustomed to living.

Relying on shares to provide this income is dubious, because shares generally only pay dividends twice a year. That's a long time between passive income pay days. Fixed-interest income on your savings might pay monthly, but the returns are pitiful and sometimes don't even keep pace with inflation.

At first glance, property seems to be a powerful wealth creation vehicle. However most property investors look for capital growth over cashflow returns, and as such, need to keep working until they can access the capital growth to supplement their lifestyle. But capital gains are unreliable and can take time to accumulate, which makes using them a hit-and-miss source of financial freedom. In practice, capital gains are often used to trade up to a better lifestyle, rather than as a replacement for a salary.

## Money Trees Do Exist!

I've always been fond of the idea of having my own personal money tree that would sprout dollar notes instead of leaves. For the first 26 years of my life I was lead to believe that money trees were about as real as Santa Claus or the Tooth Fairy. Well, I'd been savagely misled because money trees do exist, just not in the form that many people expect.

Acquiring positive cashflow properties that provide passive income is like buying your own miniature money tree. Month after month you'll enjoy watching your money tree sprout fruit in the form of a passive income return. Your hardest decision will be choosing how to divide up the profits; either reinvesting to build your empire (planting more money trees) or spending your money on lifestyle expenses (eating the fruits of your labours).

Your profits won't necessarily be massive. For example, in one of our smaller deals Dave and I put down $9,000 to receive a net passive income of $395 a month – forever. However, our choice of reinvesting this money and taking advantage of the benefits of compounding returns means that if we can average a 15% return then after twenty-five years a mere $395 per month will grow to $1,281,194. That's an entire money forest!

If you're thinking this all sounds great but you don't have a spare $9,000 lying around then you'll find Chapters 13, 14 and 18 very interesting as they outline low-cost strategies that allow you to buy property with little or no 'money down' (to use words made popular by Robert G. Allen).

## Chapter 11 Insights

### Insight #1:

If you want to invest in property to plug a shortfall between what you currently earn and what you currently spend, then you have little chance of long-term success.

You must first fix your money problem, which is a lack of control over what you spend rather than a problem of earning too little.

### Insight #2:

Make sure you have a plan for how you'll use your positive cashflow otherwise you may be tempted to spend the lot.

It's also critical to have a strategy for how you plan to repay your debt too.

### Insight #3:

Threatening tenants rarely achieves anything constructive. Instead, providing a reward can help you create a tenant for life or, in the very least, a regular and reliable source of long-term cashflow.

### Insight #4:

Sometimes deals that look so-so at first glance can be made into attractive investments if you can negotiate creative terms.

### Insight #5:

Net positive cashflow of $50 per week might be aiming a little high. Not all deals will offer this sort of return, especially when you're starting off and you're looking for anything that is cashflow positive.

## Chapter 11 Insights *(cont'd)*

### Insight #6:

When you allocate a portion of your profits to a different class of assets, such as shares, then you create diversification which is a hedge against having all your eggs in the one investment basket.

### Insight #7:

Provided you invest astutely, property delivers an excellent source of passive income. Shares and low interest bearing deposits usually don't.

### Insight #8:

How many properties can you afford to own that lose money? How many properties that make money can you afford to own?

### Insight #9:

Money trees do exist – I own over 130 of them!

# PART II – SUMMARY

There are three reasons why you might invest in property – to make money, to save tax and out of a love of landlording.

Hopefully the information in Part II has highlighted that choosing to save tax is a decision that results in a *certain* loss today for only the promise of a *possible* profit tomorrow. That sounds like a risky gamble to me.

The two types of profit accessible to property investors are capital gains and/or recurring positive cashflow returns. An investor with a capital gains focus usually adopts a long-term strategy and, as such, is happy to keep working and wait for prices to rise. This was not appropriate for me because I wanted to stop working as soon as possible.

Positive cashflow returns occur when you have more cash inflow than cash outflow. I don't include non-cash tax deductions (such as depreciation) in my calculations, as I feel that doing so provides a misleading result.

When all the hype is brushed aside, a successful investment strategy must be able to be replicated in order for it to be effective. If 92% of investors only own one or two properties, I have serious reservations about the true wealth-building results of the strategy the majority of property investors are using.

The only limitation on upsizing your profits will be issues of affordability, which is why it's critical that all your investments should make money as soon as possible.

# Strategies for Making Money in Property

# INTRODUCTION TO PART III

Now that you're aware of the different ways to make money in real estate, as well as the positive and negative gearing models, this section will focus on the following specific property investing strategies:

➪ Buy and Hold (Chapter 12)

➪ Wraps (Chapter 13)

➪ Lease Options (Chapter 14)

➪ Renovations (Chapter 15); and

➪ Flips (Chapter 16).

Your choice of which strategy to implement depends on two factors:

1. The profit outcome you want to achieve (i.e. capital gains and/or positive cashflow returns); and

2. The needs of the person who'll be paying you money in exchange for the use or ownership of your property.

I've summarised these two points in the Property Profit Matrix opposite.

## Maximising Your Returns

I've found that the most profitable deals are made when you tailor the needs of the person using your property to the appropriate strategy, rather than the other way around.

For example, if I can find a client who wants to buy a property off me under a wrap strategy, then my cashflow return will be higher than if I had chosen to simply rent it out (using the 'Buy and Hold' technique).

| Property Profit Matrix | | |
|---|---|---|
| **Strategy** | **Potential Profit Outcome** | **Needs of the Occupier/Purchaser** |
| Buy and Hold | • Rental income<br>• Gain on sale | Tenant (place to live). |
| Wraps | Positive net cashflow | Home buyer (place to own). |
| Lease Options | • Rental income<br>• Gain on the exercise of the option or else sale | Tenant/home buyer (place to live now and the opportunity to buy at an agreed price later). |
| Renovations | Increased rental income | Acquire renovated property. |
| Flips | Capital gain | Acquire property at agreed price. |

If you already own property then the key to increasing your returns is to better serve the needs of your clients. For example, if you have a tenant then look for ways to increase the rent that also provide your tenant with more enjoyment of your property.

A good example is the installation of ceiling fans in a house that has poor ventilation. If the tenant agrees, once the fans are operational you can justify an increase to the rent; it's a win-win outcome where you have more rent and the tenant has a better quality of life.

### A Word of Caution

Part III is an outline, as opposed to a complete guide, to five strategies that can help you to maximise your property returns.

My aim is to help you to appreciate that there's a lot more to the world of real estate investing than simply buying a property and renting it out. If you're interested in finding out more about these strategies then I encourage you to visit my website and ask questions in the discussion forum at:

www.PropertyInvesting.com/forum

With this in mind, let's start by looking at the most common way that people invest in real estate – the 'Buy and Hold' technique.

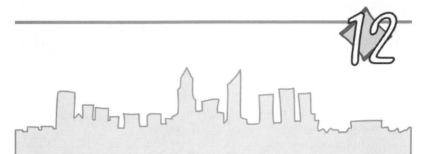

# Buy and Hold – Tenants from Hell or Partners in Wealth?

### Investor's Summary: Buy and Hold

#### Aim:

Under this strategy you buy a property and then hold onto it while it (hopefully) appreciates in value. In the meantime you seek to attract tenants who'll pay rental income.

#### Ways to Profit:

1.  *Capital gains* (provided your property appreciates in value); and/or

2.  *Positive Cashflow:* When the cash you receive as rental income is more than the cashflow expenses associated with owning the property.

## Investor's Summary: Buy and Hold *(Cont'd)*

**Your Client:**

The person living in your property is called a tenant. He or she pays rent in return for the use of your property over the term of the lease.

**Regulated by:**

⟱  The written terms and conditions of your rental agreement (called a lease); and

⟱  Established residential tenancy laws enforced by dedicated tribunals. Your rights as a landlord of a commercial property must be enforced via the court system.

**Service Providers:**

Rental managers, who charge a fee (normally based on a percentage of rent, between 5% and 10%) for managing the tenant and property related issues.

**Other Comments:**

A proven way to invest in property with established procedures for enforcing both tenant and landlord rights.

The 'Buy and Hold' strategy is a very easy way to invest in property since there's an established market of renters who demand shelter – it is one of the necessities of life.

## THE FOUR STEPS TO BUY AND HOLD

Before you can rent a property you must first own it. Figure 12.1, opposite, illustrates the steps to acquiring and establishing a buy and hold property.

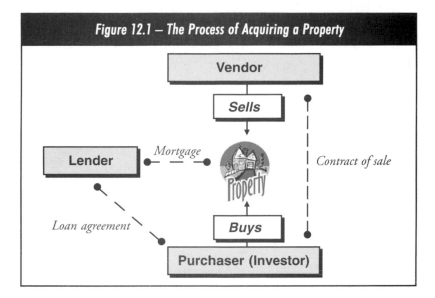

Figure 12.1 – The Process of Acquiring a Property

## Step 1:

In order to buy a property you will first need to sign a 'Contract of Sale', which is a legal document drawn up by the Vendor's (seller's) solicitor outlining the price and terms of the sale.

## Step 2:

Unless you plan to pay cash, once you've signed the Contract of Sale you'll need to organise finance. Your lender will want security – usually in the form of a first mortgage over the title of the property. The terms and conditions of the finance are contained in the loan agreement.

## Step 3:

During the settlement period your solicitor will complete a number of checks to ensure that the property is not encumbered by legal restrictions (caveats), and that any existing mortgages are discharged. You will become the new owner once the title of the property is transferred into your name.

## Step 4:

As the new owner you're entitled to all the income generated by the property, but you'll also bear the responsibility for paying loan interest and property expenses too. This is illustrated by Figure 12.2 below.

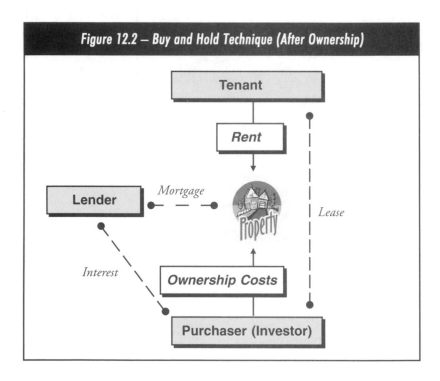

Figure 12.2 – Buy and Hold Technique (After Ownership)

Your client (or the source of your income) using the 'Buy and Hold' technique will be the **tenant**. A tenant pays you an agreed periodic rent in exchange for the use of your property. The terms and conditions of a tenant's occupation are outlined in a **lease**.

If you don't have the marketing skills to attract potential clients and/or you don't want the hassle of dealing with tenants, you can appoint a **rental manager** who will happily charge you a fee for doing the work on your behalf.

# ISOLATING THE REAL ASSET

I was taught in accounting school that an **asset** is something that, when used, generates income. Furthermore, if you could put an asset in its best operating environment, then you stood to maximise your income earning potential.

That's great theory as an accountant, but as a property investor I had to learn how to apply this definition in a practical way. In doing so I made an important discovery that resulted in me questioning what I'd previously been taught. The discovery was:

### Steve's Investing Tip

When it comes to property, the asset definition changes depending on the profit outcome you're trying to achieve.

## The Asset Definition if You Desire Capital Gains Returns

Accountants the world over would look at Figure 12.1 (page 187) and conclude that the assets in such a property investment are a combination of the land and buildings. However, as a property investor, I perceived that buildings depreciate with use and require ongoing maintenance. On the other hand, land appreciates with little or no effort, so, if I want capital gains returns, it makes sense to primarily focus on the qualities of the land, which is why 'location, location, location' (see page 93 for more information) is seen as critical.

The best way to maximise my capital gains returns would be to secure the right property in the right area. The conclusion to draw is that if you're seeking capital gains returns, your focus should be on the land, then the building. The tenant is given little, if any, attention.

## The Focus of the Capital Gains Investor

| | |
|---|---|
| **Outcome:** | Make money |
| **Achieved when:** | Your asset appreciates in value |
| **Strategy for capital appreciation:** | Property investing |
| **Primary asset:** | Land |
| **Secondary asset:** | Building |
| **Ancillary item:** | Tenant |

## The Asset Definition if you Desire Positive Cashflow Returns

A radical change in thought is needed when you're a positive cashflow investor, because the reliability of your income stream (and thus your ability to achieve financial independence) depends on the quality of the tenant you attract.

With cashflow as our focus, the accounting definition needs to be politely refined so that we recognise the tenant as the primary asset, the building (where the tenant lives) as the secondary asset and the land (where the building is located) as the ancillary item.

In a practical context, as a positive cashflow investor you don't care so much where the property is located, so long as:

1. The numbers stack up and it's likely that you'll earn a positive cashflow return; and

2. It's inhabited by a good tenant who regularly pays rent.

### Summary

Irrespective of which investment outcome you desire, the land, building and tenant are all important variables upon which your success is dependent. However, you must choose whether you want capital gains or positive cashflow returns, since your decision will determine which of the three components are given the majority of your time.

## The Focus of the Positive Cashflow Investor

| | |
|---|---|
| **Outcome:** | Financial Independence |
| **Achieved when:** | Passive income is more than lifestyle expenses |
| **Strategy for earning passive income:** | Property investing |
| **Primary asset:** | Tenant |
| **Secondary asset:** | Building |
| **Ancillary item:** | Land |

## Steve's Investing Tip

A 'Buy and Hold' investor must choose which is more important – capital gains or positive cashflow returns, and then focus on properties that deliver the required outcome.

The remainder of this chapter is allocated to looking at tenants in more detail.

# WHO'S DOING WHO A FAVOUR?

Which of the options in Table 12.1, below, best reflects your opinion?

| Table 12.1 – Multiple Choice (Circle Your Answer) | |
| --- | --- |
| **Question: In Your Opinion, Who is Doing Who a Favour?** | |
| A | The landlord is doing the tenant a favour by providing a place to live. |
| B | The tenant is doing the landlord a favour by paying rent. |
| C | No-one is doing anyone a favour. |
| D | I don't know... I just want to keep reading (see page 81). |

Of the people to whom I've asked this question, the majority of those who answered 'A' had a capital gains focus and saw the tenant as a means to an end. Those who chose 'B' were more intent on earning cashflow returns and viewed the tenant as an investing partner.

I believe it's the tenant who does the landlord a favour. I could own over 1,000 properties, but without reliable tenants providing a regular rental income, my goal of financial independence would be little more than a dream. Don't get me wrong though... the land and building are still important, but they're not as important as the source of the cashflow.

## Steve's Investing Tip

Properties are inanimate objects without bank accounts... Tenants – who are living breathing humans – are the ones with the chequebooks.

## Passive Investing is not the Same as Passive Income

It takes a lot of hard work to find and buy an investment property – there's the constant looking, dealing with agents, organising finance... by the time you've actually settled, you might feel like you're entitled to a well-earned rest. Unfortunately, this is not the case.

### Steve's Investing Tip

Investing is not a passive activity – it requires ongoing effort.

Many investors make the mistake of thinking that all the hard work is behind them once they've signed a contract to buy a property. In truth, anyone can sign a contract, but it takes real expertise and much effort to maximise the profitability of your assets.

## Rental Managers

Your asset is said to be on autopilot when you have a reliable tenant and no serious maintenance or other issues. Investing is easy and the rent cheques keep coming in with a minimum of effort. During these times you'll find that one rental manager is as good as another and it might make sense to go with a cheaper option rather than pay a premium for a service that's not needed.

However, when times are tough, a good rental manager can be worth his or her weight in gold. And this is the problem... you never know when you're about to hit real estate turbulence. So how do you know when to pay for the services of a premium quality rental manager?

Well, it depends on whether you're a passive or active investor at heart. A passive investor is someone who believes that things will look after themselves. Sadly, left to their own devices, such people will have a hard time making a success out of property investing.

If you're a passive investor then it will be essential for you to use a pro-active rental manager to counterbalance your own happy-go-lucky approach.

On the other hand, if you're the sort of person who takes control of a situation and makes things happen, then you can get away with a cheaper rental manager provided you're willing to put in the effort when required to monitor and correct your property as needs be. Now, it would be a mistake to correlate the commission a rental manager charges with his or her level of expertise. What you need to do is interview multiple rental managers and try to decipher whether or not they have the skills which you lack.

## Steve's Investing Tip

You can still be a passive investor and make money, but only if you have a pro-active rental manager on your team.

An example immediately comes to mind. In one of our rental properties, the tenants recently decided to vacate with about six months left to run on their lease. It turned out that they'd split up and no longer wanted to live together. Anyway, they had been good tenants for about two and a half years and when they left they recommended friends of theirs to take over the lease. Well, that's not entirely right... our old tenants didn't so much recommend their friends as they did inform us that friends of theirs were now living in the property and responsible for future rent payments.

Now a passive investor might have said "Yeah, no problem" and hoped that the new tenants were as good as the old ones. If things went wrong, the passive investor might be tempted to complain that he or she tried to do the right thing but was taken for a ride.

Passive does not mean the same thing as stupid. Would you hand the keys of your $100,000 prestige car to a complete stranger? I didn't think so. Then why would you treat the keys to your $100,000 property investment any differently? Clearly, a tenant with no bond and without the proper checks moving into our property was far less than a satisfactory outcome. Especially when some of our independent inquiries revealed that the guy who our new female tenant was living with was (allegedly) a local druggie. Furthermore, they had been kicked out of their last place for not paying the rent.

Sensing that this property had well and truly come off autopilot and was headed for a nasty crash landing, I immediately started taking corrective action. However, my biggest problem was that because possession is nine tenths of the law, once tenants have moved into a property (whether legally or illegally) then it's not easy to get them to move out.

There was no point trying to alienate the tenants by ranting and raving, because if I did that then there would be no chance of receiving any money off them at all. So, instead of fighting the system, I sought a solution that worked *with* the system.

In conjunction with our rental manager we agreed that, given the unusual circumstances of the new lease arrangements, if we were going to evict them then by the time the whole process was complete, it might take up to six months.

Our answer was to get them to sign a new six-month lease on the conditions they:

1.  Complete an application form and sign all the necessary paperwork

2.  Pay a bond; and

3.  Pay the correct amount of rent on time.

The plan was that if the tenants fell behind in their rent, then we would immediately seek to terminate the new six-month lease which would be a lot easier to enforce than the old lease (which didn't even have their names on it).

The tenants agreed to points (1) and (3), but when it came to the bond, they couldn't afford it since their bond on their other property was forfeited to pay for the rent in arrears. Rather than jump up and down though, I said that it wasn't a problem so long as they paid their bond by agreed instalments on top of their rent.

To date there have been no problems, however this situation requires constant monitoring since any neglect at my end will surely be seen by the tenant as a sign that the initial 'tough' rules have begun to slacken.

## Steve's Investing Tip

Don't confuse passive income with doing nothing. Never forget that you're the one with the money on the line.

For two and a half years while the old tenants were in the property we had nothing but investment bliss. Yet out of nowhere we hit a bad patch of tenant turbulence which required that I quickly wrestle back control to keep my property income from crash landing. It may not be perfect, but there's a saying that I've come to agree with, which is:

## Steve's Investing Tip

Things will always work out best for those people who make the best of how things work out.

# TENANTS FROM HELL

Tenants come in all shapes and sizes and from a diverse range of backgrounds. The majority are just normal people who want a neat and tidy place to live; however, a small fraction of tenants will cause you nothing but trouble. Every landlord's nightmare is to be landed with a tenant from hell – someone who never pays rent and trashes the property.

I invite you now to turn to Appendix C (page 369) and read a selection of 'tenant from hell' stories contributed by members from the www.PropertyInvesting.com community.

## Avoiding Tenants from Hell

It's not possible to completely eliminate the chance that you might inadvertently rent your property to a bad tenant. In my experience even good tenants can go off the rails if their life circumstances change. Yet you can mitigate or reduce the risk of renting to a bad tenant by:

### 1. Completing the Proper Checks (Due Diligence) Over the Tenant

When you rent your property you're making a decision to trust your tenant to look after it. As I mentioned before, you're essentially handing the keys to a very valuable asset over to (usually) a complete stranger. It's essential that you:

1. Try and find out as much as you can about your tenant; and then

2. Test the accuracy of the information he or she provides.

A critical point in Marlene's tenant from hell story (page 375) was that she went to the trouble of checking her potential client's references only to discover "It was just a friend pretending to be the tenant's employer".

My auditing background tells me that the more evidence you gather, the more informed your decision will be. Never just accept a tenant in desperation just because you need money to cover your property expenses – there's no guarantee that a tenant signed up hastily and without the proper check will ever pay you a dollar in rent. If you'd like to know more about the due diligence process that I follow when selecting a tenant and rental manger, visit:

www.PropertyInvesting.com/BuyerBeware

*The message: The more you leave to chance, the higher the chance that something will go wrong!*

### 2. Being Vigilant in Retaining Control

It's terribly naive just to assume your investment will run on autopilot. If I was running a manufacturing business and never bothered to look after the most important machine on the factory floor, then I'd be asking for trouble.

So it is with passive landlords who find a tenant and then ignore their asset believing that everything will be OK. Without ever checking (but just assuming) that things are running as they should, early warning signs go unheeded and only once there's a complete breakdown (when it's usually far too late) is urgent action taken.

The lesson from Leslie's tenant from hell story (page 378) was to never just assume the money is on the way. Continued follow up is critical, as is documenting everything you agree to.

*Again, the message is: The more you leave to chance, the higher the chance that something will go wrong!*

### 3. Inspecting Your Asset Regularly

The best person to watch over your asset is you. You know the condition it was in when you bought it, and you're the best judge to determine whether or not the tenant is treating it with the respect it deserves. This was the lesson in Charlie's tenant from hell story (page 369). While he took his life into his own hands, he nevertheless retained responsibility for doing regular inspections, despite the fact that he also used a real estate agency to veto his potential tenants.

*Again, the message is: The more you leave to chance, the higher the chance that something will go wrong!*

### 4. Taking Immediate Corrective Action

It's rare that a tenancy problem will sort itself out unless you take corrective action. If you're a landlord who adopts a 'fingers crossed' approach to your investment then you're setting yourself up for much financial heartache. The theme of all the tenants from hell stories is that problems are only resolved by:

1. Recognising the issue; and then

2. Taking corrective action.

When you find something wrong, confront the issue directly. The longer you take, the bigger the problem you'll have to deal with later on.

*Again, the message is: The more you leave to chance, the higher the chance that something will go wrong!*

## Partners in Wealth (the Steve McKnight Approach to Landlording)

It would be a mistake to think that all tenants are out to cause mischief. The vast majority of renters are happy to pay their rent on time provided they can:

▷ Have a neat and tidy place to call home; and

▷ Deal with a reasonable landlord.

### The Big Stick Approach Doesn't Work!

Tenancy laws are written to favour the tenant rather than the landlord. For example, before you can start proceedings to evict a late paying tenant in Victoria, you must wait at least 14 days. In other words, tenants can pay their rent up to two weeks late and there's precious little you can do about it.

Some landlords jump up and down and threaten their tenants with eviction or other nasty outcomes. I call this the 'big stick' approach – but it's all bluff because when push comes to shove there's little or no backup available from the authorities.

Be very careful with what you threaten to do. Tenants either know their rights or they will quickly establish them. If you break the law, a disgruntled tenant may make it his or her mission to cause you maximum pain.

### Win-Win Outcomes

I've come to understand that the best way to get the result you desire is to offer a reward or incentive system that provides the tenant with a benefit for doing above and beyond what's required.

By focusing on a win-win outcome, I'm able to regularly achieve above-market rents while also reducing the risk that my properties will be vacant for long periods of time.

The way it works is quite simple – the tenant is given an incentive for paying the rent on time and keeping the property in a neat and tidy condition, which is really his or her obligation under the lease anyway. If the tenant does not meet his or her obligations then the incentive is taken away.

A great example is movie tickets. Let's imagine that the rent is due on the 15th of each month. Now, if the tenant wanted to string you out, he or she could wait up until the 29th of each month before paying and there's not a lot you could do.

However, let's say that you make it a rule that the rent has to be paid **prior** to (rather than **on** or **after**) the 15th in order to qualify for two free movie tickets. All of a sudden the offer of an incentive makes the effort of paying the rent worthwhile, and at what cost to the investor? Two free movie tickets will probably set you back around $20 per month (if you use movie money), which is $240 per annum.

Only you can decide if $20 per month (which comes out of your positive cashflow profits anyway) is a price you're willing to pay to have a happy tenant who pays the rent early. But please remember that if you plan to fund your financial independence on passive income derived from the tenant, then a regular and reliable income stream will be fundamental to your success.

To me, $20 a month seems like an outrageous bargain to secure a loyal customer – especially when you consider that a rental manager will charge you one week's rent plus advertising to attract a new tenant. Sure, tenants move on but it's not uncommon for a client to ask me if I have another property (bigger, smaller, etc.) that better suits his or her needs before seeking a new place to live with another landlord.

### Finding Ideal Tenants

In my mind an ideal tenant is someone who:

▷ Demonstrates an ability to pay the required rent

▷ Has an established rental history of living in the one place for several years; and

▷ Wants to treat their rental property like a home.

Without doubt, the best way to find an ideal tenant is to seek a referral from someone who you already regard as the sort of person you want to live in your property. We all like to associate with like-minded people, so it's likely that friends and associates of an ideal tenant will also be ideal tenants in their own right too.

You might like to offer an incentive for the referral. As I've mentioned, most agents require one week's rent as a reletting fee, so you could provide at least this to one of your contacts who supplies a good quality lead who ends up renting your property.

If you don't know anyone who would make an ideal tenant, then Plan B is to rely on potential clients generated via normal marketing channels (running classified ads or putting a 'For Lease' sign at the front of the property). If you can, it's a good idea to conduct an interview with your potential tenants in the place where they currently live, since this is how you should expect the tenant to live in your home.

### The Essence of Successful Landlording

I regard my tenants as partners in my wealth, as without them, I'd need to go back and work in a job. This does not mean that I'm passive with my investments – it means that I'm respectful of both my own and my tenant's rights. It's important to understand that landlording is a people business – if you don't like dealing with people then find something else to keep you happy.

## SUMMARY

'Buy and Hold' is a property investing technique where you purchase a property and then rent it out while hoping for capital appreciation. The amount of your capital gain returns depends on the quality of the location, whereas your rental return will depend on the calibre of your tenant.

There are good and bad tenants in any market. You can avoid your investment falling into the wrong hands by leaving as little as possible to chance.

## Chapter 12 Insights

### Insight #1:

If capital gains are your desired investment outcome then you'll need to focus on location, location, location. However positive cashflow investors need to pay closer attention to the income yield and the quality of the tenant.

### Insight #2:

Are you a passive investor? If so then you'll need to employ a proactive rental manager to compensate for your relaxed style. Two passives don't make for a happy outcome.

### Insight #3:

You wouldn't hand the keys to your $100,000 prestige car to just anyone. By the same token you shouldn't just hand over the keys to your investment property without first completing some due diligence to determine the quality of your potential tenant.

### Insight #4:

Rather than just relying on a rental system that clearly favours the rights of a tenant, to achieve the outcome you desire it's important to offer additional incentives. Ideally you'd provide rewards for helping the tenant treat the property like a home and not just a rental property.

### Insight #5:

I firmly believe that you'll attract the tenant that you deserve. Put in minimal effort and you'll find tenants who share the same relaxed attitude when it comes to paying the rent and looking after the property.

# Wraps (Vendor's Terms): Become Like a Bank

## Investor's Summary: Wraps

### Aim:

Instead of selling your property for a lump-sum cash settlement, another option is to sell it by instalments or a series of payments over an agreed timeframe.

When you do this you become more like a financier, as the majority of your profit is earned as interest and most of the risks of ownership pass to your client.

### Ways to Profit:

*Positive Net Cashflow:* Occurs when the instalment repayments you receive from your client are higher than your loan repayments.

## Investor's Summary: Wraps *(cont'd)*

### Your Client:

Someone who would like to own a property but, for a variety of reasons, can't access traditional finance.

### Regulated by:

⊅ The terms and conditions you offer as set out in the contract of sale.

⊅ The Sale of Land Act (or equivalent) in each state.

⊅ Possibly the Consumer Credit Code (CCC).

### Service Providers:

While not a necessity, the easiest way to receive your instalment repayments is by direct debit, which is why it's a good idea to establish this facility with your client's bank.

### Other Comments:

There's an increasing debate about the ethics of wraps with a minority of shysters giving the whole industry a bad name. The key to success is to always create a win-win outcome and to focus on people rather than profit. Wraps are legal in every state except South Australia (where only the government can offer vendor's finance).

When vendor's finance arrangements (a.k.a. 'Wraps' – short for 'wrap around mortgages') are handled the right way (with a genuine intention to create a win-win outcome), the technique offers an excellent return for the investor and also provides the client with the opportunity of a lifetime.

Vendor's finance is a creative technique that must be tailored to the needs of your client. Let's take a closer look at how it works.

## WHAT IS A WRAP?

When you decide to sell a property you have two choices:

▷ **Option 1** is to sell for a lump-sum cash amount, broken down into a deposit and the balance payable on settlement. For example, selling a property for $100,000 based on a $10,000 deposit and the balance, $90,000, being due in 60 days time. This option is the way that the majority of property is sold.

▷ **Option 2**, which is not as well known, involves breaking down the amount owing into a series of instalment repayments over an agreed timeframe, instead of receiving a lump-sum cash payment. For example, you could take the same $100,000 property and sell it on the basis that you receive a $10,000 deposit and the balance on vendor's terms, which might be 1,300 weekly repayments (i.e. 25 years) of $173.86. If you're not paid out earlier, over the term of the contract you'll receive $226,019 (1,300 x $173.86).

While the nitty gritty varies from state to state, the fundamentals behind a vendor's finance arrangement are:

1. Your client has beneficial ownership of the property.

2. You retain legal ownership because title to the property remains in your name until your client makes his or her final payment due under the contract.

3. Just like a bank does not pay the repairs or rates on a property that it finances, all ongoing ownership costs become the responsibility of your client.

4. You become more like a financier than a traditional landlord in that you don't receive rent – you just make a

margin on the difference between the repayment you receive from your client and the repayment you make off your loan.

5. You lock in your profit at the beginning of the contract, so your client is the beneficiary of any capital appreciation above and beyond his or her purchase price.

A great way to expand upon the concept is by discussing the four phases of a wrap transaction within the context of a real-life wrap example.

## THE FOUR PHASES OF A WRAP TRANSACTION

### Phase 1: Acquire a Property

Before you can sell a property on vendor's terms you first **must** own it, which means the title of the property must be in your (or your investment entity's) name. As such you'll also need to organise appropriate finance, as your client can only sign a contract to buy from you once you've settled on your purchase.

### Steve's Investing Tip

A critical point to note is that once you've sold a property under a wrap, you are not allowed to refinance your loan.

To illustrate how the numbers unfold in a wrap transaction, I've reproduced the real-life details of one of our first vendor's finance deals in Table 13.1 opposite.

In addition to these figures, there were other closing costs (stamp duty etc.) of $2,051.40. Table 13.2, opposite, is a summary of the final figures.

| Table 13.1 – One of Our First Deals | | |
|---|---|---|
| **SETTLEMENT STATEMENT** | | |
| To: Purchase Price | | $49,500.00 |
| To: Purchaser's Solicitor Costs and Disbursements (Current Bill) | | $509.16 |
| To: Purchaser's Solicitor Costs and Disbursements (Prior Bill) | | $287.25 |
| To: Rate Adjustment | | $554.81 |
| By: Deposit Paid | $1,000.00 | |
| By: Loan Monies From Financier | $37,251.60 | |
| By: Balance Required To Settle: | $12,599.62 | |
| Total: | $50,851.22 | $50,851.22 |

| Table 13.2 – Summary | |
|---|---|
| **INITIAL CASH DOWN** | |
| Deposit (20%) | $9,900 |
| Closing costs | $7,102 |
| **Total Cash Needed** | **$17,002** |

We acquired the property on the 22nd of September 2000 and sold it on vendor's terms a month later.

**Summary:**

In the example given, Phase 1 covered the period up until our property purchase settled – i.e. the title was transferred into our name.

## Phase 2: Sell the Property

The person who we sold this property to on vendor's terms was found after answering a classified ad that I ran in the local paper. The ad read:

```
    Own Your Own Home for Less than
              $120 per week

            Stop renting now.

  Owner wants to sell this neat and tidy 3 Bdr
       family home with large backyard.

           Close to school and shops.

       Lock up garage. Flexible terms.

  Can help with the deposit and finance too.
            Call now [mobile no.]
```

If you're just beginning, running a classified ad is an excellent way to find customers. However, the best source of potential clients is referrals from your existing customers who have tried and are satisfied with the vendor's finance service that you offer.

Anyway, one of the callers who rang about the ad didn't want to buy the property on offer. Rather she was interested to see if I could buy the property that she currently rented and which had just been made available for sale. Mrs G. (I'll not mention her name for confidentiality reasons) was a middle-aged lady that ran her own successful business and had a very good credit record.

She'd approached several lenders to try to buy the property, but due to her age and the fact that she was self-employed, her loan application was rejected.

Naturally, Mrs. G. was initially sceptical and she had plenty of questions to ask. I explained that we buy property and then offer it for sale on vendor's terms; she'd make her repayment to us, and then we would make our repayment to the bank. After I'd reassured her by outlining exactly how we make our profit (down to the last cent) and how she could pay me out at any time, she asked if I would buy the property and then sell it to her on vendor's terms.

## Steve's Investing Tip

It's critical that you adopt a policy of full and complete disclosure. I send my clients a summary of what the property cost and an outline of how much money I stand to make. If your client isn't comfortable that you're making money, then you won't be able to build a win-win deal.

## Making Money in a Wrap

The profit you make in a wrap transaction is derived from two components:

1. An *interest margin*, which is the difference between the interest rate your lender charges you and the interest rate you charge your customer; and/or

2. A *price margin*, which is the difference between what you buy the property for, and the price at which you offer it for sale.

A question that I'm asked a lot is "How do I know how much to charge as my margin?" At first glace, it might appear that the answer depends on:

⇨ Your minimum required return on investment; and

⇨ How much you are risking by undertaking the investment.

However, practically speaking, the margin you should charge depends largely on how much your client can reasonably afford to repay. The key is to tailor the terms of your finance to create an outcome where everyone wins.

### Steve's Investing Tip

The amount that your wrap client can reasonably afford determines how much profit you can charge as a margin.

### Interest Rate Margin

For no good reason, other than it seemed like a fair amount, our standard interest rate margin is plus 2% on what our lender charges us. In unusual cases, Dave and I reserve the right to vary this interest margin, depending on the unique circumstances of our client. In reality though, there's only been one occasion where we have varied beyond our usual plus 2%.

This occurred when we wrapped a property to an ex-bankrupt who went broke as a result of a failed marriage. Within the boundaries of making sure that it was still comfortably affordable, we charged him a plus 3.5% interest margin for the first year (because it was a bigger risk) and then reduced the rate back to plus 2% thereafter.

### Price Margin

When Dave and I began wrapping we were buying properties for around $44,000 and then selling them for $65,000. At first glance this is nearly a 50% profit, but there were some important additional factors that made this markup appear more reasonable.

First, our purchase price needed to be increased to reflect our closing costs and loan set up fees. By the time we'd paid these charges and arranged a new contract for the sale on vendor's terms, $44,000 was closer to $50,000.

Second, the price margin is not a profit that is made as a lump sum on day one. Instead it's earned over the term of the contract – usually 25 years. So in the example of Mrs. G., if the contract goes for the full term, we make $840 per annum ($21,000 ÷ 25 years). Put another way, the property needs to appreciate at just 1.91% per annum and our client will make back the price margin.

What the price margin really offers is a minimum profit in the event that your client refinances early in the contract and you are paid out.

### *What's a Fair Price Margin?*

This is a difficult question to answer. Charging too little or too much can turn a good deal sour for either the investor or the wrap client. The majority of your profit in a wrap is derived from the interest margin, so what you add as a price premium just needs to make the effort involved in setting up the deal worthwhile, in the event that your client decides to refinance early in the contract.

### Keeping it Affordable

The critical success factor in a wrap transaction is keeping your client's repayments within affordable guidelines. You can do this by varying the interest and/or price margin, and tailoring the wrap to meet the specific circumstances of your client.

For example, in constructing the terms for Mrs. G. we made it a point to keep her weekly repayments much less than the $130 per week she paid to rent the exact same property. Being a reasonable credit risk, we set our interest margin at plus 2%, which meant that her initial interest rate was 9.5%. We then decided that, in this case, a price margin of around 25% would be fair, so we put a circle around $63,000 as a possible selling price.

However, before making this formal, Dave and I went back to check that the repayment under these parameters was affordable. Our client was able to access the $7,000 First Home Owner Grant and offered a deposit of $6,500 with the other $500 being allocated to paying her costs for independent legal advice. Using a financial calculator, I determined that a loan of $56,500 ($63,500 – $6,500) over 25 years at 9.5% interest came to $113.62 per week, which was well inside the $130 guideline. Tables 13.3 and 13.4, opposite, summarise the numbers from this example.

Even though we could have charged more, we felt that at this price we were leaving room should interest rates go higher and we also had to remember that our client had to pay for all the rates, repairs, insurance etc.

### Summary:

Phase 2 covers the sale of your investment property on the terms and conditions you create. Remember to let affordability determine your margin and if your profit is too low, don't be tempted to squeeze the client for more – that's *not* going to produce a win-win outcome.

## Phase 3: Cashflow

Once you've sold your property on vendor's terms then you've created the facility to receive net positive cashflow for the duration of the contract. It's wise to encourage your client to pay by using a direct debit facility straight into your loan account to make the whole process as automated and as easy as possible for all concerned.

During the cashflow phase you'll need to continue to monitor your investment in addition to completing some administration in order to prepare periodic loan statements, which are needed under the Consumer Credit Code.

| Table 13.3 – Preliminary Numbers on the Wrap Example | | | |
|---|---|---|---|
| **OUR PURCHASE** | | **OUR SALE** | |
| Purchase Price | $49,500 | Sale Price | $63,000 |
| Deposit (20%) | $9,900 | Deposit | $6,500 |
| Closing costs | $7,102 | Closing costs* | $500 |
| Initial cash needed | $17,002 | Total | $7,000 |
| Less client's deposit | ($6,500) | | |
| **Net Cash Needed** | **$10,502** | **Total Cash Needed** | **$7,000** |
| Bank loan | $39,600 | Vendor's finance | $56,500 |
| Interest rate | 7.5% | Interest rate | 9.5% |
| Loan term | 25 Years | Loan term | 25 Years |
| **Weekly Repayment** | **$67.38** | **Weekly Repayment** | **$113.62** |

**\*Note:** In a wrap completed in Victoria, the only closing costs a client pays at the time of entering into a wrap is for independent legal advice over his or her purchase. Stamp duty is payable when the title transfers into the new owner's name which will happen at the end of the contract.

| Table 13.4 – Cash on Cash Return on the Wrap Example | |
|---|---|
| **OUR CASH ON CASH RETURN** | |
| Weekly cash in | $113.62 |
| Weekly cash out | ($67.38) |
| Net cashflow | $46.24 x 52 |
| Annual net cashflow | $2,404.48 |
| Net cash needed | $10,502.00 |
| **Annual Cash on Cash Return** | **22.90%** |

*Summary:*

Phase 3 is simply the duration of your vendor's finance contract.

## Phase 4: Cashed Out/Termination

Your wrap contract ends when either:

1. You receive your last repayment, which can happen:

    ⇨ At the scheduled end of the contract, or

    ⇨ Earlier if your client decides to refinance or sell the property.

2. You need to rescind the contract because your client defaults on his or her payment obligation and you need to take back possession.

# WRAP QUESTIONS ANSWERED

Vendor's finance is an advanced property investing strategy – similar to what options trading is to the stock market. There are plenty of pitfalls for the novice or unwary investor and it's easy to make expensive mistakes. Before using this technique there are many issues that you need to consider and it is beyond the scope of this book to discuss them all.

### Steve's Investing Tip

If you'd like more information about the wrap technique then please visit:

www.PropertyInvesting.com/strategies/wraps

## The Human Nature of Wraps

The success or failure of your wrap investment depends entirely on the quality of the client who buys your property on vendor's terms. If you have a good client then you can expect a minimum of fuss. But, on the other hand, the reverse is also true – a bad client will mean plenty of investing headaches.

### A Bad Wrap Experience

While Dave and I try hard to make a success of all our wrap investments, even the best made plans sometimes fail. Once we sold a property to a couple who, on first impression, seemed perfectly normal. They had good credit records, an established rental history and could demonstrate that the instalment payments we offered were comfortably affordable. Everything was going well until one day they just stopped paying. We phoned them regularly but could only leave messages on their answering machine. We also sent letters asking them to contact us. As a final straw, Dave dropped in to see them. They said that they regretted having fallen behind and promised to pay extra to catch up. And for a while they kept to their word and did just that.

However, before too long, their payments ceased again and a stone wall of silence greeted our every attempt to contact them. Left with little option, we sent them a letter explaining that unless they kept to their word, we'd have little option but to rescind the contract, in which case they'd need to find somewhere else to live.

That approach at least prompted them to phone the office. Rather than looking to work through the issue though, Dave and I were threatened with having our heads punched in, our homes blown up and our wives assaulted.

Sometimes a person who can't afford to stay can't afford to leave either. In a last-ditch offer to create a win-win outcome, Dave (bad cop) explained that we had $2,000 to spend, either in legal fees to enforce our rights or else to help them relocate to another property. The offer of cash changed everything and while tense, the couple agreed to move on and return to renting (strangely, they moved into a property which cost more in rent than what their repayments to us had been). We handed over $2,000 cash the day they moved out and then spent another $1,000 cleaning up the property before seeking a new client who wanted to buy the property on vendor's terms.

In hindsight the lesson I learned from this experience was that a person with a 'victim mentality', that is, someone who feels that the world owes them a favour, is not a person that you want to have as a client.

### A Good Wrap Experience

One of our wrap clients is a couple with three children. They came to our attention when Dave was sitting in a real estate agent's office looking for properties to buy that came with existing tenants. The agent mentioned that this couple were concerned about losing their home if it was sold to a buyer who also wanted to live in the property. They had approached the bank to seek finance in their own right, but had been rejected on the basis that they were contractors without an established employment record.

Dave asked the agent to approach them to see if they would be interested in buying the property off us on vendor's terms, provided we could keep their repayments within affordable limits. After asking questions and seeking independent legal advice, Dave met with the family and outlined how vendor's finance works. Seeing the chance to own a home on fair terms, they sensed this was the opportunity of a lifetime.

Shortly after accepting our deal (i.e. during Phase 3), the parents received a call from their child's school wanting to know the reason for the tremendous turnaround in their son's behaviour. Whereas before he was unsettled and disruptive, he was now attentive and a good class contributor. We later heard that the day after we'd sold them the property on vendor's terms, the boy ran to school yelling "We don't have to move! We don't have to move!"

Today, just three years into a 25 year contract, the recent boom in prices has resulted in their house being worth much more than the price they paid for it. Do we feel upset that we might have charged too little as a price margin? No. At the time we entered this deal the terms were fair for everyone and it's pleasing that, with the benefit of hindsight, we can say that there was a genuine win-win outcome.

A properly constructed wrap deal has the power to transform lives. This example, again, underpins the importance of focusing on the needs of people first, and letting the profit take care of itself.

## Your Wrap Client Base

You'd be making a huge error in judgement if you believed that the only people interested in vendor's finance were those with dubious credit histories. For example, one of our potential clients who answered an advertisement had a $45,000 compensation payout after being injured at work. He wanted to by a $65,000 house, yet because he was unable to work and his only income was from a disability pension, all the major lenders quickly rejected his loan application. Yet to me, a $45,000 deposit meant that by the time I'd added on my margin his loan repayments were just $70 per week – a fraction of his pension and far less than the $200 per week he paid to rent his current home.

Here's a list of people that a major lender may reject but who might, nevertheless, be a good credit risk:

▷ Self-employed business owners

▷ Employees who have not been with an employer long enough

▷ People who are paid in cash

▷ Employees with a disjointed employment record

▷ People who have received a worker's compensation pay out

▷ New Australians

▷ People who have one or two credit blemishes on their credit records

▷ Ex-bankrupts (who went bankrupt for personal reasons)

▷ Short-term unemployed workers, such as seasonal employees; and

▷ Older citizens (they are often ignored by the banks).

But be warned – there's a tendency for people to overstate what they can afford to repay. You won't be doing anyone any favours by creating a deal that places your client on the financial red line. Be sure to consider the impact of a rise in interest rates and help your client to quantify the likely extra costs for the rates, insurance etc. Just because there's a dollar to be made doesn't justify going ahead at all costs. You need to be satisfied that you're offering a true win-win outcome.

## Steve's Investing Tip

While it's not realistic to expect that all your deals will turn out as planned, if you avoid the warning signs or ignore your gut feeling, then financial disaster won't be too far away.

Wrapping is a niche market. You're looking for clients that can demonstrate that they're either good credit risks but don't qualify for regular finance, or alternatively, they might have had one or two black marks on their credit file yet be able to demonstrate that they have learned their lesson and are ready to move on.

# THE CRITICAL SUCCESS FACTORS IN A WRAP

## It's All About People

While the essence of a wrap is that the investor becomes more like a financier than a traditional landlord, the source of the cashflow is the same – it comes from the pockets of everyday people.

One of the early mistakes Dave and I made was to focus far too much on just getting a deal over the line rather than meeting the needs of our wrap client base. That's when we discovered that the quality of our investments depended almost entirely on the calibre of the person living in the house. When we shifted our focus to fulfilling our clients' needs, rather than just our own, we achieved a level of success and personal satisfaction that we never thought possible.

### Steve's Investing Tip

Focus on people and let the profits take care of themselves.

## Build Win-Win Outcomes

Dave and I once had the opportunity to buy a property that one of our wrap clients desperately wanted, which was located next door to his best friend. The agent selling the property knew this as well and inflated the sales price by an extra $10,000. Even buying at this price and adding our margin, our client could still afford the repayments, but only just.

Stepping back from the deal for a moment, Dave and I began to question whether or not we were creating a true win-win outcome given that the property was clearly overpriced. After a lot of thought we declined to proceed, but instead of leaving our client in uncertain territory, we networked hard and were able to find him a loan (albeit on a slightly higher interest rate than we were offering) with a non-conforming lender.

Not all deals will bring dollars directly into your pocket, but if you create enough win-win circumstances then your success will be a matter of time, not a matter of luck.

## Play by the Rules

The three never-break rules of wrapping:

▷ *Keep repayments affordable* – never place your client on the financial red line.

▷ *Full disclosure* – to both your client and to your financier.

▷ *Compliance* with all the laws.

As the wrap laws in each state are slightly different, you're going to need to complete further research before launching into your first vendor's finance deal. While www.PropertyInvesting.com provides an excellent resource, there are some specific laws that you should research, namely:

### A. Privacy Laws

You need to be careful about privacy laws when seeking information about potential wrap clients, particularly when doing a formal credit check.

### B. Consumer Credit Laws

Whether wrapping falls under consumer credit laws is open to debate, but why risk being caught in an argument that's easily avoidable? In most states it's a matter of procedure (which means filling in forms) to comply with the consumer protection laws. Be sure to complete your due diligence before launching in to a deal.

### C. First Home Owner Grant

If eligible, your client may be able to use his or her First Home Owner Grant to partly fund his or her deposit. At the time of writing the grant was immediately accessible in Victoria and New South Wales, but was payable after one year in Queensland and Tasmania. Check with the local state authority responsible for administering the grant in your area.

## The Arguments for Vendor's Finance

When you decide to wrap you decide to invest in people. Presenting a person with an opportunity to own his or her home is, in many ways, being in the business of delivering dreams. Providing you wrap the right way, which is putting people before profit, you'll create the potential for a win-win outcome – an outcome where your client gets a house and you make money in the form of regular ongoing positive cashflow.

If you create a deal that's affordable then you'll find wraps to be relatively maintenance free. There's no requirement to study stock charts or make sure all your ostriches are in the right paddock. All you need to do is keep a watchful eye to ensure your clients meet their minimum requirements under the vendor's finance contract.

Wraps are an established way of making money. There is no promise of getting rich quick. In my opinion it's not only a fair reward for the risk involved and the capital contributed, it's also a great way to invest in property and create ongoing positive cashflow returns.

## The Arguments Against Vendor's Finance

Wraps do have weaknesses too. While they provide positive cashflow returns, it takes a lot of time and effort to set the deal up in a win-win way. You really must enjoy dealing with people to get a benefit from wrapping. If you're primarily interested in money and returns, try trading stocks.

Another fair criticism is that it takes many wrap deals to provide enough cash to enable you to become financially independent. I have never advocated the use of wraps as a 'get-rich-quick' scheme. If you're looking for a quick fix to your financial problems, vendor's finance isn't the answer.

As wraps have a finite life, you must accept that one day your interest in the property will end. That's why it's important to take some of your positive cashflow and reinvest it in other investments designed to keep meeting your financial goals (as outlined in Step 4 of the Positive Gearing Model on page 164).

## THE FINAL WORD ON WRAPPING

I wouldn't be where I am today without using wraps. With limited funds to invest, wraps allowed Dave and I to buy multiple properties in a short amount of time. It's an excellent investment tool, but is only sustainable if you build win-win outcomes.

## Chapter 13 Insights

### Insight #1:

In a wrap transaction you become more like a bank and less like a traditional landlord. The majority of your profit is derived from your interest rate margin and you pass nearly all the costs of ownership on to your client.

### Insight #2:

Provided your clients meet strict criteria, vendor's finance offers a relatively high return for the risk involved. Avoid people with a 'victim mentality' and *always* ensure your client can comfortably make his or her repayments.

### Insight #3:

It's not just the financially challenged who'll be interested in vendor's finance. There's a huge number of people in every market who want to own a home but fail to meet the major bank's strict lending criteria.

### Insight #4:

Wrapping is a volume business. If you only plan to do one or two then you may find the effort too much for the return. But once you get started you'll quickly discover that it's a strategy that can help you to fast-track your financial independence.

### Insight #5:

Vendor's finance is about investing in people. If you can't create a win-win outcome then it's better to avoid the deal rather than proceed knowing that it's likely you'll encounter financial headaches in the not too distant future.

# Lease Options:
# The Best of Both Worlds

## Investor's Summary: Lease Options

### Aim:

A lease option, also known as a 'rent to buy arrangement', is a combination of a residential lease with a call option.

It provides the tenant with an opportunity, but not an obligation, to purchase the property for an agreed price, on or before an agreed date.

### Ways to Profit:

1.  *Positive net cashflow:* Occurs when your rent is higher than your interest and property ownership costs.

## Investor's Summary: Lease Options *(cont'd)*

### Ways to Profit *(cont'd):*

2.  *Capital gains:* If your client exercises his or her call option then you'll make a capital gain – the difference between your sale price under the option agreement and what you originally paid for the property.

### Your Client:

Someone who'd like to rent a property today, while also retaining the right to purchase it at a later date.

### Regulated by:

🗷 The written terms and conditions of your rental or occupation agreement (called a *lease*, or in some states a *license to occupy*).

🗷 The written terms and conditions of your option contract.

🗷 Where applicable, established residential tenancy laws enforced by tenancy tribunals.

### Service Providers:

To automate the collection of your rental income you may like to use the services of a rental manager who will charge a fee for managing the tenant and property related issues.

### Other Comments:

Lease options are an attractive alternative for people who would like to own a home in the future, but are happy renting for the time being. In Queensland and New South Wales, a *license to occupy* is used instead of a residential lease.

In the process of following up leads (people who responded to our classified ads), we'd occasionally meet good quality people but, because of their circumstances, providing vendor's finance would not have resulted in a win-win outcome.

For example, some clients did not have the necessary deposit, or alternatively, a large part of their regular income included government rent assistance, which would cease if they owned rather then rented. Dave and I could see the potential in helping these people, but in order to do so we needed to implement a different investment strategy. That's when I devised a 'rent to buy' plan that we nicknamed 'HomeStarter'.

## OUR 'HOMESTARTER' APPROACH

For the clients who wanted to own a property but had no deposit, we offered them the opportunity to live in one of our investment properties on the basis of a slightly higher than normal market rent.

In return we'd channel $50 per month ($600 per annum) into a notional holding account. Furthermore, if our client did what was required for 12 consecutive months, we'd provide an additional $600 bonus.

There was a catch though. The balance in the holding account could only be used to match, dollar for dollar, the money the tenant had independently saved and wanted to contribute as a deposit when buying the property off us on vendor's terms.

If the tenant paid the rent late, didn't keep the property in a neat and tidy condition or decided not to proceed with the purchase, then any money in the holding account was forfeited.

HomeStarter worked well up until the introduction of the First Home Owner Grant, at which point those eligible for the grant were able to gain instant access to a deposit. This has largely made the HomeStarter program redundant, however, if the grant is withdrawn then I can foresee it becoming relevant again.

# THE MORE FORMAL LEASE-OPTION MODEL

There's a more formal lease option model based on a system that works well in the United States. It contains two components:

1.  A call option that allows (but does not compel) the tenant to purchase the property at a future date for an agreed price; and

2.  A residential lease over a property.

Let's look at these two concepts in more detail:

## The Call-Option Component

The call-option component provides the tenant or occupier with the right (but not an obligation) to buy the property, on or before a future specified date, for an agreed value.

In exchange for this right, the investor charges a once off non-refundable call-option fee, usually determined by the perceived risk to the investor, but not normally more than a few thousand dollars. Should the tenant or occupier decide to exercise his or her option to buy the property then his or her call-option fee is then credited against the agreed purchase price under the option agreement.

## The Residential Lease/License to Occupy Component

Until the date when the option must be exercised, the person living in the property has much the same obligations as a tenant. That is, they must pay the rent on time and in return the landlord must maintain the property in good repair.

The rental payment set by the lease-option investor is usually at a market premium (say plus 20%). This may appear a little draconian at first glance, yet a portion of each rental payment is deducted from the agreed sales price under the option contract.

This may all sound a little complicated, so let's look at how a lease option works using an example contributed by professional investor Tony Barton, Australia's leading lease-option expert.

## A Contribution by Australia's Foremost Lease-Option Expert – Tony Barton

*Hi, my name's Tony Barton and I'm pleased to be able to contribute this information about how I've profited from lease options.*

*I started investing in property at pretty much the same time as Steve and Dave. In fact, I can share a little secret and reveal that we were even at the same breakthrough investing seminar back in May 1999.*

*Whereas Steve and Dave adopted wraps as their niche, I turned to lease options and have since created many opportunities where everyone in the deal has profited.*

*My niche is investing in three, four, or five-bedroom "cosmetically challenged" family homes on 500-800 square metres of land. Ideally the property will have a carport or garage, be fenced, close to public transport and other important amenities.*

*Most of my clients fall into the demographic of your average blue-collar, working-class family, earning less than $45,000 per annum. For one reason or another, usually their lack of ability to save money for a deposit or a bad credit history, my clients cannot access finance to buy their own home using conventional lending means.*

*I write this to illustrate that I invest in a specific market both in terms of the houses I buy, the areas where I invest and, most importantly, the people I aim to help.*

*Typically I find houses in outer urban areas of Victoria, where the population is greater than 15,000 persons and prices for the average home are about 30% of Melbourne's median home value.*

*Affordability is crucial in determining where I buy my houses. It would be ridiculous for me to try to place a family of four that earn*

*$35,000 per annum into a house that is worth $300,000 and expect a positive long-term outcome. It's important to match all the pieces in the investing jigsaw together in order to create (as Steve says) "win-win outcomes" for everybody.*

*As a summary, my lease-option strategy provides middle-of-the-road families with the opportunity to enter the housing market without needing to enter into large amounts of debt or come up with a substantial deposit.*

*The lease-option strategy has allowed me to acquire multiple properties without necessarily having to use further cash outlays.*

*For example, as the lease is a long-term contract and my clients have the intention of one day owning the property, they often make substantial improvements to the cosmetically challenged state of the property. Even though they pay and do the work (with my approval), I'm able to borrow against the additional equity they are contributing to the property and then use that money to buy more properties.*

*Of course, in order to do this in an ethical manner, I need to provide my client with full disclosure. However, working through this issue, because my clients have a fixed, agreed purchase price at the time of the contract, any improvement to the value of the property also benefits them.*

*If you can appreciate this point then you'll begin to see the power of lease options for everyone involved in the deal.*

## An Example

*In November 1999 I acquired a property (coincidentally in Ballarat, where I understand Steve and Dave also started) for $54,000 (including closing costs).*

*Having run my own classified ad and found a client base that wanted to avail themselves of my lease-option services, I then structured the following deal:*

➢ *Call-option price of $68,850 that the client could exercise on or before 30 November 2024 (i.e. over the next 25 years)*

D A base weekly rent of $170 with increases for inflation and upwards movements in interest rates; and

D An option fee of $2,000.

Between November 1999 and May 2002 the person living in the property made his rent payments as required and renovated his home with my permission. He did a thorough internal repaint, landscaped the gardens and also put in a $4,500 split-system air conditioner.

In May 2002 he decided to exercise his option, arrange for alternative finance and cash me out. After deducting his option fee and the appropriate amount from his weekly rental (which I calculate using a formula), his final option exercise price was reduced to $64,000.

While disappointed to lose my income stream, I was delighted to later find out that the bank had valued his property at $95,000.

The result was a win-win outcome that Steve so rightly points out is critical. In addition to a capital gain of $10,000 I earned when my client exercised his option, I also enjoyed a regular positive net cashflow income of approximately $70 per week for two and a half years. Table 14.1, overleaf, shows a summary of the numbers.

## A Bad Deal Turned Good

While everybody hopes that their investments will have a happy ending, I've learned far more and made substantial amounts of money from making mistakes. In short, deals that turn sour offer the best learning possibilities and allow for you to finetune your investing system.

Let me share one such 'bad' experience.

When I first started buying houses I bought as many as I could afford. Actually, I had the whole system for buying properties pretty much mastered. However, where I fell down was finding **clients** who wanted to live in the properties under my lease-option strategy.

One house I'd acquired sat vacant for 120 days and the negative cashflow associated with having to pay the loan interest was *hurting my profitability. As I was eager to have it rented as soon as possible, my eagerness led me to put clients into the property without doing the stringent checks that I do today.*

| Table 14.1 – Summary | |
|---|---|
| **INITIAL CASH DOWN** | |
| Deposit | $10,200 |
| Closing costs and legals | $3,000 |
| Initial cash needed | $13,200 |
| *Less* option fee received | ($2,000) |
| **Net Cash Needed** | **$11,200** |
| **ANNUAL CASH ON CASH RETURN** | |
| Net weekly cashflow | $70<br>x 52 |
| Annual positive cashflow | $3,640 |
| Net initial cash needed | ÷ $11,200 |
| **Annual Cash on Cash Return** | **32.50%** |
| **PROJECT CASH ON CASH RETURN** | |
| Net cashflow, 30 months<br>(June 1999 to November 2001) | $9,100 |
| Capital gain | $10,000 |
| Total positive cashflow | $19,100 |
| Net initial cash needed | ÷ $11,200 |
| **Project Cash on Cash Return** | **170.54%** |
| **Annualised Projected<br>Cash on Cash Return** | **68.22% p.a.** |

*These clients didn't have an established rental history and I requested a slightly higher than normal option fee of 4% of the purchase price ($3,200) to compensate for the additional risk. Having purchased the property for $78,000, I set their option price at $102,000 which they could exercise at anytime during the term of the lease (which was 25 years and 51 days). The periodic rental was set at $195 per week.*

*As the clients appeared both enthusiastic and grateful for the opportunity, and they certainly appeared to have the ability to easily afford the rent, I decided to approve their application without properly investigating their lack of rental history.*

*A few months into the lease agreement I received a number of phone calls at my office from disgruntled neighbours in the street, to complain about late night parties and noise coming from the house.*

*The once quiet street had been turned into a car park where multiple cars were parked in the driveway, front lawn and nature strip. In fact, anywhere with enough spare land had either a parked car or the sum of a car's dismantled parts.*

*I made initial enquires with the tenant who promised to "keep the peace" with the neighbourhood and remove the cars from where they were not allowed to be under the terms of the lease. Progress was immediate as the tenant did everything I requested promptly after our telephone conversation.*

*However, three months further down the track, I began to receive more irate telephone calls from the neighbours. It seemed the property had become a halfway house and the noise, parties and cars were back in even greater numbers.*

*I took more of an interest and decided to telephone the tenants to tell them I would be coming to do an inspection in 48 hours.*

*Even though my client's payments were in advance, upon arrival at the house, the noise, cars and even more strangely – my clients had all disappeared without a trace.*

*What they did leave behind though was a huge general mess both inside and outside the house.*

*Everything needed cleaning – the ceilings, the carpets, the walls, the windows. There was a hole in one of the walls in the kitchen where, apparently, the tenant had been completing some creative cooking.*

*While I was initially alarmed at the cost of cleaning the house and the necessary repairs (luckily these were covered by insurance) the whole experience taught me to:*

1. *Never rent a property to someone without an established rental history; and*

2. *Always pay a rental manager to handle the inspections and rent collection in order to free up my time to help more people, rather than having to take on the burdensome task of managing real estate.*

*Within three weeks of the property being cleaned, repainted and repaired I was able to lease-option it to a new tenant, a couple with an excellent long-term rental history.*

*They loved what they saw and moved into the property, paying a new call-option fee ($2,500) and, since I had spruced up the house, they agreed to a rent that was $10 higher than what my last tenant paid. I was also able to increase the option exercise price to $112,000, so in the end, I actually had a better performing investment once I was able to put the bad experience behind me. Table 14.2, opposite, is a summary of how the numbers on the deal turned out.*

*My final piece of advice is to reinforce the need to see lease-optioning as an investment in the person first and the property second. If you can set up a win-win outcome then you'll find the lease-option technique to be a relatively hassle-free way to earn substantial investment returns.*

# THE DIFFERENCE BETWEEN A WRAP AND A LEASE OPTION

The fundamental difference between a wrap and a lease option is the status of the person occupying the property. In a wrap transaction your client signs a contract to buy the property and is making repayments. Under a lease option, there's the opportunity to purchase at a future date but no obligation. Until the option is exercised the occupier pays rent.

| *Table 14.2 – Summary* | |
|---|---|
| **INITIAL CASH DOWN** | |
| Deposit | $15,600 |
| Closing costs and legals | $4,680 |
| Initial cash needed | $20,280 |
| *Less* initial option fee received | ($3,200) |
| **Net Cash Needed** | **$17,080** |
| **PROJECTED ANNUAL CASH ON CASH RETURN** | |
| Net weekly cashflow | $97 x 52 |
| Projected positive cashflow | $5,044 |
| Net initial cash needed | ÷ $17,080 |
| **Annual Cash on Cash Return** | **29.53%** |
| **AMENDED ANNUAL CASH ON CASH RETURN** | |
| New net weekly cashflow | $107 x 52 |
| Projected positive cashflow | $5,564 |
| Net initial cash needed (Deducting 2nd option fee of $2,500) | ÷ $14,580 |
| **Annual Cash on Cash Return** | **38.16%** |

**Steve's Investing Tip**

Under a wrap there is a contract signed for the purchase of a property whereas under a lease option, there's only the right, rather than an obligation, to buy.

Clients buying using the lease-option strategy will only become entitled to receive the First Home Owner Grant once they exercise their right to purchase the property.

# CRITICAL FACTORS IN A LEASE OPTION

The factors that determine the success or otherwise of a lease option are pretty much the same as those affecting a vendor's finance contract, namely:

## Pre-Qualifying Leads

The reliability of your income stream depends entirely on the quality of your lease-option client. Like wraps, lease-option agreements can last for up to 25 years, which is a long time to be investing in a person. It's critical that you research the needs and abilities of potential clients to ensure that you:

▷ Don't 'max out' your client by placing them in a property where they can only just afford to pay the rent. Conditions that exist today won't prevail forever, so when you invest for the long-term you need to allow some leeway for increases in market rent and inflation adjustments.

▷ Check the details of your potential client's previous tenancy. It may be tempting to do a deal with just about anyone who's interested, yet that could be a massive mistake. The amount of financial distress you suffer is inversely proportional to the amount of time and effort you invest to ensure you have a quality client. You don't want someone with a checkered rental history and who occupies a prime place on the tenant black list.

☞ Be sure you know who'll be living in your property and specify this in the lease agreement. Relatives, friends and pets of your client make may make for unwanted additions.

## The Right Property

While the real asset in a lease option is the person, the underlying property is also important. You may not need a five-star home, but it's certainly wise to only buy properties that are structurally sound. Empower your client to make cosmetic changes to his or her heart's content (subject to you first agreeing of course) but as far as structural problems go, expensive repairs may mean that your client loses interest in the property and leaves rather than stays for the long-term.

The lease-option technique works for houses at all price ranges provided the rent can be set at a level that delivers a positive cashflow return to the investor and this is within affordable limits for the client.

## Win-Win Deals

The details outlined in Tony's earlier example are only one of an infinite number of ways that a lease option can be structured.

### Steve's Investing Tip

Successful lease-optioning is not so much dependent on the property, but the person who will become your client.

### Know the Laws!

It's critical that you know the laws in the area where you plan to invest. For example, in some states you're not allowed to pass on the costs of rates etc. to the tenant, which means that you need to approach this issue from a different (yet perfectly legal) angle in order to overcome it. Be sure to get appropriate legal advice before jumping into the deep-end of the investing pool.

## THE FINAL WORD ON LEASE OPTIONS

A lease option is a valuable investment strategy for a niche market of potential clients. It's appropriate to use when your clients want to own their home one day but, for the time being, are happy just to rent.

By using a lease option, the investor receives a guaranteed long-term, above-market rental return and almost entirely eliminates the possibility of crippling vacancies. The client obtains peace of mind by knowing they have a secure lease with the added bonus of eventually owning the property, if they so desire.

### Steve's Investing Tip

The key to sustainable investing is to only venture into deals where there's a chance for everyone to win.

## Chapter 14 Insights

### Insight #1:

A lease option is a strategy that combines a residential lease with an option for the tenant to buy the property at an agreed price, on or before, an agreed date, as negotiated at the beginning of the deal.

### Insight #2:

The rent charged is usually set at a market premium, perhaps up to 20% higher. However, a portion of the rent is then credited against the option price provided the client goes ahead and purchases the property.

### Insight #3:

The client is charged a once-off, non-refundable option fee at the beginning of the tenancy to help cover the investor's initial deposit and legal costs. This fee is also deducted from the option price if the client decides to purchase the property.

### Insight #4:

A great way to encourage the tenant to increase the equity in the property is to complete some general cosmetic upgrades. Because title is in your name, you're allowed to borrow a portion of additional equity, which you can then use to fund the deposits on other investment properties.

### Insight #5:

Just like under the wrap strategy, the strength and reliability of your cashflow with a lease-option strategy depends entirely on the quality of the person – rather than the property – you invest in.

# Renovations... Mould to Gold, or Good Money After Bad?

## Investor's Summary: Renovations

### Aim:

When you complete a renovation you aim to add more value (either actual or perceived) to the property than the actual cost of completing the upgrades.

### Ways to Profit:

1.  *Increased Cashflow:* Through higher market rents which a renovated property should attract.

2.  *Capital Gains:* When the value added is more than the cost of renovations.

## Investor's Summary: Renovations *(cont'd)*

### Your Client:

You, as you want to maximise the return on your investment.

### Regulated by:

⏩ Council regulations to the extent that planning permits are needed; and

⏩ State laws restricting owner-builders and home handypeople.

### Service Providers:

You can either do the renovations yourself or employ contractors such as builders, painters, plumbers etc.

### Other Comments:

Provided you're the right kind of person (someone who is either good with their hands or excels at project management), renovating properties will be an exciting and rewarding challenge. It can be as simple as painting a room or as complicated as taking a house back to its basic frame and then rebuilding.

# THE JOURNEY CONTINUES...

Chapter 5 ended with Dave and I purchasing our first investment property – a three-bedroom weatherboard home in West Wendouree. It was a few more months before Dave and I began to actively look for more properties. We had to wait for our business savings account to replenish a little and for our first property to settle so that we had both confidence and the knowledge of how the process of buying houses would unfold.

We eventually committed to returning to Ballarat. However, this time Dave and I also planned to bring our wives and make a day of the whole trip. As our accounting business was busy, we left on a Saturday morning and, driving in separate cars, agreed to meet up in Ballarat for morning tea. We arranged for Micky G, the real estate agent who'd sold us our first property, to schedule more inspections, including a few houses that we had not been able to get through on our last trip.

Once again (this was now surely more than a coincidence) it was the last house that Mick showed us that we found to be the most interesting. The property was an unusually shaped Federation weatherboard house. It had four bedrooms with two living areas – one of which was a large upstairs loft. The property was within easy walking distance to the city mall and was situated on a massive corner block of land. A possible option that Dave and I immediately identified was to subdivide the backyard and sell it off to a developer.

Yet not everything was positive. The exterior of the house needed repairs, the grounds were a jungle, and student tenants had run riot inside, turning everything they'd touched to grunge. There was more dust than wool in the carpets, all the window sash cords were broken and new light fittings were needed throughout. All in all, the property was screaming for some urgent tender loving care.

Mick advised us that the house had been passed-in at auction the week before as it had failed to meet the vendor's reserve (minimum sale price) of $83,000.

When Dave and I looked at the property we saw huge potential. All our wives saw was hard work and they suggested that the rejection by the local market was a sign to leave this deal alone. Hang on! We were the experts and not easily dissuaded, so we convinced them this house was a great opportunity waiting to be harvested.

In an effort to negotiate, we submitted an offer of $78,000 but Mick was adamant the owner wouldn't take anything less than

$83,000. With other buyers looking through the property at the same inspection time, we didn't want to miss out on the deal, so we agreed to pay full price.

Our 'back of the envelope' plans were to spend three months and $20,000 renovating the property and then quickly sell it for what Mick said would be a good price – around the $130,000 mark (after allowing for sale costs). Dave and I signed the contract to purchase our second investment property on the 27th of July 1999 with a 30-day settlement period.

## Seeking Solutions

By this time, two months on from our first purchase, Dave and I had managed to replenish our business savings account, but our bank balance was not anywhere near large enough to pay for the property and all the renovation costs.

Another possibility was for Dave and I to access our emergency personal cash; Dave could redraw about $40,000 off his home mortgage, and Julie and I had a private bank account balance of about $30,000. While we could have organised an investment loan and kept the majority of our personal savings intact, we were reluctant to do this because we were only planning to do a three-month project.

Jumping through the hoops to organise a short-term mortgage would be expensive, both in terms of time and money, so we decided to go down a different path and look for a project partner.

The obvious choice was my father, who'd just retired from his job after 40 years and was looking for a project to sink his teeth into. Although not a builder, Dad is certainly capable of doing minor home renovations and possessed an array of power tools that would put most tradesmen to shame. Even more importantly, he had the time and money to throw at the project.

## Pear Shaped

Dave and I showed Dad our budgeted figures and convinced him that this was a good opportunity to make some quick cash. Once we'd established an informal partnership (we shook hands), it was down to the business of renovating. We were able to secure early access to the property, which allowed us to begin renovating during the settlement period. (The tenants had moved out.)

I'm here to tell you that as renovators, Dave and I make far better accountants. Every time we lifted a hammer or a paintbrush, all we seemed to do was create more work.

Dad, who crowned himself 'one coat Macca', boasted how he was a skilled painter. Sadly, it turned out that he wasn't as blessed as he'd led us to believe. By the end of the job we'd renamed him 'one more coat Macca', as several of the rooms had to be painted three times after we'd run out of his custom-tinted paint. It was impossible to match up the same paint shades, so we had to restart again from scratch.

Instead of taking three months, we ended up allocating every weekend for six months to the job of stripping back wallpaper, painting, landscaping and repairing window sash cords.

And all we did was the cosmetic work. The major tasks – like putting in a new kitchen, polishing the floorboards, laying down cork tiles, painting the exterior of the house, landscaping the front garden, fixing the roof and fitting marble hearths to the fireplaces, were all left to expert subcontractors.

At the end of the project we were 50% over budget in dollars and 109% over budget in time. It was mid-January 2000 and the total cost of the house after repairs and closing costs had ballooned to $111,402. Exhausted and frustrated at earning no income, we all agreed to sell the property as soon as possible and put the whole experience behind us.

We'd had a run in with Mick's boss, so we went with another agent in town who was impressed with what we'd done and said that we should "put a circle around $140,000 as a fair sale price." Our fully renovated dream home sat on the market without any interest at all until, on the 2nd of March 2000, an out of town buyer offered us the pitiful sum of $125,000.

Even worse – we'd later discover that the agent we chose (he seemed like a good negotiator from other dealings we'd had with him) actually told the potential purchaser to submit a low offer as the vendors "were starting to get a little desperate". The whole process had been a disaster. Not only had we channelled much more money into the house than was budgeted, we had a fool of an agent, and I was sick to death of the smell of fresh paint. Being upset at the treatment we'd received, I couldn't bear the thought of paying a fool a commission and so we rejected the offer and listed the property with another real estate agent. The innocent purchaser was left confused. The agent had told him the deal was pretty much stitched up when, in fact, we hadn't ever agreed to his offer, much less signed a contract.

Finally on the 21st of March our new agent coaxed an extra token $2,555 out of the same purchaser, and we agreed to sell. We all breathed a collective sigh of relief. Table 15.1, below, is a summary of the details.

| Table 15.1 – Numbers on Our Second Property Investment | | |
|---|---|---|
| | **EXPECTATION** | **EVENTUAL OUTCOME** |
| Project length | 90 days | 188 days |
| Purchase price | $83,000 | $83,000 |
| Closing costs | $3,000 | $2,821 |
| Renovation cost | $17,000 | $25,581 |
| **TOTAL COST** | **$103,000** | **$111,402** |
| Sale price | $140,000 | $127,555 |
| Sale costs | $7,000 | $7,364 |
| **Net After-Sale Proceeds** | **$133,000** | **$120,191** |
| **PROFIT** | **$30,000** | **$8,789** |

Being accountants, the one thing we did do well was keep track of the numbers. After sales costs, we made the total profit of $8,789.20 or $2,929.73 each. When you convert this sum back into an hourly rate and factor in the risk, we'd have been better off flipping burgers for McDonald's.

## Learning the Lesson

I have no doubt that another investor with more experience in decorating and renovating could have made more profit out of this opportunity. But for us, rehabilitating houses was not an area of expertise. I often wonder how many great deals passed us by as we spent our time painting walls and digging gardens.

Once you find your niche you'll discover that it comes naturally to you. It may be that you're a born landlord, or you may like the challenge of renovation. You might even have what it takes to be a successful property developer. It doesn't matter what your niche is, so long as you stick with it and learn from your mistakes.

### Moving On

Towards the end of renovating the property another deal came up – the opportunity to transform two adjoining houses on separate titles in a much better area. I was keen to proceed if we could negotiate a low deposit and secure a six-month settlement period, however Dave wisely torpedoed my enthusiasm suggesting it would be better to wait until we'd sold our existing renovated property before we looked to do a similar project.

What Dave and I needed to discover was that we weren't renovators. However, the only way we could find this out was to first attempt a project and discover whether or not we were skilled at the strategy. I certainly don't regret buying this property. I was able to share some great father-son bonding time with Dad, build a database of reliable tradesmen and learn a lot more about how much potential problems cost to fix. Dave and I were not afraid to do other renovation projects. However, we did discover that we needed to employ or hire other people to do the work. Our hands are skilled at holding pens, not hammers.

## THE SECRET OF RENOVATION SUCCESS

### Steve's Investing Tip

The secret to renovation success is to **always maintain control**.

The critical success factor in any renovation is control over:

1. *Time*

   You'll either need to spend the time doing the renovation work yourself or spend hours co-ordinating a team of contractors to get the job done for you; and

2. *Money*

   Renovations can be very expensive and, as I learned, a budget can easily blow out of control.

Time and money blowouts will cripple even the best planned projects. If you don't have a lot of experience completing renovations then it's critical to pay someone to check over your budgeted timeframe and numbers. Luckily you can pay a builder, or for bigger projects, a quantity surveyor to do this for you.

### Avoid Making the Same Mistake Twice

After our property had eventually been sold, Dave and I did go back and look at the other renovation opportunity we had found, but only on the basis that we wouldn't be the bunnies that did the work. This time, unlike our first renovation project, we invested $280 and engaged a builder to look through the house to provide us with an estimation of what it would cost to renovate. When the builder told us that we'd be mad to proceed, we quickly ended negotiations.

There's a saying: life's lessons keep repeating until you learn them. For me, I had to learn that finding and sticking to my niche was far more important than chasing potential quick profits.

Sooner or later you'll be attracted to a deal that promises fast cash or amazing returns. Your greed gland will start secreting and you might be tempted to stray from your niche. Trust me, don't do it. Learn from my mistake. It doesn't matter how boring or routine your niche becomes, you won't go broke if all you do is keep making money. Another valuable lesson that Dave and I learned, which was more than just an investing tip, was to pay more attention to what our wives told us to do.

## Chapter 15 Insights

### Insight #1:
Don't be afraid to try something new provided that you feel it's within your area of expertise – just try to avoid making the same mistakes twice.

### Insight #2:
It would have been easy for Dave and I to say that, since we didn't have the money in our business, we couldn't afford to buy any more property. There is *always* a way when you think in terms of "How can I?" rather than "Can I?"

*Cont'd...*

## Chapter 15 Insights *(cont'd)*

### Insight #3:

Unless you're a skilled renovator, it is far more sensible to pay other people to complete the work, provided the numbers in the deal show that you'll make your required profit. Time is your most valuable asset and when your head is in a paint tin, it's hard to see the opportunity of a lifetime that might be crawling past outside.

### Insight #4:

Some real estate agents are better to buy from while others are better at handling sales. Unfortunately, the only way to tell is with experience.

### Insight #5:

Please don't think that every deal we touch turns to gold. While we've never lost money on a property transaction, it has sometimes been very close. Even though we only made $2,929.73 each on our second purchase, the experience was of far more value.

There's no seminar that could have taught us as much practical information and, as such, this renovation was one of our biggest learning experiences.

### Insight #6:

Life's lessons keep on repeating until you learn them. What lessons have you needed to repeat lately?

# Flips: Quick Cash... but Beware

## Investor's Summary: Flips

### Aim:

To acquire a property and then on-sell it to another party before having to settle on the purchase.

### Ways to Profit:

*Capital Gains:* The difference between the price you pay to buy the property and what you can sell your interest in the contract for.

### Your Client:

You, as you're seeking to make a quick lump-sum gain.

## Investor's Summary: Flips *(cont'd)*

### Regulated by:

⓭ State-based stamp duty legislation; and

⓭ State-based legislation governing the sale of land.

### Service Providers:

For a commission, real estate agents may be able to find a client who would be interested in taking over the purchase of the property.

### Other Comments:

Flipping properties sounds great in theory, but trying to implement this strategy is a lot more difficult than what you might expect, especially in a booming market.

# MYTH AND REALITY

If you're someone who wants to make a start in real estate and you have a lot of time but very little money, flipping houses might seem like an attractive option. With time on your side, you can search for 'diamond in the rough' deals – properties you can acquire at a significant discount because the vendor has an urgent need to sell. The concept appears straightforward enough:

**Step 1:** Find a house that would be suitable as a flip (i.e. a property at a discount, or a situation where you can negotiate a long-term settlement).

**Step 2:** Buy it.

**Step 3:** Sell it to someone before having to close on the deal.

**Step 4:** Set up simultaneous buy and sell settlement dates so, after solicitors swap a lot of paper, you receive a lump-sum cash profit and the person buying off you obtains the property title in their name.

Table 16.1, below, is an example.

| Table 16.1 – Flip Example | |
|---|---|
| **Your Purchase:** | |
| Purchase date: | 15 September 20XX |
| Purchase price: | $150,000 |
| Settlement date: | 15th January 20XY |
| **Your Sale:** | |
| Sale date: | 20 October 20XX |
| Your sale price: | $180,000 |
| Settlement date: | 15th January 20XY |
| **Your Profit:** | |
| Buy/sell margin: | $30,000 |
| Closing and sale costs: | ($10,000) |
| **Total Profit:** | **$20,000** |

While it may seem simple, in reality there is much more to the process of flipping. Bargain properties, especially in a booming market, aren't that easy to find and there's another problem... flipping properties in Australia seems to attract double stamp duty which seriously erodes potential profits.

## My Experience

Dave and I have never completed a flip, although we did have the opportunity to test the strategy. In April 2002 we signed the contract to buy a block of 21 positive cashflow units on the

Sunshine Coast in Queensland for $530,000. Our problem was that, as usual, we didn't have enough money right then and there to buy the property. With a huge positive cashflow return, we didn't want to miss out so we tried to negotiate creative terms – which, in this case, involved a six-month settlement period.

The vendor agreed and we signed the contract to purchase the property. In September, as settlement time drew nearer, the agent faxed us a press clipping saying how property in the area had boomed and hinted that we could quite easily sell the property for up to $700,000.

If Dave and I decided to sell then after closing and sale costs we stood to make about $130,000 – not bad for just signing a contract and waiting while a property boom happened around us. Whilst it was tempting, we didn't take the bait and instead we went on to acquire the property on the basis that we were looking to secure ongoing cashflow rather than a once-off capital gain.

### Steve's Investing Tip

For a theoretical example of the numbers involved in a flip transaction visit:

www.PropertyInvesting.com/strategies/flips

## CRITICAL FACTORS IN A FLIP TRANSACTION

The critical success factors in a flip are:

### Finding Undervalued Properties

Finding cheap properties, especially in a 'hot' market where prices are rising daily and properties are selling quickly is no easy task. However, like most creative investments, the time you allocate to sourcing opportunities will have a direct impact on your success. If you're already stretched for time because you're working long hours in a job, then flips are unlikely to feature greatly in your property investing portfolio.

On the other hand, if you have lots of time then it may only take one or two lucrative deals each year to potentially replace your normal salary.

## Finding a Buyer

To be a successful flipper you must dispose of your interest in the contract before having to settle on the property. In other words, you are acting as a private broker by seeking to pass on the property to another person.

While you might be able to locate a cheap property, your eventual success remains dependent on finding someone who wants to buy it off you. That's why it's critical for flippers to maintain a database of investors who are time-poor but are happy to pay for you to bring them deals.

## Affordability

If you can't flip the property before settlement date then you'll have to buy it. This means that you have to be conscious of the financial implications on your wealth creation plans should this happen.

## Profitability

Flipping in Australia is not as straightforward as it might seem. There are two issues that I can immediately think of that will impact on the profitability of a flip. They are:

### 1. Stamp Duty

You may find that even though you dispose of your interest in the contract before settlement, you will still be liable to pay stamp duty on your purchase. The folks that drafted up the stamp duty legislation included some catch-all clauses so that if you acquire a property stamp duty is levied regardless of whether or not you on-sell it during the settlement period.

While there *may* be ways around this, such as buying an option to purchase the property rather than agreeing to buy the actual property, the legalities are complex and you should consult a lawyer before setting up a flip deal.

### 2. Capital Gains

You should also be mindful that if you buy and sell a property within a 12 month period then you won't be eligible for the 50% capital gains tax discount. This means that if you're already paying tax at the top marginal rate then up to 48.5% of your profit will be redirected back into the government's tax coffers.

### A Suggested Solution...

If you ever come across what you believe to be a great deal but don't have the resources to buy it in your own right, then a third party might be interested in 'buying' it off you. Dave and I often pay spotters fees of several thousand dollars if we end up purchasing a property that we sourced as a referral from someone else. If you know about a deal and want to make some quick cash (that won't attract double stamp duty!) then use the forum at www.PropertyInvesting.com to look for a buyer.

## THE FINAL WORD ON FLIPS

Flips, otherwise known as quick-cash deals, seem like a very good idea on paper. In reality though, there are many dangers that need to be mitigated, and a lot of time needs to be invested before you'll see the fruits of your creative endeavours. I feel that flipping is a strategy that would work far better in a buyer's market, where there are many motivated sellers who might be willing to accept creative alternatives. In a seller's market – where the vendor calls the shots – seeking to negotiate a discount on price, or asking for unusual settlement terms, won't be popular if properties are being listed and sold within a matter of days.

In any event, a potentially more attractive alternative is to sell the details of the deal to an investor in return for a spotter's fee. That way you don't physically have to sign a contract or come up with a deposit, and there's no risk that you'll be left having to acquire the property if you can't find another buyer.

## Chapter 16 Insights

### Insight #1:

Flipping properties is a strategy designed to earn quick cash profits rather than ongoing positive cashflow.

### Insight #2:

It's a strategy that's difficult to use successfully in a market that has rapidly booming prices and where vendors are asking for quick (30-day) settlement periods.

### Insight #3:

Any profit you earn is likely to be heavily eroded by the impact of stamp duty and also capital gains tax.

### Insight #4:

Nevertheless, for people who are time rich and money poor, sourcing properties and then selling them to investors for a spotter's fee can be potentially lucrative.

You can do this without having to sign the contract or pay a deposit in your own name. If you're looking to earn a spotter's fee, use the forum at our site www.PropertyInvesting.com to look for potential buyers.

# SUMMARY OF PART III

Other than property development, the five main ways to profit from property are:

1.  Buy and Hold (Chapter 12)

2.  Wraps (Chapter 13)

3.  Lease Options (Chapter 14)

4.  Renovations (Chapter 15); and

5.  Flips (Chapter 16).

## How Do You Know which Strategy to Use?

When Dave and I began our property investing we quickly established wrapping as our preferred niche. In fact, we became so focused on vendor's finance that we forgot about trying to master any of the other strategies.

On reflection, this was too narrow an approach and who knows how many great deals passed us by because we only knew how to make a profit from wraps? Today I know that the key to making money is to find solutions to problems. The flexibility to be able to implement five property investing strategies gives you the knowledge to solve a lot of problems.

The two types of problems you may encounter are:

### 1. People Problems

The first way to solve people problems is to focus on the needs of everyday people, which is done by meeting a vendor's needs (if you're buying) and a client's needs (when you sell). Adopting a people focus means that you tailor the circumstances of your offer in such a way as to solve a person's problems.

For example, if you have a client who wants to own rather than rent, you might first try to construct a wrap deal that accommodates his or her needs. If you can't do this then you might try to offer a lease-option alternative. If that fails then perhaps you could use the 'Homestarter' model I created to secure your client as a long-term tenant while he or she works to improve his or her circumstances.

My father worked in truck sales all his life and often handled his clients' finance applications. In an industry known for its rough and tumble nature, Dad said that the three things (he called it 'the Three Cs') he always looked for were (in this order):

1.   *Character* – that the people seeking finance appeared to be honest and trustworthy. If there was any indication that they were trying to pull a shifty then Dad would listen to the discussion, but would always later refuse the application.

2.   *Capacity* – many of Dad's customers could 'talk the talk' but, at the end of the day, all that mattered was hard evidence of an ability to repay.

3.   *Credit* – the final qualifying criteria was the customer's credit history. Dad firmly believed that history was a good yardstick for expected future performance.

When it comes to evaluating tenants and potential wrap or lease-option clients I can recommend adopting 'the Three Cs' approach. Only when you can gather evidence that all three criteria can be met should you proceed with investing in the person.

### 2. Property Focus

The second approach to making money from real estate is to start with a property and, if you seek cashflow returns, find a person who's interested in either renting or owning it. If you're after capital gains then you can look to flip or renovate the property.

# CONCLUSION

Whichever option you use, the critical observation to make is that at the end of the day it will be a person who's the source of your profit – either providing positive cashflow or buying your renovated or flipped property.

As such, maximising your property return is a matter of matching the right person and property to the right strategy. The more investing strategies you know about and can implement, the better your chances of maximising your return.

**Steve's Investing Tip**

Maximising your property return is a matter of matching the right person or property to the right strategy.

# Applying the Knowledge

# INTRODUCTION TO PART IV

So far I've outlined so much theory that, provided you retained and understood it, you would easily qualify to become a recognised expert on the topic of real estate investing.

However, while you could be classed as a theoretical guru, unless you can translate what you know into an investing profit, you'll be forever destined to trade your time in exchange for money by working in a job.

## Steve's Investing Tip

All the knowledge in the world is useless unless you have a practical context in which to apply it.

Now, as we draw to a conclusion, Part IV is dedicated to providing information that will help you to answer important questions, such as:

▷ How can I turn my theory into practice?; and

▷ Do I have what it takes to be successful?

# Planning for Success

It was the end of November 2000 and Dave and I were meeting at my house to discuss the latest developments in our accounting and property investing businesses. Both areas were progressing well, despite our lack of a formal business plan. This day, however, was going to be a watershed – a defining moment that would demonstrate the power and importance of having a plan.

Dave and I owned two investment properties at the time and, based on a net return of $50 per week, we calculated that we needed to acquire a further 26 properties at which point our investment income would cover our rather basic lifestyle requirements. While we wouldn't be living like kings, we'd at least be well on the way to being free from the need to work in our accounting practice.

It all seemed pretty easy on paper when we broke down the responsibilities for buying our targeted 26 properties. Dave would need to acquire ten deals, while I would need to find and buy 16 houses. This was all on top of our work obligations to our accounting clients, plus the ongoing (and increasing) management involved as we purchased more properties.

Having read about effective goal setting, Dave and I understood the importance of establishing a deadline. For no good reason we chose the end of February 2001 as our target, which gave us 90 days – less the Christmas and New Year's holidays – to get busy. We then further broke down this timeframe into the number of properties we had to buy each month. Table 17.1, below, shows our targets.

| Table 17.1 – Our Plan For Acquiring 26 Houses in 90 Days | | | | |
|---|---|---|---|---|
| | **Dec.** | **Jan.** | **Feb.** | **Total** |
| Dave | 2 | 4 | 4 | 10 |
| Steve | 4 | 6 | 6 | 16 |

The going was by no means easy, especially since the whole country generally shuts down from around the 15th of December until the 15th of January each year. When we tallied up our purchases at the end of February we'd only acquired 18 properties. While a little disappointed that we fell short of our goal, to average a new property every five days was still an impressive effort.

Our lesson from this experience was that impressive results can be achieved when you:

⤷ Think big

⤷ Set a goal

⤷ Break it down into mini steps; and

⤷ Take immediate and massive action.

Without a plan we managed to achieve slow and steady progress, yet when we took the time to set some goals – challenging goals – even though we fell short of our expectations our results were very impressive.

If you don't have a plan and are wondering why you have trouble gaining momentum, now you have your answer. If you're achieving good results without a plan, just think of what you could achieve if you formalised your commitment and set some objectives outside your comfort zone.

# THE PATH OF LEAST RESISTANCE

I invite you to complete an important practical exercise to illustrate the path of least resistance.

## Step 1:

Take a pen and place a dot in the top-middle of Figure 17.1. Write the word 'NOW' to the right of the dot. This first dot symbolises your current position on your road to financial independence.

It doesn't matter how old you are, how much money you have in the bank, your marital status or anything else – we just need a point of reference from which to move forward. Yesterday is gone forever, let's focus our attention on tomorrow.

**Fig. 17.1 – Your Path of Least Resistance**

Map your path as directed.

## Step 2:

Next, draw a second dot in the middle of the bottom of Figure 17.1. Write the word 'FUTURE' to the right of it. This second dot represents your ideal wealth creation position at some point in the future, perhaps many years from now.

## Step 3:

Having completed Steps 1 and 2, you know where you are as well as having an idea of your destination too. You also have some idea of what direction you need to head in. Your next step is to identify your path of least resistance, which is the shortest distance between the two dots.

Have a go at trying to draw the path of least resistance between the 'Now' and 'Future' dots in Figure 17.1.

## Step 4:

After you've drawn your path of least resistance go back and draw three small squares evenly spaced along the line between the 'NOW' dot and the 'FUTURE' dot. Write A, next to the first square, B next to the second and C next to the third. These are your milestones of achievement.

No doubt the distance between where you are now and where you want to end up in terms of wealth creation will be a considerable distance apart. It's wise to set milestones that provide reassurance that you're making headway towards your ultimate goal.

### Be *Guided* but not *Taught*

Your journey to financial independence isn't something you can achieve overnight. The lessons you must learn take time and must be *experienced* rather than *taught*. However, you can be guided along your path by people who have already walked the road you're travelling. The best advice I can offer is that your success is dependent on developing a realistic goal, turning it into achievable milestones, and maintaining the necessary focus for as long as it takes for you to achieve success.

## A Major Battle

A major psychological battle must be fought on the road to financial independence well before a dollar of passive income is ever earned. The powerful emotions of greed and fear are our biggest enemies. We all know, in our heart of hearts, that get-rich-quick schemes don't work, but we're still attracted to the chance of making a quick profit because we want something for nothing (greed). We're also afraid of missing out (fear) on an opportunity that other people seem to be cashing in on. Instead of applying the necessary focus, we become distracted and unknowingly follow the path of *maximum* resistance.

I'll use the example of a hypothetical client – let's call him Andrew – to illustrate the path of maximum resistance. Andrew is committed to creating wealth. He knows where he's at today and even better, knows how much income he needs to become financially independent. His preferred strategy to make money (at the moment anyway) is positive cashflow property investing.

Andrew begins on his journey and soon discovers that sourcing positive cashflow property is harder than it first seemed. With continuing work pressures, he finds it difficult to find the time to look for deals. As fate would have it, a letter arrives in the mail from a seminar company outlining how to make a fortune trading shares using a patented 'black box solution' that boasts an amazing 99% success rate.

Frustrated about property being such hard going, Andrew pays $2,000 to attend a two-day seminar where the black box system is outlined and then tested with a number of pre-worked examples. Based on the historical information given, a starting account balance of $30,000 was turned into $60,000 in just six months.

Impressed with the ease of use and happy that it didn't require a lot of his time, Andrew paid a further $5,200 to subscribe to a year's supply of weekly online wealth building reports as generated by the magic black box. Three months later, and after an extensive paper trading exercise where he theoretically made $5,878, Andrew places his first trade and makes an impressive $544 in just three hours. The next day he breaks even and the day after he makes a further $950. Growing with confidence, Andrew becomes less stringent about applying the 16 rules that came with the reports and begins to rely more and more on his own judgement. He is becoming fixated with the stock market and every chance he has, he's online checking the latest prices and seeing whether or not he's making or losing money.

That's when he begins to lose, not a lot, but enough money over a consistent timeframe for Andrew to question whether or not trading shares is really for him. After a correction to the stock market, the reliability of the magic black box reports are questioned and Andrew becomes disillusioned. Returning to what he knows best, Andrew throws himself back into his work.

Several more months pass and then one day Andrew's flicking through the pages of a magazine and notices an advertisement about the great returns and tax advantages that arise from investing in olives. Sensing that there is no harm in looking, Andrew sends off the application form to receive a prospectus. He also books in to attend an introductory free seminar.

Not being a fool, and feeling a little burnt by the 'black box solution' experience, Andrew does some research and discovers that a government organisation has issued a warning that the prospectus prior to the one that Andrew received contains some potentially unreasonable assumptions.

Confused and frustrated about wasting his precious time, Andrew abandons the idea of olives and again focuses on his major source of income – his job. Soon after his hard work is rewarded with a promotion to a managerial position and a pay increase. Yet when you take out the additional tax and superannuation, there's not really a lot more pay, but there is a significant obligation to put in more hours, including weekend work.

A few months pass by and then one night while relaxing in front of the TV the phone rings. It's Simon, an old friend from high school. They talk about old times for nearly an hour before agreeing to catch up at Simon's house for dinner where they'll also discuss how Simon and his wife make an extra $1,000 per week from their home-based business.

The dinner was delightful and the company pleasant. As the dishes were being cleared away, the topic moved on to the business opportunity and Andrew's friend outlined how he and his wife were making a lot of money using a multi-level marketing organisation emanating from the United States. Knowing that an extra $1,000 a week would be more than handy, Andrew eagerly signs up, pays his joining fee and buys the first month's motivational books and tapes. All he needs to do to earn $1,000 per week is to buy $100 worth of product from the wholesaler and every month sign up two new people under him and then help the people he signs up to sign up more people.

He allocates each Tuesday night to inviting guests from his circle of friends over for dinner, and every Thursday night to attending a networking and motivational event. Andrew has mixed success. A few of his friends are interested, but most are quite rude and question his morality in mixing business with friendship.

He perseveres and achieves solid results until his work wins a big tender and all managers are required to work an additional 12 hours per week for at least the next six months. When the contract ends, Andrew is so exhausted he books a three-week holiday to the Whitsunday Islands.

When he returns he's invited to play indoor cricket on Thursday nights. This used to be the night he went to his once-a-week network marketing debriefing, but he's happy not to get involved again since the effort he was allocating was not translating into the extra dollars he was hoping for. Simon called twice and left messages on the answering machine but Andrew didn't bother calling back. Simon never called again.

More time passed by and Andrew's team wins the indoor cricket championship. One of his team-mates is a real estate agent, and, over a beer one night, starts talking about how property prices are primed to really take off. This rekindles Andrew's interest in property, but this time he's planning to make money like the people on his favourite reality TV show, where they renovate houses and sell them off for a substantial profit in only a matter of months.

Andrew starts looking for suitable real estate and eventually buys a property for $200,000. Over the next six months he spends every available second of his non-working life renovating. He uses his life savings of $50,000 to pay for the costs before putting it back on the market and selling it for $310,000.

Delighted with result, but burnt out after spending his weekends renovating, Andrew reinvests his profits back into another property – an off-the-plan apartment in town. A major factor in his decision is the fact that he has to pay a large slab of his renovation profits in tax, so he's looking for a more tax-effective opportunity.

All is going well until Andrew's work fails to win three major tenders and, unfortunately, he is retrenched. If he leaves by the end of the week then the company will pay him $20,000 on top of the sick leave and annual leave he's owed.

Sensing the opportunity for a break, Andrew takes the redundancy package, only to find that people with his skills aren't in demand and it's tough to secure a job interview, let alone a position. His negatively geared property soon starts to niggle his hip pocket nerve and he decides that, given he no longer has a job, he can't afford to keep his investment apartment.

Contacting the agent he bought it off, he lists the property for sale and is lucky that a buyer comes along and offers what Andrew paid for the property. After agent's commission and interest payments, Andrew loses about $20,000.

Times are starting to get tough and instead of applying for management positions, Andrew starts submitting his resume for rank and file jobs. He is starting to really see how dependent he was on his job. This is a worrying realisation because Andrew made himself a promise that, unlike his father, he wouldn't be working until 60 or relying on the pension in retirement.

Just last week Andrew received two lucky breaks. Firstly, he was offered a job. It carried less salary than he previously earned but he was under no obligation to work weekends. Secondly, he was reading the paper when he noticed an article explaining that organic food was becoming more and more popular. There was a 1800 number to call to find out how to make money as a distributor.

Hardly able to contain his excitement, Andrew is planning to take the job and call the number to see what needs to happen for him to become a distributor. He's telling anyone who'll listen that he thinks this is his next big opportunity.

Andrew's path is shown in Figure 17.2. He is similar to the many people I meet who express an interest in wealth creation. He has the passion and he's certainly intelligent – all he lacks is focus. Instead of having a path of least resistance, he lurches from opportunity to opportunity and ends up travelling a great distance only to end up frustrated.

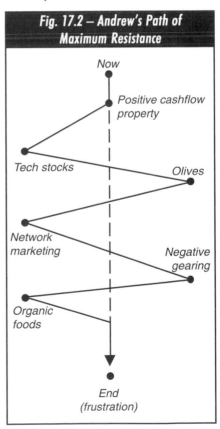

**Fig. 17.2 – Andrew's Path of Maximum Resistance**

Now

Positive cashflow property

Tech stocks

Olives

Network marketing

Negative gearing

Organic foods

End (frustration)

Any of his chosen paths could have created wealth – provided he applied himself and stuck with an investment strategy. By switching from one strategy to another, all Andrew achieved was a path of maximum resistance.

### Steve's Investing Tip

Uncertainty and lack of focus are the downfall of many investors.

## Your Personal Wealth Creation Plan and Path of Least Resistance

I'd like to help you to create your own personal wealth creation plan and, in doing so, identify your path of least resistance when investing in positive cashflow real estate. All that's required is that you complete the following four steps and fill in Tables 17.2, 17.3 and 17.4.

### Step 1: Where Are You Now?

| Table 17.2 – Current Income Details | | | |
|---|---|---|---|
| | **YOU** | **YOUR SPOUSE** | **TOTAL** |
| Total salary and other non-passive income | $ | $ | $ |
| Passive income | $ | $ | $ |
| **Total Income** | $ | $ | $ |

## Step 2: What's Your Ultimate Money Goal?

| Table 17.3 – Future Income Details | | | |
|---|---|---|---|
| | **YOU** | **YOUR SPOUSE** | **TOTAL** |
| Total salary and other non-passive income | $ | $ | $ |
| Passive income | $ | $ | $ |
| **Total Income** | $ | $ | $ |

## Step 3: By What Time?

| Table 17.4 – Your Deadline |
|---|
| **Insert Your Deadline:** |
| *Day:*          *Month:*          *Year:* |

## Step 4: Complete Your Money Goal

Now bring together Steps 2 and 3 to complete your money goal.

**My Money Goal**

Annual passive income of $_____

by _____.

Only once you've decided how much passive income you require and by what date can you begin to frame an answer to the next question, which is "What's the best way to get there?"

# MEASURING SUCCESS

It was early 2000 when Dave and I used the four-step template to set our own money goal. The figure we came to was $500,000 per annum ($250,000 each) in net passive income on or before the 9th of May 2004 (my 32nd birthday). At the time we made our goal, $500,000 per annum in net passive income seemed about as achievable as trying to climb Mount Everest with no training.

Yet as we gained experience and grew in confidence, we began to overcome the insurmountable by setting milestones (our A, B and C on the path of least resistance) linked to the number of properties we acquired. Our philosophy was quite simple – the more positive cashflow property we owned, the bigger our annual passive income figure became and the closer we edged to our financial goal.

## You Can Do the Same

If you assume that each positive cashflow property you buy will earn you a conservative average of $30 per week in net passive income, then you can translate your passive income back into the number of properties you need to acquire (see Tables 17.5 and 17.6 opposite).

I can certainly understand how the thought of buying over 50 properties can be very, very daunting. But if you break the big goal up into mini goals, say ten properties per year over five years, then all of a sudden the goal appears much more achievable.

# MAKING THE NECESSARY SACRIFICE

If you decide to use positive cashflow property to fund your financial independence then you can expect your journey to be difficult and to require significant sacrifices. In my case I lived off a monthly allowance of $400 derived from my wife's salary while the majority of the profits Dave and I earned in our business were reinvested back into buying more property.

| Table 17.5 – Current Income Details | |
| --- | --- |
| **TRANSLATING FINANCIAL INDEPENDENCE INTO THE NUMBER OF PROPERTIES NEEDED** | |
| **Your Goal in Annual Passive Income** | $ |
| *(52 weeks per annum)* | ÷ 52 |
| **Your Goal in Weekly Passive Income** | $ |
| *(Your property averages $30 positive cashflow per week)* | ÷ 30 |
| **Number of Properties Needed** | |

| Table 17.6 – Quick Reference Translating Financial Independence into the Number of Properties | | | | | |
| --- | --- | --- | --- | --- | --- |
| Passive Income | $50,000 | $70,000 | $90,000 | $110,000 | $130,000 |
| # Properties | 32 | 45 | 58 | 71 | 83 |

Julie and I chose to rent rather than own a home as our weekly rent expense was cheaper than making loan repayments. Most of my friends and family have been living in their own home for several years; Julie and I have had to suffer the hassle of rental managers inspecting our place every six months and the possibility of being told to move on when our lease expired.

It's impossible to say what you'll need to sacrifice and I can't promise that adopting a positive cashflow approach will make you an overnight millionaire, but with patience, commitment and delayed gratification you can become rich enough to buy back the time you'd otherwise spend working in a job.

**Steve's Investing Tip**

Financial independence does not arise by fluke or by chance. It is earned.

## How Long will it Take?

Only you can answer this question, however I'm reminded of a true story that might help you understand that whatever the timeline, it's something that *you* decide rather than something that's decided for you.

Before we set up our own accounting practice, Dave and I were employed as managers in a small firm of chartered accountants. One of the last clients we worked on was an electricity company in the process of becoming privatised. There was plenty of money to be thrown at contractors, and given that the CEO was friends with one of the partners, the job of writing internal tax manuals was created and awarded to our firm. Dave and I were both confident that the documents, which we spent weeks at the company's site writing and billing over $150 an hour for, would never be read. The task wasn't a lot of fun since the employees all knew they were about to be retrenched. Motivation levels for everyone plummeted to new lows with each day that passed.

There was ample time for Dave and I to reflect back on our own employment positions in the firm we worked for, and we came to see that our jobs were no long-term certainties either. That's when the idea for Bradley McKnight – Chartered Accountants was born. At least we were assured of job security when we worked for ourselves.

Dave and I began to wonder how long it would take us to set up the necessary infrastructure, at which point I grabbed a marker pen and assumed a lecturing position in front of the whiteboard.

"Dave, as I see it we have two choices", I said.

I drew a stick figure at one end of the whiteboard and a finish line at the other end. "We can either sprint to our goal." I said pointing to the diagram I'd just drawn. "Or, we can hurdle it and do it the hard way." As I said this I drew another stick figure under the first one and a series of hurdles leading up to the finish line.

"Which one will lead us to our goal the fastest? Sprinting or hurdling?" I asked

Dave replied "Sprinting, obviously".

"Exactly!" I exclaimed. "So let's remove as many of the hurdles as we can *before the race begins* and we'll get to our goal even sooner."

Over the course of several years of investing together, Dave and I have often reflected back on this conversation. What we've found is that many of the hurdles we've been forced to jump have not only slowed us down, but they were left there by *choice* rather than by necessity.

Take some time to consider what's holding you back. Is it something that can be easily overcome, or are you inadvertently making life unnecessarily hard for yourself?

## The Plateau Effect

The plateau effect can occur at any time – sometimes even before you've purchased a property. It's characterised by a distinct feeling that you're stuck in a rut, resulting in immense trouble gaining momentum. For most investors the plateau effect is preceded by one of the following events:

⇨ The lack of a long-term investment plan.

⇨ Cashflow shortfalls given that you have existing property investments that are negatively geared.

⇨ Unlimited imagination, but very limited finance.

⇨ An inability to locate deals.

⇨ Negative experiences with current investments.

⇨ Fatigue or boredom with the idea of property investing when once it was exciting and exhilarating.

Unfortunately, without immediate correction, the plateau effect can be fatal, which helps to further explain why so many property investors own so few properties. If you're suffering from the plateau effect right now then I'm a messenger of both good and bad news.

OK, first the bad news. *Everyone* experiences a property-investing plateau sooner or later – no-one is immune. Now the good news! The plateau can be overcome provided you adopt the right attitude and seek assistance where necessary. A plateau arises from the combination of a lack of knowledge, limited time and/or a shortage of money.

For example, when Dave and I began investing we found it very tough to find finance for multiple properties given that we'd only been in business for a few months. We tried everything until Dave was on the internet one night and saw a banner advertisement saying "Desperate for finance? Click here." Dave couldn't click the ad fast enough and that's how we found our first mortgage broker, who went on to source our first five deals.

Yet up until then, several months passed and it would have been easy for us to give up or to at least put our plans on hold for six months while we saved more money to prove our creditworthiness. Instead, we kept trying to maintain the momentum needed to purchase multiple properties.

A vital point to remember is that you can *always* help yourself by taking action, whether it be ringing up to source finance, or calling agents and asking them about the properties they have available for sale. The worst thing you can do is to accept the reasons for your lack of momentum, as this will justify a decision to stop trying.

An even poorer option is to assign control of an element critical to the success of your investment to someone who does not have an interest in seeing it come to fruition. Relying on someone to make things happen on your behalf is a sure way of stalling.

### Steve's Investing Tip

Your only certainty is that by doing nothing, nothing will happen.

If you're experiencing the plateau effect then you're probably also severely frustrated because you know it's possible to make a lot of money in real estate, but you just can't seem to locate all the pieces to the wealth creation jigsaw. Stick at it though, success will come in time.

### Steve's Investing Tip

Find like minded investors at:

www.PropertyInvesting.com/forum

No doubt there will be many investors who have been through your situation before and can offer assistance or, at the very least, encouragement. Going it alone will make your life unnecessarily complicated.

## THE NEXT STEP

I can distinctly remember the slogan at one of the places where I worked as an accountant. It was a picture of a yacht with a caption underneath that read "How do you know where you're going if you haven't charted a destination?" Well, before you ever invest in a property, you must first decide why it is that you want to make money. Once you have a reason for investing, you can start to target investments that will help you achieve your goals.

Investing without an outcome in mind will create two results:

1. You'll follow the path of maximum resistance; and

2. Eventually you'll plateau out.

If you haven't already done so, go back now and complete the planning exercises in this chapter. This book can only help you to the extent you help yourself.

## Chapter 17 Insights

### Insight #1:

Only once you know where you are now, and where you want to go, can you plot the quickest path to get there.

### Insight #2:

Achieving financial independence is by no means easy, but it's also no fluke. By breaking down your financial goals into a number of positive cashflow properties you'll start to see your goal as more than just a dream.

### Insight #3:

If you think you know all the theory about goal setting but you're investing without any kind of plan then, I'm sorry, but you don't currently have what it takes to achieve massive success. You might be achieving some good results, but these will only ever be a tiny fraction of what you could achieve if you had better focus.

### Insight #4:

Despite driving a manual car for many years now, I still very occasionally stall from time to time. It's like that with investing too. Expect periods when times are tough and progress is slow. Understand that the way through these difficult periods is to continually take action – even when you can't be bothered or are just about ready to give up.

# 18

# Finding the Money to Begin Investing

If you've established your investing goals and feel that investing in property is your path, then congratulations – this step alone separates you from the majority of property punters who are simply out to make money without any real reason or purpose for doing so.

Your next step is to try to find the cash needed to pay for the deposit, closing costs or perhaps even renovation expenses (if that's your strategy of choice) on an investment property. The source of cash to pay for all these costs can be a combination of:

1. Your savings; and/or

2. Your equity; and/or

3. The money raised from public or private financiers.

## YOUR SAVINGS

It doesn't matter how much you earn, what's important is how much you keep. Being able to pay for the deposits and closing costs as you acquire more and more properties will require your savings account to be regularly topped up. Let's look at two ways that you can increase your savings.

### 1st Savings Booster Strategy:
### Earn More Money (Without an Increase in Spending)

American author Robert Allen's excellent book titled *Multiple Streams of Income* contains many great ideas for creating additional sources of money. Dave and I were already applying Allen's philosophy as we sought to grow our business income *at the same time* as we sped up our property investing activities. We did this by diversifying our business interests.

When we started, our only source of business income was our accounting fees, which we reinvested into buying property while living off meagre allowances from our wives' salaries. This was OK in the beginning but, as we changed our plans to buy more and more property, we realised we'd need more and more money to pay for the deposits and closing costs.

Our second source of income became the income that our positive cashflow investments provided. Then in late 1999, I began to write a newsletter outlining my crazy property ideas (I continue to write a newsletter at www.PropertyInvesting.com). Before long, a number of subscribers asked for a seminar, which I held in February 2001. This generated more income which we used to buy more property. Today our business interests include:

↦ A substantial portfolio of positive cashflow real estate

↦ Two web businesses, which run 24 hours a day, seven days a week; and

↦ Our original accounting practice.

Our plan is to acquire further streams of income in order to continue to bring money into the business to pay for deposits on more real estate. This all sounds magnificent for us, but can *you* also build yourself an empire, especially if you're an employee? Of course you can! If two boring old accountants can do this then just imagine what you are capable of! It may not be easy, but I'm certain you can do it.

It's important to note that if you increase your spending at the same rate as your income then you will not achieve a better financial position. The increase in your income needs to either trickle (or better yet, gush) into your savings account – not be spent on maintaining an excessive lifestyle.

## 2nd Savings Booster Strategy: Control Spending

Remember the story of my financially challenged neighbour? Her problem wasn't that she earned too little, rather that she spent too much! Dave and I were careful that we practised what we preached by applying the same prudent spending controls to our own business that we'd advised our clients to adopt in theirs.

We did this by keeping overheads as low as possible – firstly by working from home and later by being careful that we paid for the expansion of our businesses with reinvested profits rather than borrowed money. For example, we held off on a new computer system until we could pay for it out of recurring positive cashflow rather than using hire-purchase financing.

Be careful that you balance the expenses of today with having enough funds to pay for the assets you plan to buy tomorrow. If you have trouble controlling the amount of money that leaves your wallet or purse (including credit cards) remember that every dollar you spend is making someone else rich, while keeping you at work.

If you're investing to try to earn more money to fund a lifestyle beyond your means, then go back and re-read Chapter 2 in conjunction with Appendix A.

## Steve's Investing Tip

If it's dollars you can't keep, you'll always struggle just to make ends meet.

# YOUR EQUITY

Just because you don't have savings doesn't necessarily mean that you can't begin to invest in property. If you have access to equity then you can still make a start towards building your property empire. Equity, sometimes also called 'net worth', is the difference between the value of your assets and the total of your liabilities, or perhaps more bluntly, what you have left over when you pay out all your debts.

For example, if your investment property was worth $300,000 and you had a $120,000 mortgage, then your equity would be $180,000 ($300,000 − $120,000). The largest untapped source of equity for many people is their home. Take my friend Allan for example.

## Redrawing Equity

Allan runs the very professional Baker Street Recording Studio in Melbourne and nearly all of his available cash is spent maintaining and upgrading his equipment. He likes the idea of property investing, but believes his lack of cash prevents him from buying anything.

Allan bought his home for $320,000 with an initial mortgage of $256,000. Now, after repayments and the passage of time, he owes $230,000. As shown in Table 18.1 opposite, despite his lack of cash, Allan could access up to $26,000 in the form of redrawn equity and use it to pay for deposits and closing costs on a potential property investment.

| Table 18.1 – Allan's Available *Redrawn* Equity | |
|---|---|
| Allan's property value | $320,000 |
| Bank's maximum lend* | 80% |
| Bank's maximum loan | $256,000 |
| *Less* Allan's current loan | $230,000 |
| **Equity Available for Redraw** | **$26,000** |

**\*Note:** The maximum amount that a financier will provide depends on its credit lending policy.

There are some substantial benefits in using equity, including:

### The Velocity of Money

Allan currently pays interest at 7% per annum on his mortgage. As such, provided he can invest and earn an after-tax return of more than 7%, he is really accessing his equity at no cost.

### Interest Deductibility

Interest on your home loan is not normally an allowable income tax deduction. However, provided you apply the redrawn funds to certain investing activities (such as buying investment property), then you can claim a deduction for the interest on the redrawn component. I'll touch on this issue again later on page 293.

### Generally Easily Accessible

With the evolution of more flexible loan products, it's now much easier than ever before to redraw your equity. All that's usually required is for you to fill in a few forms and perhaps pay a few loan fees. In fact, since borrowing more money provides additional profits for loan companies, many financiers allow you to redraw without extra fees.

## Refinanced Equity

However, be mindful that there's a huge difference between redrawing equity, which is quite easy, and refinancing equity, which can be more problematic. By *redrawing* equity you're borrowing back the loan principal you've previously repaid.

On the other hand, *refinancing* your equity means you're seeking to have your property revalued which will allow you to borrow previous principal repayments plus a portion of any independently assessed capital appreciation.

To illustrate the point let's imagine Allan's house increased in value to $400,000. If he could refinance, his available equity would be $90,000, as shown in Table 18.2, below.

| Table 18.2 – Allan's Available *Refinanced* Equity | |
|---|---|
| Allan's property value | $400,000 |
| Bank's maximum lend* | 80% |
| Bank's maximum loan | $320,000 |
| Less Allan's current loan | $230,000 |
| **Equity Available for Redraw** | **$90,000** |

**\*Note:** The maximum amount that a financier will provide depends on its credit lending policy.

Unlike redrawing equity, there's a lot more red tape involved when you try to refinance your loan and this makes the process potentially expensive and time consuming. Furthermore, it's wise to remember that refinancing your equity carries an element of risk. Higher debt means bigger interest repayments and, for many investors, the thought of risking the family home means they'd rather not touch the equity and still be able to sleep peacefully at night. Nevertheless, if sensibly invested and diligently monitored, the risk of losing your home can be dramatically reduced, and this can mean that the benefits of refinancing may outweigh any potential downfalls.

# A COMMENT ON THE TAX DEDUCTIBILITY OF INTEREST REDRAWS

In Australia, property investors are allowed to claim a tax deduction for costs associated with earning assessable income, but only to the extent that these costs are not of a private nature. This means that if you borrow money to buy an investment property then the interest that you pay on the borrowed money is a tax deduction – as are the council rates, insurance costs and expenses that qualify as repairs and maintenance.

## Tax Deductibility of Interest on Borrowings

This is a bit of a minefield but, generally speaking, it's the reason for borrowing money that determines whether or not you can claim a deduction for the interest. Let's look at two examples using Allan as an illustration.

> **Example 1:** Allan borrows money to finance the purchase of his home (principal place of residence). Even though he may regard it as an investment, the tax authorities view it as a private matter and the interest is not deductible.

> **Example 2:** If, instead of being Allan's principal place of residence, the property was rented out to a tenant then, so long as Allan intended for his investment to make money, the interest on his loan would now qualify as a tax deduction.

## Interest Deductibility on Redraws/Refinancing

Unfortunately, the discussion needs to become a little more complex. Let's imagine that Allan decides to refinance his home to access all of his $90,000 equity (as shown in Table 18.2).

Provided Allan applied all of the $90,000 to acquiring income-producing assets then, even though his house is a private asset, he should nevertheless be able to claim a tax deduction for the interest applicable on the redraw: $6,750 ($90,000 x 7.5%). The interest on the remainder of his loan ($230,000 x 7.5%) would not qualify as a tax deduction.

On the other hand, if Allan had decided to invest $70,000 in assets and then spend the remaining $20,000 on an all expenses paid trip around the world, the interest on the portion he spent on his holiday ($1,500 or $20,000 x 7.5%) would not be deductible. Of the total $24,000 per annum that Allan would pay in interest, $18,750 of it would be non-deductible, as shown in Table 18.3, below.

| Table 18.3 – Summary of Allan's Loan and Interest Portion | | |
|---|---|---|
| | **LOAN PORTION** | **ANNUAL INTEREST AT 7.5%** |
| Allan's loan | $320,000 | $24,000 |
| Private portion | | |
| – House | $230,000 | $17,250 |
| – Trip | $20,000 | $1,500 |
| **Subtotal** | **$250,000** | **$18,750** |
| Investment assets | $70,000 | $5,250 |
| **Total** | **$320,000** | **$24,000** |

### Repaying in After-Tax Dollars

The true cost of meeting the interest payment is worsened by the fact that, having lost its tax deductibility status, Allan must now repay the money using after-tax dollars. If Allan was on the top marginal tax rate then he'd have to earn $36,408 ($18,750 ÷ [1 − 0.485]) to have $18,750 in after-tax funds.

## The Bottom Line

The idea of redrawing or refinancing your loan works well provided you plan to use the funds for investment purposes. However, if you plan to use your equity to pay for living expenses then you'll lose the tax deductibility of the interest on the additional loan.

That's why I believe that the argument for funding your financial independence using equity is both flawed and dangerous. Once you've retired and you have little or no salary income, I would have thought that the last thing you'd want to do would be to create a situation where you have substantial loans of which an increasing portion of the interest must be funded from pre-tax earnings.

I guess this summarises the difference between the hype that sells property and the reality that investors must come to grips with at the coal face of trying to make money.

### Steve's Investing Tip

Interest on mortgage redraws is not deductible where the loan funds are spent on lifestyle expenses.

# THE MONEY RAISED FROM A PUBLIC OR PRIVATE FINANCIER

The final source of cash for your investing can be money lent by a private or public financier.

## Public Financier

Provided you can meet their lending criteria, banks and major lenders will be more than happy to provide money to finance your property acquisitions. The two critical pieces of information a bank will try to ascertain are:

1.  How much money do you want to borrow as a percentage of the value of the property?; and

2.  What is your ability to repay?

The lender's risk increases as you borrow more money compared with the value of your investment (this is called the **loan to valuation ratio**, or LVR). The industry benchmark is if you keep to an LVR of 80% or less then you should have relatively few problems.

If you're seeking finance then I suggest you use the services of a mortgage broker to help you shop for the right loan for your circumstances. This will save you a lot of time and it's usually a free service as the broker is paid a commission from the lender. Just bear in mind the lack of independence here by keeping abreast of the interest rates and fees associated with the loan.

## Private Lenders

Another potential source of money is private lenders – people with cash who are looking for above-market returns. Some private lenders will just require a set return, however a few might be interested in becoming your investing partners and sharing the risks and rewards of the investment. There are plenty of people in the marketplace labelled 'time-poor, money-rich' because they have a lot of cash but little time to invest. That's why, if you have the time but not the money (that is, you're time-rich, money-poor), teaming up with a money partner could take your investing potential to new heights.

Where do such people exist? A great place to start is to approach your accountant and see if he or she knows anyone who might be interested. Another idea is to attend seminars and network with the attendees – I've seen this happen successfully many times.

## Steve's Investing Tip

Just because you don't have the funds to invest doesn't mean you can't make a start. There's always a way to solve a problem.

# HOW MUCH MONEY DO I NEED TO GET STARTED?

This is a common question I'm asked. The answer is that it depends on:

1. What type of property you plan to buy. Generally the more expensive the property, the more money you'll need.

2. Your planned investing strategy (see Part III). Some strategies like wraps or lease options can be structured so that little, if any, money is needed.

3. The purchase terms you negotiate or the way you structure the deal. If you can negotiate a second mortgage or use investors to put up the money then you could structure a low or no money down deal.

## Being Creative

In Chapter 16 I mentioned that Dave and I purchased a block of 27 units on the Sunshine Coast for $530,000. While we ended up settling on the deal (as opposed to flipping it), the agent still calls us from time to time to see if we're interested in selling.

While it's an excellent investment, all of our properties are available for sale provided the price is right and we have another opportunity offering a better yield. Our unofficial price for this property is 'offers above $800,000'. The agent rang at the time of writing and said he had a buyer who had made the following verbal offer:

⇨ $600,000 cash; and

⇨ $150,000 in e-bank dollars (like barter dollars, I think).

You have to take your hat off to whoever made this offer. Assuming that they didn't have the necessary funds, they are still trying to think creatively to get the deal across the line. Sadly, while we're always open to creative deals, in this case $150,000 in cash would go a long way further than $150,000 in e-bank dollars!

While it *is* possible to buy property with no money down, I generally suggest that having access to either cash or savings of at least $10,000 will help you get started quickly. However, the critical success factor in your property empire won't necessarily be money, it will be a combination of your psychology and your creativity.

## HOW TO BUY PROPERTY WITH LITTLE OR NO MONEY DOWN

It was best-selling American author Robert G. Allen who, with the publication of his book *Nothing Down for the 90s* popularised the phrase 'nothing down'. In its simplest form, nothing down means being able to purchase a property without needing to fund the deposit or, in the ideal circumstance, any closing costs either.

Note that I have deliberately chosen to use the word 'fund' rather than 'pay' because, as an investor, you cannot avoid these costs, only seek to defer them or else have someone pay them on your behalf. The way you structure this outcome becomes the method you implement to successfully negotiate a nothing down deal.

As you would expect, nothing down deals are enormously popular with investors who don't have a lot of cash to invest. If this sounds like you then before you become wildly excited by what I've just written I'd like to remind you of the lesson from

Chapter 2 – namely that if you lack cash now you're likely to have a spending rather than an earning problem.

That said, let's look at eight strategies you can implement to potentially acquire a property with little or no money down.

## Strategy #1: 100% Plus Financing

These days, trying to organise finance has never been easier. Some lenders are even happy to finance you 100% plus of your purchase price (including closing costs) on the basis that you can offer additional security above and beyond the first mortgage of your investment property.

If you decide to use this strategy then be mindful that with bigger debt comes more risk. Furthermore, your investments also need to retain their positive cashflow status or else you begin to jeopardise your chances of achieving financial independence.

## Strategy #2: Use Equity Before Cash

A different variation on the 100% financing theme is to redraw or refinance your equity and then use that to pay for deposits and closing costs.

This is possibly a neater finance solution, as you will avoid any cross-collateralisation of properties or, put simply, you will not stand to lose your home if your investment property folds.

## Strategy #3: Vendor Finance

In Chapter 13 I outlined how you can offer wrap services to your clients. Well, you can also ask the vendor whom you're buying off to sell you his or her property on vendor finance too and then rent it out under a buy and hold investment strategy!

While not the norm, this practice is not unusual in commercial and rural properties. The bottom line is you'll never know unless you ask.

## Strategy #4: Second Mortgage

If the person you're buying from isn't interested in providing vendor finance, then he or she might be willing to carry back a second mortgage to reduce or eliminate the need for a deposit.

For example, let's say you buy a house for $200,000 on the basis that your financier provides a loan for 80% of the purchase price in return for a first mortgage over the property. This being the case, you'll need to pay a deposit of $40,000 on top of closing costs such as stamp duty, solicitor's fees etc.

You could go back to the vendor and ask him or her to take back $40,000 of the purchase price as a second mortgage that you will repay as a lump sum at the end of five years. In the meantime you'll pay interest on the second mortgage at, say, home loan interest rates which will provide a much better return for the vendor than if he or she had the money sitting in a term deposit.

The terms and conditions of the second mortgage will be whatever you can negotiate.

## Strategy #5: Long Settlements

If the market where you're buying is experiencing rapid growth then an effective low down strategy is a long-settlement period with a view to refinancing before taking possession.

For example, let's imagine that you purchased a property for $250,000 on the basis of a 90% lend. You don't have the $25,000 plus needed for a deposit and closing costs, so instead you negotiate a nine-month settlement period with a low initial deposit of, say, $1,000. During this time the property increases in value to $300,000. The bank revalues the property and gives the green light to lend on the higher (current market) value.

You can access the equity of $45,000 (90% of $50,000), which pays for your deposit of $30,000 plus all the closing costs too.

Be careful though... the key here is to get the lender to finance based on the current higher value rather than the initial contract price. Most lenders require at least six months to have elapsed before they'll even consider doing this.

## Strategy #6: Improve and Refinance

This takes the long settlement idea to a further extreme. Renovation doesn't necessarily have to involve a full-blown, 'knock down walls and add a second level' project. Often minor updates and cosmetic alterations will suffice.

For example, let's say you bought using the long settlement strategy outlined above. Also included in your purchase terms was a clause saying that you had the right to early access to complete renovations.

You then carry out the renovation during the settlement period (without paying any interest since you don't yet own the property) and then when the job is completed, you get the lender to value the property on the post-renovation status.

Provided your renovation has added more perceived than actual cost you'll benefit from being able to borrow more money.

## Strategy #7: Money Partners

If you don't have money or a good credit history then rest assured that there are other people who exist that do have the funds and are more than willing to be your money partner – at the right price. In such a relationship, you provide the time and your money partner delivers the cash. Profits and losses are then normally split 50/50.

## Strategy #8: Sell the Deal

If you do have a lot of time but not a lot of money then you could begin establishing a pool of savings to buy in your own right by becoming what's known in the industry as a 'bird-dog'. This involves finding deals and then selling the details to an investor in return for a payment. It's an excellent way to kick-start your property investing career if you lack experience or money.

# THE NOTHING DOWN ESSENCE OF SUCCESS

The essence of a successful nothing down deal is that you never let a "No" stop you from making progress. Instead you seek a way to approach the problems that will inevitably appear from a different angle where your lack of cash necessitates some creative (but always legal) negotiation and/or financing.

## Chapter 18 Insights

### Insight #1:

There are three potential sources of money to fund your property investing acquisitions – your savings, your equity and public or private financiers.

### Insight #2:

If you have the time and money to complete a deal in your own right then I would suggest that you invest for yourself rather than sharing the profits.

### Insight #3:

The amount of money you need to get started depends on the value of the real estate you intend to acquire and the property investing strategy you plan to implement.

### Insight #4:

Providing you have room to negotiate, there is always a way forward that is only limited by your creativity.

### Insight #5:

If you have solid money habits but just happen to be temporarily short of cash – you can still invest in property. Just seek out a money partner who has the resources you lack.

# Deal Shopping and Deposits

Another common question I'm asked is "Where do you find all your good deals?" Here are six sources that I regularly use to find positive cashflow deals:

## 1. The Print Media

Surprisingly simple, many of the properties that Dave and I have acquired have been advertised for sale in the newspaper. One of the largest deals we've done was sourced from an inconspicuous, four-line classified ad in *The Sunday Age*.

## 2. The Internet

These days you can shop for property from the comfort of your own home using the internet – the good websites even allow you to set up search parameters to quickly locate opportunities.

## Steve's Investing Tip

There's an extensive list of excellent websites available at:

www.PropertyInvesting.com/links

## 3. Real Estate Agents

Agents earn commissions by selling properties, so as a potential buyer you'll be greeted with enthusiasm – but only if you come across as genuine. I should point out that real estate agents will generally be more helpful during a flat or down market. In a boom market, when property sells itself, agents generally hit the cruise button and, unless they see an easy sale, won't be so willing to show a new investor the ropes.

## 4. Investment Groups and Seminars

Sometimes deals are advertised through investment groups and contacts met at seminars. Usually the conversation starts with "I've come across this deal..."

## 5. Pounding the Pavement and Networking with Locals

One of the best ways to locate properties is to get out and pound the pavement in the areas where you plan to invest. While out and about, ask the locals if they know of anyone who is thinking of selling. More aggressive marketeers might think about doing a letterbox drop mentioning that they're private investors interested in purchasing property.

### The Importance of Asking a Local

If you're investing in an area that you don't know well then don't be afraid to ask a local for help – just be humble, respectful and appreciative of the need for information that can only be gleaned by asking someone who grew up, or has lived in the area for a long time.

For example, when we were renovating the property outlined in Chapter 15, Dave and I spent every weekend in Ballarat for roughly six months. Anyway, there was an intriguing block of vacant land a few doors up the road; it was the only site on the street that hadn't been developed.

One afternoon shortly after settlement I went to introduce myself to the neighbour. His name was Alfie and he'd lived in the Ballarat region most of his life – about 60 years. I pointed to the vacant block up the road and asked him if he knew anything about it. It turned out that he knew quite a lot.

Alfie said that there was an abandoned mine in the middle of the property that had been 'capped', a process of pouring in concrete to prevent cave-ins. Over the years there had been a few owners who would buy the property without doing the proper research, seek to build on it and submit plans to the local council, only to have them knocked back because the land around the abandoned mine was still unsafe.

A few months later I was walking up the street to the Milk Bar and noticed that the vacant block was up for sale as a 'Rate Recovery Auction'. Apparently the owner had deserted the block and now the local water board was seeking to recoup a substantial debt, comprising past water rates and interest penalties, by selling the property.

Unfortunately I wasn't in town when the auction was held, but soon after I was tidying up our front yard when a car pulled up in front of the vacant land. The driver and passengers got out and started walking around the block. Sensing that these guys might be in some danger, I went to warn them only to find out that they were the new owners.

When I asked them whether or not they knew the property was an abandoned mine site, their faces went a horrible shade of white as they realised that they had just bought a lemon. A few months later the property was back up for sale. If only they'd asked the neighbours before buying...

## 6. Think Outside the Square

While a great opportunity occasionally lands in your lap, the best deals really need to be massaged into existence. To do this you need to work hard to find a solution that meets the needs of the vendor – which might sometimes require a creative outcome.

## Summary

Finding property deals is a lot like fishing. If you only have one rod in the water with one hook on it, you'll only ever catch one fish. However, many rods with many hooks might see you find many deals. Of course, those people without a line in the water will either go hungry – or alternatively need to shop at the fish market, where the product isn't as fresh, the choice is limited and the middleman's margin adds to the price.

# A WORD ABOUT DEPOSITS

The standard deposit on a property acquisition is 10% of the purchase price, so if you don't negotiate anything to the contrary then that's what you'll pay. It's important to understand there's no law that says you *have* to put down a 10% deposit, so if you have a limited amount of savings then reducing your deposit might allow you to buy more properties.

In Chapter 17 I outlined how Dave and I planned to buy 26 properties in 90 days. Our target properties were priced around the $50,000, but we didn't have a spare $130,000 (26 x [$50,000 x 10%]) lying around to pay for 10% deposits.

Rather than giving up on our goal, Dave and I thought about possibilities for how we could proceed. That's when we decided to focus on the wraps strategy, because we knew that we could recoup a lot of the capital needed as deposits from our clients.

Solving the lack of deposit capital became a matter of timing – we had to settle and on-sell one property before settling on another. The way we did this was to stagger the settlement dates to be at least two weeks apart. By this time we could on-sell the property and bank our wrap client's deposit.

A large part of our success came when we only put down a minimal deposit, because if Dave and I had to pay the usual 10% downpayment then our investing capital would have restricted us to about ten properties. As our goal was not ten but 26 properties, Dave and I immediately made it an official 'office policy' to only offer $1,000 deposits, which all of a sudden meant we could afford downpayments on 30 properties!

When an agent came to us with a sale contract that had the standard 10% deposit, we'd just smile as we put a line through it and wrote $1,000 in its place. Understandably, some real estate agents were uncomfortable with the lower deposit. When this occurred we'd just explain that, as professional investors, we were interested in buying multiple properties and needed to protect our capital base in order to afford as many as possible. We'd place a lot of importance on how we were looking to buy *multiple* properties. Sometimes you could visibly see the impact of this emphasis. The agent would complain, look grumpy, but then as it sunk in that buying multiple properties meant several commission opportunities, resistance melted away to enthusiastic understanding if not total endorsement.

Only once have we dealt with an agent who was reluctant to accept our new 'office policy' on deposits. The purchase price was $48,000 and the agent was playing games when he wrote that our deposit would be $10,000. Frustrated and not wanting to be taken for a fool, Dave thought he'd teach the agent a lesson by putting a line through $10,000 and writing $100. While we expected it to be questioned in which case we'd allow an extra zero to be added to make it $1,000, we never heard anything of it, and a new record-low deposit was set.

A word of caution is needed here. Low deposits will not save you from the need to come up with more money later. While you can get away with an initial low deposit, when it comes time to settle on the property you'll still need to come up with the difference between your initial deposit at the time of signing the contract and what the bank will lend you, plus you'll also have to pay for the closing costs too.

To illustrate the point I've reconstructed one of our actual settlement statements in Table 19.1 below.

| Table 19.1 – Settlement Example | | |
|---|---|---|
| **PURCHASER'S SETTLEMENT STATEMENT** | | |
| To: Purchase Price | | $40,000.00 |
| To: Purchaser's Solicitor Costs and Disbursements (Current Bill) | | $486.64 |
| To: Purchaser's Solicitor Costs and Disbursements (Prior Bill) | | $285.25 |
| To: Bank Cheque Fees | | $18.00 |
| To: Rate Adjustment | | $179.45 |
| By: Deposit Paid | $1,000.00 | |
| By: Loan Monies From Financier | $29,557.60 | |
| By: Amount Provided by You | $10,411.74 | |
| Total | $40,969.34 | $40,969.34 |

If you take a moment to look back at Table 19.1, opposite, you'll note that our purchase price was $40,000. By changing the deposit to $1,000, we avoided having $3,000 of our money earning a zero per cent return during the settlement period, which maximised our cash balance for other deposits.

Our low deposit 'office policy' eventually caught up with us on settlement day. We only sought 80% finance, which in this case meant a loan of $32,000. By the time stamp duty and loan costs were deducted from this balance, the money our financier contributed fell to $29,557.60

In order to take possession of this property we needed to come up with an additional $10,411.74. Adding on the deposit of $1,000, the total cash we needed was $11,411.74, yet this was then reduced by $8,000, being the deposit our wrap client paid us. So all we needed to acquire the property was a little under $3,500, as shown in Table 19.2 below.

| Table 19.2 – Summary of Net Cash Needed | |
|---|---|
| Initial deposit | $1,000 |
| Further capital needed | $10,412 |
| Client's wrap deposit received | ($8,000) |
| **Net Cash Needed** | **$3,412** |

Dave and I scrounged and saved every cent we could to gain the funds necessary to pay the deposits and closing costs. It wasn't easy going, but when the going got tough we worked harder than ever to get the deals across the line.

You can leave a downpayment of whatever you like, but just remember that in order to settle you'll need to come up with the necessary net cash as shown in Table 19.3 overleaf.

## Steve's Investing Tip

The amount you leave as a deposit is your choice and while 10% is the industry standard, there's no reason why it has to be this high.

| Table 19.3 – Net Cash Needed At Settlement | |
|---|---|
| Purchase price | $ |
| *Plus* closing costs | $ |
| Gross cash needed | $ |
| – Initial deposit | ($        ) |
| – Money your lender is providing | ($        ) |
| – Miscellaneous deposits/receipts | ($        ) |
| | |
| **Net Cash Needed** | $ |

## Chapter 19 Insights

### Insight #1:

There are many ways to source potential property investments, from the mainstream (using real estate agents) to the unconventional (doing letterbox drops).

### Insight #2:

The more sources you use to find deals, the greater the chance of locating something that meets your requirements.

### Insight #3:

It will take time to start up your network of contacts and to search for deals. If you don't have the time then seriously consider partnering with someone who does under a joint venture agreement.

### Insight #4:

The deposit you offer is always negotiable. You don't have to tie up your investment capital earning a 0% return. If you encounter resistance to leaving a low deposit then just say "Well, that's our 'office policy' to ensure we can continue buying more property. Say, just on that, do you have any others like this available for sale?"

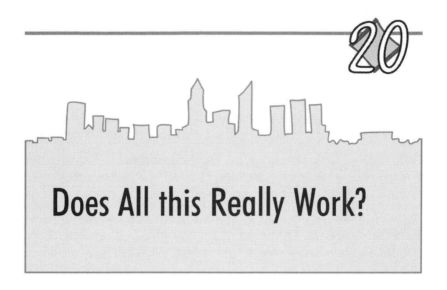

# Does All this Really Work?

So far I've shared the journey that Dave and I have enjoyed along the road to real estate success. Applying the knowledge outlined in this book, we've acquired 130 positive cashflow properties in three and a half years – so for us, the information has been proven to not only work, but work well. Dave and I have not been alone in our success. Included in this chapter are three testimonials from people who have seen, heard and implemented our ideas on positive cashflow investing.

## 1. YOU'RE NEVER TOO OLD TO INVEST –
### A Message from Brian Cavill

*Take it from me – you're never too old to start investing. I was 16 when I left school in 1963 to commence a career as a butcher. By 1974 I was married with a son and a daughter. Business wise I had bought my first butcher shop, which I later sold in 1982 for what I thought was enough money to never have to worry about working hard ever again.*

*Since I'd worked hard for 19 years without a holiday, I took six months off work and reflected upon my success to date. I thought we'd made it. Our family had substantial savings and enjoyed a very comfortable lifestyle. Seeking to maximise our profits I decided to invest the lot in a trust company for six months at 17% interest.*

*Five weeks after investing every hard-earned cent I'd saved, the trust company folded after operating for 118 years. It was supposed to be Australia's oldest and most reliable; we lost the lot.*

*To start again we decided to sell our flash car, campervan and some other assets. I returned to what I knew best and in 1983 I bought another butcher shop, taking on my son as my apprentice.*

*The shop was supposed to be taking $3,500 per week, but by the Wednesday of the first week, all that had come through the door was $35. I was looking for a way out, but my solicitor advised that going to court was unlikely to provide the result I was looking for.*

*My options were to either walk away or try to turn things around. We had no money and my confidence had been reduced to zero. I found myself on the floor of the butcher shop fridge crying out for help to the God I believed in, but didn't know. I sought forgiveness for stuffing up and for trying to do things my way and on my own. I cried out for His help and guidance, acknowledging I could no longer do it alone. When I finally arose from the fridge floor, I felt amazingly calm and knew that everything was going to be all right.*

*During the next six years I continued to work hard. Years later, after I had accepted Jesus into my life, I came to realise it was the peace of God that had touched me. Without knowing it, He began to impact my thought processes and I was beginning to walk through an amazing journey of transformation.*

*Discovering I had a gift for massage, I became involved with a local football club – first as a sponsor then as a sports trainer. In 1987 I sold the butcher shop with takings of around $6,000 per week. I established a full-time massage practice at a gymnasium at 40 years of age.*

*For the next ten years, with the support of my wife and family, I built a successful massage practice. My skills were widely recognised and I was appointed masseur for pro-golf in Victoria until 1990 when I resigned to concentrate on the new centre we'd built at the back of our home.*

*As I studied my Bible, I began to pray for financial wisdom. Now, what I'm about to say next is sure to sound a little crazy. Butchering was predominantly a cash business and without much effort I had been able to cheat the taxman to the tune of about $28,000. Anyway, I really felt that the way back to prosperity was to first clear my conscience.*

*While understandably a little nervous, I wrote the tax department a long letter and attached a cheque, only to have it returned because the system didn't cater for such honesty. However, a few attempts later, the government did keep the money and that was the end of the matter.*

*It was time to start again and I sought advice from many financial experts who all seemed to indicate that private superannuation was the right vehicle to take me to retirement. However, having gone through the experience of losing all our money in the trust company, I refused to follow this advice.*

*Instead I bought a negatively geared property to supposedly ease my tax burden. While it certainly did this, we still had to find the money each month to put back into the property.*

*We were working hard, had a successful business and didn't waste money, yet we couldn't seem to do anything other that just survive. A large slab of our money still went to pay our taxes. What were we doing wrong?*

*I continued praying and came across the story of the three servants (Matthew 25:14).*

## The Three Servants

*Paraphrasing, the master went on a journey and gave three of his servants an amount of money (called a talent). One servant received five talents, another received two talents and the third received only one talent.*

After one year the master returned and went to see what the servants had done with the money entrusted to them. The servants receiving the most money had managed to double what they were given and were given more.

However, the third servant decided to bury his one talent in the ground and when the master returned, he had nothing to show for it, even though he could have deposited it and earned interest. This servant was punished and thrown into prison!

"Oh, no!" I thought. Considering the amount of money that had gone through my hands, I was looking suspiciously like the wicked servant. I was more determined than ever to get money working for us, rather than us working for money.

One day I was in a book store and, like so many others, bought and read Robert Kiyosaki's Rich Dad Poor Dad, which answered some of my questions about money.

My accountant at the time couldn't offer any advice other than to put everything into super. Furthermore, my accountant went on to say that he had the same tax problems as me, which was when I realised that he had done all he could for me. As much as I liked him, I began my search for a new accountant and to my amazement every person I spoke to was still singing the praises of superannuation.

Then a mutual friend put us on to Dave Bradley, advising us that he was an accountant who was talking about the virtues of positive cashflow investing.

I'll never forget the day we met Dave. It was 1999 and he was an answer to our prayers. Dave does not beat around the bush. At our first meeting he said "If you're serious about investing then I'll consider being your accountant. But to show me you are serious there's a $2,000 a head seminar that my business partner Steve and I are attending with our wives. I strongly advise you to attend and, in fact, if you're not interested in going, then I'm probably not interested in being your accountant."

Already quite stunned, Dave dropped another bombshell. "Oh, in your case, I also advise you to sell your negatively geared property".

*I went to the seminar and went on to begin researching areas in which to invest. Not really knowing what I was doing, but having a firm resolve, I made a start in a regional area that people thought I was crazy to invest in. "Brian", they'd say, "houses there are $30,000 for good reason!"*

*There was pressure at home too. I didn't have the cash for deposits so I took out a line of credit against our home. My wife wasn't too pleased, but she reluctantly gave me the go ahead.*

*By 2000 I'd bought two houses, two duplexes, and a three-plex. On paper they were all positive cashflow. For example, after some basic renovations, the two duplexes cost a total of $88,000 and rented at $380 per week. What a fantastic return! How easy was this?*

*But, by the end of the 2001 financial year we'd had 14 tenants either shoot through or be "persuaded to leave" because they were not paying their rent. We also experienced some lengthy periods when the properties sat vacant. It's true what Steve says about vacancies – they're a silent killer of cashflow returns.*

*What was going wrong? David rightly questioned whether property investing was for me. I tended to get involved with my tenants' problems while trying to help them. I needed to adopt a firmer approach since I was perceived to be a soft touch.*

*One costly error I'd made was to think I was an ace negotiator by securing a great rental management deal. In this case, what I paid for was what I got – cheap commissions and cheap tenants.*

*It was around this time that Steve and Dave refined their strategies and due diligence templates to transform their ideas into a replicable system for successful investing.*

*Steve would regularly come for massages (he calls me 'Brian the Butcher') and began to influence my thinking. As I reset his ligaments he'd say things like "win-win solutions", "solving problems", "invest in people" and "think creatively".*

*Taking Steve's advice and seeking his help as a mentor, I spent the rest of 2001 turning things around. After owning the three-plex for just six months we on-sold it (and the problems) for a good profit.*

*I networked to find the best rental agent in the area and she found us good paying tenants for the duplexes. We also finally managed to source a quality tenant for one of the houses. We wrapped our second house.*

*Things were back on track thanks to my friends and mentors Dave Bradley and Steve McKnight.*

*So what have I learnt? I thank God for the journey I'm on and give credit to my leader in life and all matters – Jesus Christ. I've come to realise that there's a price to pay in life. You either learn from costly mistakes, or you keep repeating them.*

*Acquiring good money habits has been fundamental to my success. If you're not getting the results you desire, whether it be in your marriage, your diet, family or finance – then look to change.*

*I'm also very much guided and influenced by Steve and Dave. My wife, who all the time has been uncertain about the strategy I'm adopting, attended one of Steve's amazing seminars and now has a greater understanding of where we are heading, and more importantly, why it's critical to do something different.*

*I'm thankful Dave and Steve are our mentors and accountants. Other critical members of my investing team include solicitors, bankers, insurance agents and real estate agents. In fact, if the people we're using cease to become willing team players then we'll find someone else.*

*Finally, we're always looking to build a win-win outcome.*

*Where are my wife and I today? Our first wrap fell over because our client stopped making repayments. In response we had to repossess the house and then look to wrap it to another person.*

*As a result I have tightened up our due diligence process and now have several other successful wraps. Prices in the area where we invest have more than doubled, so we took the opportunity to sell everything that was not wrapped for some quick cash.*

*Even with all the early mistakes and challenges, it's been really exciting. Becoming financially free whilst helping people to own their own home is a great way to invest.*

*It's been special to be a part of what Dave and Steve have achieved in such a short time. It's a real privilege to be able to learn from them and to count them as friends.*

*It also continues to amaze me that every successful business owner or investor, whether they realise it or not, uses principles laid out in the Bible. The principles of giving, of sowing and reaping, principles of integrity, of having your money work for you which are all common themes of success.*

*Today we're researching new areas and with our refined investing system in place, we will continue to build our portfolio of properties. Our financial freedom is no longer a question of if but when. We have a plan and are firmly on the way to achieving our goal.*

*Yes. Financial independence is possible. Even for this old bloke. With the right team leader and the right team you can do it too.*

## 2. PERSISTENCE PAYS
### – A Message from Andrew Deering

*As a former full-time share trader, I can certainly understand it when those who love stocks suggest I've turned to the dark side of the force by becoming a staunch advocate of property investing. However, the stock market wasn't delivering the investment results I was looking for. Sure, I was making money by trading shares, but the novelty of my trading system was wearing thin. I was spending quality time at the screen instead of with my wife and kids.*

*So there I was, at the end of another day, staring aimlessly at my computer screen and rubbing my temples in frustration, wondering how the market could dare to not react in the way I thought or predicted it would or should. That's when I experienced something of an epiphany. I came to realise that I started trading to earn extra money so that I could work less. However, all I'd done was earn enough extra money to encourage me to work more in the hope of upsizing my profits. Something had to change!*

*Now, being a voracious reader I'd devoured tonnes of information about share trading and wealth creation in general. One email that consistently stood out from the pack was a monthly newsletter written by Steve McKnight which praised the virtues of cashflow positive property investment.*

*While I'd been to the author's website and found the information very interesting, I'd never taken it as anything more than a good read that was of very little practical use for someone like me, who was interested in the stock market.*

*Yet on the day of my epiphany I raced back to my computer's email inbox and called up every McKnight email I'd ever received. I re-read them all, this time in a completely new light. Re-evaluating my goals, I saw that my trading system was dependent on me, but to work less I had to take me out of the picture. I came to realise that the more my strategy relied on me, the more time I had to spend at the computer screen. Was there another option?*

*Steve claimed that he bought houses that made money from day one. His philosophy was that you could spend the time once and receive a lifetime of cashflow. This was different to my trading system that required me to be present everyday to 'pull the trigger'.*

*Furthermore, when it came to property I was much more familiar with negative gearing than I was with positive gearing. I had implemented the same strategy with my stocks by borrowing money to invest and claiming the interest as a tax deduction.*

*Steve's criticism of tax savings as a reason to invest suddenly took on new meaning as I realised that I'd been trying to make money by losing money! Was I mad? I was beginning to see the many flaws in my wealth creation strategy.*

*I'd been receiving Steve's emails for more than a year and only now was I beginning to see the sense in his approach.*

*Lamenting all my lost time and opportunities I immediately hit the internet trying to find positive cashflow properties and more information to satisfy my thirst. But after weeks of searching, I'd found nothing and was beginning to rub my temples again in familiar frustration. My last desperate act was to write Steve an email asking for his urgent help. I was becoming adamant that his approach might work down south, but up here in Queensland opportunities did not seem to exist.*

*Offering little more than reassurance (I now understand he did this because my investing journey is more important than my investing outcome) Steve simply replied with, "Keep looking".*

*I was also trying to learn more about wrapping and whether or not it was a strategy I could use. It was an interesting concept, but who would ever need to buy a house using such a method? Having had a good job and having bought my first house at age 22, I made the mistake of being ignorant and thinking everyone else had enjoyed a similar experience. Only later did I realise that around 20% of the population were not so lucky and couldn't qualify to buy a house using traditional means.*

*As I found out more, I received a flyer advising that Steve would be speaking at a Brisbane event. Knowing that numbers would be limited, I intended to book immediately but, as luck had it, I had to work on the night of the seminar, and couldn't attend. However, I was not going to give in easily and quickly decided that I'd attend the same seminar the following night in Coolum. It was certainly worth attending as I gleaned a lot more information off Steve in person than I ever did in his newsletters. At the end of the night I invested in his Wrap Library, which promised to provide everything I needed to know to help me to start with wrapping.*

*Having a long drive back to Brisbane, I immediately started using his Wrap Library by listening to CD #1. My friend, who came with me, must have thought he was caught in a whirlwind, but he was also very encouraged by what he'd heard (thanks Micah).*

*Steve's product sent me into a new level of desire to achieve financial freedom. I listened to the audio, read the notes and then re-listened many times. I spent the next few months using every spare minute to learn more about property and trying to hunt down deals. No kidding, I literally spend hundreds of hours (just ask my wife – thanks Fiona) pounding the pavement, on the phone, or on the internet.*

*While my learning curve was exponential, I still struggled to find properties that fitted into my new investing system. This time I didn't email Steve, I called him and told him that I thought his information was interesting but wasn't applicable in my market.*

*Once more Steve provided affirmation that perhaps the problem wasn't the system but the way I was applying it. He told me other people in Queensland were using it successfully, so I could too! Not wanting to let go of my grasp on financial independence so easily, I again hit the pavements. Finally I bumped into a property that met my criteria.*

## My First Rental

*I decided that I had been looking enough and I was going to buy a house. The agent I felt most comfortable with had shown me a property two weeks beforehand which I felt was 'the one'. Upon calling her I found that there were already two offers in and that I needed to offer above $72,000 to have a real chance. This was my first buy so I blindly trusted the agent and offered $73,000.*

*I went home that day and was struck with what I had just done. "What if they want more?", I thought, "What if I can't rent it? What if…?" The terror was setting in.*

*I got a call the next day congratulating me on my purchase. I didn't know whether to jump for joy or jump off a building as it was such a big investment for my mindset at the time.*

*Then the fun began. I needed to organise a building inspection, organise finance and many other details associated with buying a house. I felt like a blind man in a razor factory afraid to go too far or touch too much in case I made a fatal mistake. After a month of sleepless nights the deal was settled and the property was tenanted the next day.*

*Wow! All my fears subsided and I realised that it really wasn't that hard after all. I was lucky that the agent was honest and it was a good investment but since then I have been more strict in doing my own due diligence to ensure a property is of a minimum standard.*

## Repeating the Process

*After I'd completed my first deal I knew that I could translate my theoretical system into practical money making. It was as if a light had come on in my head. The next trick was to upsize my investments and acquire even more properties.*

*I acquired my first property in May 2002 and by the end of February 2003 I'd purchased seven more. I'd earned once-off profits of around $35,000 together with an annual passive income of approximately $6,000.*

*Of these deals, one was a wrap, two were renovations and the remaining were buy and holds. I'm keenly looking forward to what the future holds as I feel much more able and confident to complete more deals. Having journeyed so far I'm starting to see new opportunities every day and best of all... I no longer have to stare at the computer screen or worry about what's happening in the stock market. My success has been a combination of:*

▷ ***A great mentor.*** *It's awesome to have one or more mentors. In particular I'd like to thank Steve and my friend Andreas. Mentors turn mountains into molehills. If you haven't already done so, I'd suggest you subscribe to Steve's free newsletter at www.PropertyInvesting.com.*

▷ ***Great friends.*** *It's been fantastic to share my journey with friends who have supported me not just during the good times, but for the occasional bad times too. Thanks to Everett and Micah.*

▷ ***Family as team members.*** *I doubt I could have achieved anything if I did not have the support and encouragement of my wife (thanks Fiona) and two beautiful girls (thanks Emily-Jane and Annabelle). Hang on guys because the roller coaster hasn't finished yet.*

▷ ***A trust in God.*** *It's wonderful to know that God cares and wants the best for me. He has been my rock in times of frustration and he has helped me find my path.*

*All in all, property investing has been an absolute adventure. It has not been easy. Each week opened up new challenges and I can't remember ever being so active (mentally and at times physically). However, by the same token, I cannot remember a time when I've been so happy and had such a feeling of completeness and success.*

*My positive cashflow journey has been difficult, especially since it goes against the grain of the normal negative gearing real estate rhetoric. However the rewards are worthwhile.*

*While you don't have to be a rocket scientist, you must desire success with all your heart. If there's one thing I remember daily, it's to stop and smell the roses... but not for too long or I might miss the next opportunity!*

## 3. CHOOSING NOT TO GO TO WORK
### – A Message from Bruce Innocent

*Have you ever thought about what it would be like to be able to choose whether or not you go to work? I mean really, truly be able to think it over and then make the call without any financial considerations, because whatever you do, your family will be fed, clothed, housed, transported, schooled and entertained independent of your efforts. What if you could do that? What if...*

*As far as my contribution to this book is concerned, my story begins about two and a half years ago when my life and business partner, Denise, was seven months pregnant and about to become a full-time mum.*

*While we were both very much looking forward to becoming parents, it also meant that we were going to have to survive on just one income – which was half of what we currently enjoyed. I knew nothing about money. Mmmm – maybe that's a bit harsh, but it was true.*

*I didn't learn about it in school, and even though I had a well-paying, professional job for many years, I had enormous credit card debt. Denise was in only a marginally better situation, but I remember her saying that she always had money when she needed it.*

*On the bright side I at least controlled four properties. One of these I owned outright, but this had really only happened after both my parents had passed away and left me their home (which*

*I can tell you truthfully is far too high a price to pay for anything in this world). We lived in one and the other three were rented and losing money, but I only found this out when I finally got around to doing my tax... eight years late.*

*I was working away from home at a remote mine site, and my friend, who employed me, asked me to help out one of his workmates (Mark) by fixing a computer in his home. So, that evening, in return for a meal, I helped Mark install some huge new hard-drives for his PC. I couldn't understand why he needed all this capacity, so I asked what he was planning to do.*

*My new friend simply said "for my stock market data". A little confused I replied "What? But you're a senior metallurgist and manager? Don't you earn stacks of money already?"*

*He just smiled and pointed out that he was getting really burnt out and needed time with his partner and four children, so he was embarking on a new career.*

*At the end of our discussion he looked me up and down and said, "Here, borrow this, my brother gave it to me for a present" and pressed a copy of Robert Kiyosaki's* Rich Dad Poor Dad *into my hand.*

*I stayed up late and read almost all of it in one evening. Wow, what a mind flip! My head was flooded with thoughts: "My home is not an asset?" "So, that was the basics of reading a balance sheet?", "I can buy property that makes money?"*

*Denise and I both read the book and had our entire viewpoint on money shifted radically. It felt like my eyes had been opened for the first time.*

*That book rapidly led to other books, then onto a fantastic board game, and ultimately a website, which had a bulletin board full of American investors strutting their stuff. The trouble was, all of the nitty gritty information related only to America.*

*But after a lot of searching, buried in one of the discussion threads was a post titled "How I got out of the rat race in 11 months – in Victoria". The writer also left his email address.*

*It was the day before our child was born and I was so nervous that my fingers were shaking as I decided to get in contact with this financially free person to ask some questions.*

*As I did, several thoughts flashed by; "What if this person doesn't want to communicate? Who is it? Will he or she mind me emailing them? How pretentious was I to write? I was frightened!*

*Having gone through all of the angst I was a little surprised that not only did I receive a reply, it came back within five minutes. A few emails went back and forth, then I received:*

---

**From:** Steve McKnight

**To:** Bruce Innocent

**Subject:** Re: Real Estate Investors Network

Hi Bruce! You must either be a speed typist or have lots of time... Sadly, I'm not a speed typist and I don't have a lot of time either :-(

Just call me and I'll answer your questions one on one.

Bye

Steve.

---

*Shaking even more I picked up the phone and dialled. We spoke for only a few minutes but he told me that he and his business partner had purchased 40 properties in 11 months.*

*My mind was reeling, "40! It wasn't possible, but it **must** be – he sounded like he was telling the truth" (and of course, he was).*

*I thanked him for his time. I looked at Denise and told her about this amazing person that I had just talked with.*

*The next day some much more important events happened <grin> and I became the proud father of a bouncing (and screaming) baby boy, but that's another life-bending experience entirely.*

*When things at home settled down a little I returned to creating our new financial life. After much researching and reading, we eventually decided to go the next step and I attended Steve and Dave's first ever gathering of investors in November 2000, held at a humble baseball club in Melbourne.*

*Although Denise and I had pretty much 'sussed out' what a wrap was and had learnt a little about cashflow positive concepts, I remember being totally, totally at sea and taking copious notes on:*

➭ *The maths*

➭ *What to look for*

➭ *How to analyse a deal (they made us play a game and at one point ran an auction); and*

➭ *What to say to potential clients when they phoned up.*

*I was sleeping on a friend's couch that night and I remember staying up for hours afterwards trying to learn how the numbers worked. When I returned home I relayed all my learnings to Denise and then convinced our solicitor, accountant and banker that the wrap idea had merit.*

*We needed to take action. Even though we owned a resource written by Steve about writing classified ads, I was still scared and lacked the confidence to get my act together and place the advertisement. Denise, seeing my paralysis, did what she does best – assessed the situation and simply took over, placing one of Steve's sample ads in a local paper!*

*Then, as luck would have it, she became sick and I was juggling the job of looking after our son and answering all 65 phone calls that we received in the next two days! All my fears were ganging up on me at once.*

*Anyway, we built a list of people, sorted out an amazing list of 'how to' specifics and then went out and bought our first few houses, which our clients found for us.*

*We were so scared! It was so awesome! Our settlements all went wrong, we had written unconditional contracts, our finance fell over at the last minute and we had to use credit cards as bridging finance... but... we'd started; and that glass of celebratory champers went down very, very well!*

*I was recalling our experiences a few months later to a wonderful friend named Brenton and he said to me "Bruce, you and Denise have moved through a lot of fear."*

*In a short amount of time we completed 14 wraps in addition to a few standard buy and holds. In doing these deals we have come up against and solved a multitude of problems, which has taught us some very valuable lessons – every little problem you solve adds a little more to your confidence and allows you to solve the next slightly larger problem.*

*You try, you fall over, you learn, you try, you fall over, you learn and all of a sudden, you walk!*

*There have been good times, bad times, frustrations, disillusionment, intense learning and many successes. It's truly been an awesome ride, and as I reflect I see a mountain range of experience separating 'me now' from 'me then'.*

*So where are we nowadays? Denise and I are in the process of closing our 40th property purchase. We have, on paper at least, replaced our salary income. We control about $2 million, or so, of real estate and are planning to buy another 40 houses in the next 12 months.*

*We're not completely sure of how we'll do it, but we have the first deal almost done and believe that we can easily do the next eight.*

*I guess what I am saying here is that everyone is empowered to change their circumstance by making a choice. Successful investing is **not** rocket science – what's required is motivation, determination, a great partner, a good team and a stack of other skills that you'll only ever learn along the way.*

*Where's a good place to make a start? Simply wanting an outcome badly enough will help you to step beyond your comfort zone and take action. Immerse yourself in really **wanting** to…. That's all we did.*

*Financial independence can be more than a dream if you take the courage to give it a go.*

***Epilogue:*** *Oh, and by the way, not only did Mark (whose computer I repaired) become a stock trader – he went on to invest in the* *future's market. He rang about two weeks ago and told me about his first $100k trade. Didn't quite go as planned and he walked away with $60k profit. Not too bad I reckon! <grin>*

## Chapter 20 Insights

### Your Insight:

Use the space below to write down your own thoughts and to answer this question:

"What do I need to do in order to make property investing work for me?"

# What's Your Next Move?

As I see it, today, right now, this very instant you have a choice.

On the one hand you can continue to do what you're doing. Stop for a minute now and think ten years ahead. Imagine what your life would be like. If you work in a career, pause and look up the corporate ladder. Is the top rung a destination where you want to end up? Look around your workplace. Do the people with more seniority have the sort of lifestyle that you feel is appealing? Would you like to work as hard as they do?

On the other hand, is there another possibility that you feel is more attractive? One where you can gradually gain the freedom of your time?

All that's required is that you make a choice and decide to take action towards an outcome that you feel your heart is calling you to. Take the test in Table 21.1, overleaf.

| Table 21.1 – Multiple Choice (Circle Your Answer) | |
|---|---|
| TODAY'S DATE: | |
| **Question: What Do I Want?** | |
| A | More of what I'm doing? |
| B | Something different? |

If you work in a job and answered 'A', then I wish you the best of success with your career. In fact, I'm a little envious because I never experienced the job satisfaction that you must enjoy from your work. The advice I leave you with is to always maintain control over your finances and only invest in things that make money.

If you answered 'B', then I urge you to spend a few moments now thinking about the physical steps you need to take to harness your momentum.

### Steve's Investing Tip

The only way to transform *do* into *done* is to take action.

Make a list (do it now on the page opposite) of action steps you can complete over the next 30 days that will get your life in order and allow you to begin or expand your property investing empire.

## THE WORST-CASE SCENARIO

Dave's father once asked him what he'd do if all his investing plans amounted to nothing. Can you imagine how he responded? He said, "Dad, a 1% chance of actually achieving success is better than a 100% chance of failure, which is what I will have if I never try at all. I can always go back to doing full-time accounting."

## My 30-day Plan of Action

Write your 30-day plan of action in the space below.

Is the same also true for you? If you tried to make a go of property investing but failed, could you always just go back to what you are doing now? Sure, you might need to take a slightly lower initial salary at a new company, but so what?

It took a lot for me to abandon my career as a chartered accountant in public practice. However, I can still remember the day I finally came to terms with the fact that I really had nothing to lose, as I was already living my worst-case scenario – having to work hard for a considerably long time. Because I could always go back to doing the books for clients, I owed it to myself to at least try something different, for I knew that in order for things to change, first things had to change.

## The Answer

It's a tough ask, but if I had to summarise the secrets to my success in just one paragraph, it would read like this:

*Instead of living a comfortable lifestyle, I chose to delay my gratification and allocate my savings and reinvested profits to acquiring positive cashflow properties. I've also looked to maximise my investment returns by solving the housing needs of everyday people within the context of creating win-win outcomes.*

At the beginning of Part IV I suggested that you keep the following two questions in mind:

⮞ **Question 1:** How can I turn my theory into practice?; and

⮞ **Question 2:** Do I have what it takes to be successful?

If you haven't already worked out your own answers, I'm happy to share my thoughts.

Question 1 can only be answered by taking action. It's hard to move out of a comfort zone, but you can do it with an expectation of success provided you have a purpose and a plan, and on the assumption that you only invest in assets that make money.

As for Question 2... you have what it takes to be successful if your mind can believe that your dreams are achievable – for what the mind can realistically see, the body can achieve.

## YOUR JOURNEY

I think I've said enough. It's time for us to shake hands and part ways, for although we may share financial independence as a common destination, the road your journey must take will be different from mine. Thank-you for allowing me to share my story and experience with you. Good luck, and God bless.

## Chapter 21 Insights

### Insight #1:

Are you living in your own worst-case scenario? What's really at stake if you were to try something different?

You don't need to do anything too radical – perhaps just invest a few days into looking for property deals that make money from day one. You could start with residential property – or move straight into commercial, if that's your preference.

The worst thing you can do is nothing at all. For in the absence of change, things will always stay the same. That's also called relaxing into a comfort zone – and I can tell you that no one ever became financially independent by staying in his or her comfort zone.

### Insight #2:

Don't be fooled into a false sense of security. Becoming a real estate baron (or baroness) is a lot of hard work and there's always the chance that you'll lose money. My advice is that money can always be replaced, but time can't.

### Insight #3:

While financial independence is a nice outcome, the real adventure is the journey. I can't promise you that every day will be a good day, but I can tell you that creating win-win outcomes through property investing beats the living daylights out of doing tax returns.

# PART V:

# More of the Nitty Gritty

# Appendix A

# W.E.A.L.T.H.

Back in Chapter 2, I explained how important it was to develop good money habits in order to sustain your wealth creation activities. When trying to explain this concept to my neightbour, Jackie, I used the following W.E.A.L.T.H. acronym to reveal the necessary steps to controlling spending.

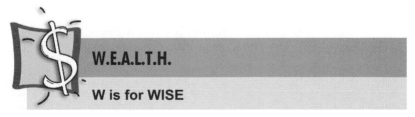

**W.E.A.L.T.H.**

**W is for WISE**

Being wise with money is a lot different to being tight. The wise realise that spending money is inevitable, so provided it's not wasted, wealth is created to be enjoyed rather than hoarded. If you want to become wise with your money then the key is to avoid impulse buying. Instead of buying on emotion, the ramifications of spending money need to be considered *before* flipping out your credit card.

Some questions you might like to consider when deciding whether or not your purchase is wise include:

▷ Would someone else regard my purchase as wise?

▷ What would happen if I didn't buy right now?

▷ Could I purchase the item at a different time or place and save money?

▷ Could I trial it first and then return it later if I was not satisfied?

▷ What guarantees does the item come with?

A good way to guard against impulse buying is to wait at least 24 hours after first seeing the product or service you want to buy.

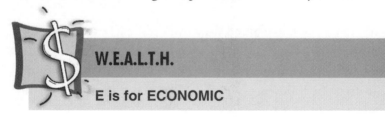

**W.E.A.L.T.H.**

**E is for ECONOMIC**

Economic also means cost-effective. It takes so much effort to earn money, it's a shame to spend it on something that has a high perceived but low actual value. One of the few topics that's stuck in my head from university is the term 'price-quality illusion'. It summarises the common myth that the higher the price the better the quality. Often multiple retail outlets sell the same clothes, made in the same factory, using the same material. All that's different is the label attached on the back (which can be sewn on in the retail store!) and sometimes more than 50% in price, depending on whether the store is a bulk outlet or a boutique.

Recently my wife and I purchased a new car – a Mazda 323. We shopped around for a good deal and just as we were about to buy we discovered that another dealership had the same type of car, brand new, but just superseded by about six months. In fact, except for ABS brakes, it was mechanically identical to the current model; all that had changed were some minor modifications to the body and headlights. However the difference in price was substantial – about 10% or $2,500. Some questions you could use to determine whether or not a purchase is economic include:

➪ Is it worth the money?

➪ Is a cheaper substitute available of similar quality?

➪ Have I shopped around to ensure that the price today is a good price?

➪ Does it have a high perceived value but a low actual or intrinsic value? Am I prepared to pay the premium?

➪ Am I paying excessively for a brand name?

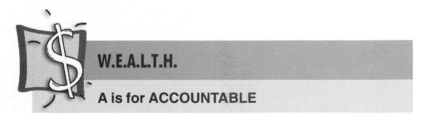

## W.E.A.L.T.H.

### A is for ACCOUNTABLE

No matter what you do, being accountable for your actions will be critical to your success. When it comes to money, accountable people retain control of their spending by tracking every dollar that leaves their wallet or purse, including purchases made using EFTPOS and credit cards. If you can't or don't want this obligation because it restricts your freedom then you're the sort of person that needs it the most.

Yes, it's a pain and a nuisance, but all you need to do is:

▷ Ask for receipts (or a tax invoice)

▷ Keep your receipts; and

▷ Record the payment to keep a tally of where you spend your money. You can do it manually or alternatively use programs such as Microsoft Excel, MYOB or Quicken.

Retaining all your receipts can also help you at tax time since a good tax accountant will find ways for you to legally claim a lot of expenses, provided you can provide substantiation.

If you're having trouble reconciling your bank statements with your cheque book then use the *free report* I've written, available at:

www.PropertyInvesting.com/accountable

Some questions you can ask to determine whether or not you're being accountable include:

▷ Am I keeping my receipts?

▷ Do I have a home budget that says how much I want to save and then works backwards to show much I can afford to spend?

▷ Am I impulsive or someone who's accountable by nature?

▷ Why do I like or hate the thought of having to be accountable?

▷ If being a millionaire required that I keep my receipts and became accountable for how I spend my money, could I do it?

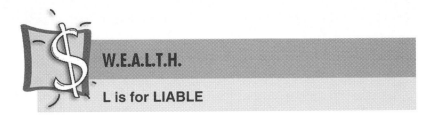

## W.E.A.L.T.H.

### L is for LIABLE

Being liable requires you to accept the responsibility that you're the one making each purchase and that you're the one ultimately responsible for determining whether or not you can afford to do so. It's tempting to use credit cards to buy something now, enjoy it, and then imagine that you can somehow repay the debt with money that you'll earn tomorrow. This is dangerous thinking!

Credit cards provide guilt-free instant gratification. But the purchase always comes at a cost, which is *at least* what you paid for it, or if you can't repay by the due date, cost plus potentially high interest charges too.

Loyalty programs that reward people for using debt have caused a change in the way consumer's view credit. I'm reminded of the story of how small monkeys are captured in the jungles of Africa – something I first read about in Robert G. Allen's book *Creating Wealth*.

Captors use heavy thick glass bottles, with long narrow necks, into which they deposit a handful of sweet-smelling nuts. The bottles are dropped on the jungle floor and the captors return the next morning to occasionally find a small monkey trapped next to a bottle. The monkey, attracted by the sweet scent of the nuts, comes to investigate. Seeking to claim the nuts for its own, the monkey reaches its open hand into the bottle and grabs its prize with a clenched fist. This secures the monkey's capture because while an open hand can reach into the bottle and grab the nuts, a clenched fist is too big to withdraw. As the bottle is too heavy for the monkey to drag away, it becomes trapped. All the monkey needs to do is to let go and escape. But those nuts are just too tempting and the monkey becomes the victim of a simple trap.

It's so easy to rack up debt and worry about the consequences later, only to become a slave to the debt when you become forced to work hard just to make ends meet. If only you could avoid that debt to begin with, then you could avoid the trap altogether.

Ask yourself these questions to determine whether or not you're being liable:

▷ If I quit work today, how long could I survive (in days) before my mortgage and other debt meant that I needed to find another job?

▷ Do I manage my credit cards, or do my credit cards manage me?

▷ What is the current interest rate I pay on all my outstanding debt?

▷ Am I really helping or hindering myself by using credit?

## W.E.A.L.T.H.

### T is for THOROUGH

Being thorough means researching your purchase to ascertain all its features and shortcomings *before* you buy. At the very least, compare the performance of your planned purchase with its nearest competitor to ensure any price premium is worth it. If you're buying a property and need a loan, being thorough requires that you calculate the ***effective interest rate*** to properly compare different loan products. The effective interest rate is the cost of finance once you have added in all the loan fees and charges on top of the interest rate.

For example, let's say you want to borrow $100,000 at an interest rate of 7% per annum. Furthermore, the loan has a

$10 per month service fee on top of a $200 per annum loan charge. While the advertised interest rate is 7% per annum, the effective annual interest rate is 7.32% per annum ([$7,000 + ($10 x 12) + $200] ÷ $100,000).

You might find it cheaper to take a higher interest rate with no fees rather than a loan with a seemingly cheap rate that's nevertheless loaded with every fee imaginable. The only way you'll know is by shopping around and comparing loans based on their effective interest rates. Some questions to ask when determining whether or not you're being thorough include:

➪ Have I identified the nearest rival and shopped around for the best deal?

➪ Do I have contingency plans in place in case something unforseen, like losing my job, occurs?

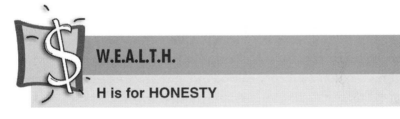

## W.E.A.L.T.H.

### H is for HONESTY

Honesty is the final criteria. Never kid yourself that spending money doesn't matter. A million dollars is just that – 1,000,000 dollar coins. A dollar that's spent haphazardly is quickly lost forever. If you don't know whether or not you can afford something then ask "How can I afford it?" and if you don't like the answer then don't buy it.

Never, ever, ever repay debt with debt, like using one credit card to pay off another. This is the sign of someone who is sinking fast. When all else fails, come back to honesty and accept responsibility for what has happened in the past then recommit to adopting a new approach to money for the future. You might need to adopt a payment plan or take drastic action to pay for your old debts, but things won't seem as bad once you've regained control.

Some questions to ask when determining whether or not you're being honest include:

▷ If I already know I should do all this money stuff, then why aren't I doing it?

▷ I can always go back to what I'm doing now – what have I got to lose by giving it a go?

▷ Why do I kid myself that I'm good with money if I'm not?

▷ If I can learn to drive a car, why can't I learn to use money effectively?

If you can follow my W.E.A.L.T.H. model then, just like my neighbour, your control over your spending will improve instantly and dramatically. The results will be impressive and your savings will begin to grow immediately, allowing you to promptly begin investing in property.

This is not just a theory – good money habits are a cornerstone for building sustainable long-term wealth. Property is how I make money and adopting the W.E.A.L.T.H. approach helps me to keep it. It's not about being tight with your money – it's about being smart with how you choose to spend it.

# Appendix B

# More on
# Negative Gearing

The text for this Appendix is taken from information I wrote for
www.PropertyInvesting.com. It has been praised for both its
detail and ease of understanding.

Often proclaimed as a property investor's best friend, negative
gearing is a concept that few people really understand. Sadly this
ignorance is causing many investors a lot of financial heartache.
Let's review the basics of negative gearing, the way it works and
how unwary investors are being willingly coaxed into buying
so-called 'assets' that are purposefully designed to lose money.

In my article entitled 'Positive Cashflow Returns Through
Property Investment' (see: www.PropertyInvesting.com/
PositiveCashflow) I explain that there are two ways to make money
in real estate – either through capital appreciation and/or via

positive cashflow returns. And in the world of property investment, the most common way that investors seek to profit is through capital appreciation, which is why location is regarded as critical to real estate success.

The preferred weapon in the fight to achieve capital gains returns in Australia, New Zealand and Canada is something called negative gearing. Negative gearing seems simple enough – buy the right property in the right location and then have the tenant and the taxman partially fund your repayments while you sit back and profit from the appreciating property value.

But can using property to make money be that simple? In a rapidly rising market, as was seen in most of Australia between 1996 and 2002, yes – it can appear to be that easy. Just hop on the escalator and ride the easy way to the top. Yet there quite are a few investing pitfalls that aren't discussed in the glossy sales 'off-the-plan' brochures, at the free seminars, or on the carefully tailored reality TV shows.

So, let's take a full "warts 'n' all" look at negative gearing to see when the time is right to use it and when it should be avoided like the plague. There's lots of hype when it comes to negative gearing. Lots and lots and lots in fact. And this all stems from the fact that quite a number of property sharks make a killing from selling negatively geared properties to unsuspecting investors.

Sadly, a lot of investors are sold on the potential outcome of owning property (hopefully making truckloads of money) without understanding the immediate consequences of their investment. Negative gearing is a strategy that provides immediate tax benefits while also offering the promise of long-term gains in the form of capital appreciation.

## TAX BENEFITS

The Australian Taxation Office (ATO) allows property investors to offset an income loss (where property costs are higher than

348

property income) incurred on a real estate investment against any other taxable income. To explain how this works we need to work through the numbers based on a typical property.

John is a taxpayer earning $80,000 per annum (plus superannuation) in a contract job for a major IT company. He is thinking about purchasing a property for $230,000 (inclusive of $7,850 in closing costs). To maximise his available tax deduction he has been able to secure 90% finance on a 25-year principal and interest loan with a current variable interest-only rate of 6.7% per annum. He makes weekly loan repayments in advance. The developer has offered a five-year rental guarantee at $250 per week ($13,000 per annum). The rates and body corporate fees total $2,000 per annum and there's also an 8% rental management commission to be paid. We are going to ignore depreciation benefits for the time being. At the end of the first year, the profitability of John's property investment is shown in Table 1 below.

| Table 1 – Rental Income Statement with One Property | |
|---|---|
| Rental income | $13,000 |
| Rental management | ($1,040) |
| Loan interest | ($13,869) |
| Rates etc. | ($2,000) |
| **Total** | **($3,909)** |

John is then able to claim the loss of $3,909 against his salary income and can reduce his overall tax bill as shown in Table 2 overleaf.

Even though John has made a loss of $3,909, the after-tax effect on his bottom line income is only $2,013 ($54,393 – $52,380).

| Table 2 – John's Position | | |
|---|---|---|
| | **JOHN WITH NO PROPERTY** | **JOHN WITH 1 PROPERTY** |
| Salary | $80,000 | $80,000 |
| Property losses | $0 | ($3,909) |
| Taxable income | $80,000 | $76,091 |
| Income tax + Medicare | ($25,607) | ($23,711) |
| **After-Tax Salary** | **$54,393** | **$52,380** |

Are you wondering why – given that this investment was going to lose money – John could possibly want to buy it? Good question! Trying to provide a sensible answer raises several key issues at the heart of negative gearing.

The short answer is that John is speculating that his *potential* capital gain will be consistently more than his *certain* income loss. This isn't out of the realms of possibility given that all he seemingly needs is capital appreciation of just 0.88% ($2,013 ÷ $230,000) per annum to at least break even. Indeed, if John had purchased this property back in 1996, then it's extremely likely that he'd be sitting on a small gold mine right now.

But trying to examine John's intention for investing actually raises many other issues that must also be considered to paint the full picture of his investment now and in the future. Let's now examine some of those issues.

## Can You Make Money and Save Tax at the Same Time?

At any given point in time you can't make money *and* save tax because the act of making money gives rise to the need to actually pay tax. This is where we need to discuss the difference between a realised and an unrealised profit/loss.

In negative gearing the loss is real in that John will physically have to come up with the after tax shortfall of his expenses over his income. This can be summarised by Table 3 below.

| Table 3 – John's Negative Gearing Loss | |
|---|---|
| Property loss | ($3,909) |
| Tax benefit at 48.5% | $1,896 |
| **After-Tax Loss** | **($2,013)** |

The consequences of this are that John will physically lose the buying power of $2,013 out of his pocket until expenses fall and/or income rises. In pre-tax dollars, the $2,013 equates to 5.19% (($2,013/48.5%)/$80,000) of his salary that he has lost from owning this property.

On the other hand, any capital gains on the property remain unrealised, and as such there is no tax to pay, until he decides to sell. John can even refinance any capital appreciation he obtains and effectively pay no tax, provided he doesn't sell!

But the problem with an unrealised gain is that you can't generally use it to fund your day-to-day lifestyle expenses. For example, you can't go into the supermarket and pay for your groceries using your capital gains debit card. Accessing your unrealised profits can also be expensive (with refinancing fees) and time consuming (with forms to fill in and sometimes lengthy delays).

Contrast the situation of realised loss and unrealised gains with cashflow positive property that has only realised income gains. Because your property income is higher than your property expenses you'll have to actually pay tax on your profit.

For example, imagine John purchased a property that had the annual outcome shown in Table 4 overleaf.

| Table 4 – Annual Outcome | |
|---|---|
| Property income | $12,000 |
| Property expenses | ($10,000) |
| **Subtotal** | **$2,000** |
| Tax payable at 48.5% | ($970) |
| **After-Tax Profit** | **$1,030** |

Unlike the previous negatively geared example, if John purchased this type of property then he'd instantly add to his bottom line. That is, he'd have more money from investing in property from day one (before any capital gains), not less.

And under both models he'd profit from any capital gains although it has been traditionally claimed that it is difficult to get both capital gains and positive cashflow from the same property.

The bottom line here is that it's not possible to use negative gearing to consistently invest in property in a way that sees you pocket more cash *and* claim a tax deduction at the same time.

## How Many Properties Can You Afford to Own?

Australian Bureau of Statistics data reveals that only eight in 100 property investors own three or more properties. If owning property was such a great idea then wouldn't it make sense to own multiple properties... say 10, 20, 30 or even more?

The reason why only 8% of all investors are able to own three or more properties is because of affordability issues. Let's return to our earlier example and imagine that John was able to buy five of the same negatively geared properties. How would his after-tax financial circumstance look? The results are shown in the Table 5 and Table 6 opposite.

### Table 5 – John's Position with 5 Properties

| RENTAL INCOME STATEMENT WITH 5 PROPERTIES | |
|---|---|
| Rental income | $65,000 |
| Rental management | ($5,200) |
| Loan interest | ($69,345) |
| Rates etc. | ($10,000) |
| **Total** | **($19,545)** |

### Table 6 – Position Comparison

| | JOHN WITH 1 PROPERTY | JOHN WITH 5 PROPERTIES |
|---|---|---|
| Salary | $80,000 | $80,000 |
| Property losses | ($3,909) | ($19,545) |
| Taxable income | $76,091 | $60,455 |
| Income tax + Medicare | ($23,711) | ($16,230) |
| **After-Tax Salary** | **$52,380** | **$44,185** |

What we can see now is that as John owns more properties his after-tax cash position is dramatically shrinking. Sooner or later John will reach the point when he can no longer afford to buy more property. His real after-tax wealth is spiralling down in ever decreasing circles, which is illustrated by Figure 1 overleaf.

Figure 1 shows that as John owns more property his after-tax pool of available cash decreases, while his losses from owning property increase. This illustrates the decrease in his purchasing power as only a maximum of 48.5% of the property loss can be claimed as a tax deduction. The remainder must be paid out of John's after-tax salary.

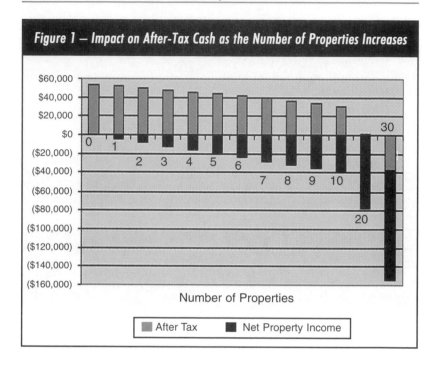

Figure 1 – Impact on After-Tax Cash as the Number of Properties Increases

The lack of sustainability is a phenomenon of negative cashflow that is rarely discussed. The outcome of this investment is that you need to keep working in order to continue to earn enough of a salary to fund the cash drain of the loss making investment.

### Five Years On...

Let's take our example of John a few steps further and fast forward five years. His property has appreciated by 40% and is now worth $322,000. His rent has increased by 10% and he now earns $275 per week, but his rental guarantee has now lapsed and he needs to allow for $1,000 per annum in maintenance. Rates have risen to $2,200. Let's imagine interest rates have remained steady at 6.7%. During the same time John's salary has risen to $90,000. His annual property income statement would now look like Table 7 opposite.

| Table 7 – Rental Income Statement with 1 Property, 5 Years On... | |
|---|---|
| Rental income | $14,300 |
| Rental management | ($1,144) |
| Loan interest | ($13,869) |
| Rates etc. | ($2,200) |
| Maintenance | ($1,000) |
| **Total** | **($3,913)** |

Based on these figures John's property has been able to hold its own in terms of profitability in that his rental increase has offset his additional expenses. Really though, allowing for inflation, he is slightly worse off as a dollar five years on buys less than a dollar at the time John bought his property.

Whereas five years ago John was $2,013 out of pocket, now he's $2,015 ($59,543 – $57,528) down, as shown in Table 8. This figure represents a minuscule deterioration, but he has earned unrealised capital gains of $92,000.

| Table 8 – Comparing Positions 5 Years On... | | |
|---|---|---|
| | **JOHN WITH NO PROPERTY** | **JOHN WITH 1 PROPERTY** |
| Salary | $90,000 | $90,000 |
| Property losses | $0 | ($3,913) |
| Taxable income | $90,000 | $86,087 |
| Income tax + Medicare | ($30,457) | ($28,559) |
| **After-Tax Salary** | **$59,543** | **$57,528** |

In summary on paper he's doing well, but in reality his purchasing power has taken a hit. Negative gearing has achieved an outcome of theoretical wealth-creation but an actual real loss in purchasing power.

## Using the Equity

John has made a paper capital gain of $92,000. If he decided to realise that gain, what options would he have?

### Selling

Assuming John sold his property for $322,000 on the last day of the tax year then his profit would be as shown in Table 9 below.

| Table 9 – Likely Profit on Sale of John's Property | |
|---|---|
| Sale price | $322,000 |
| Agent's commission (4%) | ($12,880) |
| Legals etc. | ($2,000) |
| | $307,120 |
| Acquisition cost | ($230,000) |
| Gross capital gain | $77,120 |
| 50% exemption | ($38,560) |
| Taxable Portion | $38,560 |
| Income tax at 48.5% | ($18,702) |
| After-tax profit | $19,858 |
| Add tax-free portion | $38,560 |
| **Total After-Tax Gain** | **$58,418** |

*Cont'd...*

| Table 9 – Likely Profit on Sale of John's Property (cont'd) | |
|---|---|
| Total gain | $58,418 |
| Five years (after-tax) negative cashflow | ($10,065) |
| **Net Gain** | **$48,353** |

My point here is that John's paper gain of $92,000 is quickly eroded back to $48,353 after adjusting for tax and the negative cashflow. Perhaps it's pertinent to remember that tax is only payable if you sell, in which case the impact on your net profit can be significant.

If John sold his property under these circumstances then he would have made a decent return, albeit he would have had to take a lifestyle cut in order to fund the annual negative cashflow from expenses being higher than income.

### Hold and Refinance

If John didn't want to pay tax then he needn't sell. He could approach his original financier and seek to refinance his loan to 90% of his property's new value. That is, he could access a further $82,800 [90% x ($322,000 – $230,000)].

Should John use this money for investing in other property investments then he'd qualify for a tax deduction on the additional interest. But if he did this then his annual negative cashflow would increase because he would have borrowed more money. This position is shown in Table 10 overleaf.

What John would find is that refinancing would allow him to acquire another property with no money down, but the additional interest cost would further reduce his available after-tax cash.

| Table 10 – Rental Income Statement if John Refinances and Spends Money on Investments | |
|---|---|
| Rental income | $14,300 |
| Rental management | ($1,144) |
| Loan interest (90% of $322,000 x 6.7%) | ($19,417) |
| Rates etc. | ($2,200) |
| Maintenance | ($1,000) |
| **Total** | **($9,461)** |

The worst thing that John could do would be to redraw the equity and then fund his lifestyle with the proceeds. If he did this then he would lose the interest deductibility of the redrawn amount – which would have a nasty impact on his overall wealth creation plans.

Let's look at what would happen if John redrew all of his equity to pay for an around-the-world extravaganza. This position is illustrated in Table 11 opposite.

The wash up of all this is that if John sold then he'd pocket a handsome gain – the product of steady capital appreciation while he owned the property. But if he refinanced and then reinvested the proceeds, his borrowings would increase, as would his interest costs, which would have the effect of further decreasing his net after-tax available cash.

Even worse, if John refinanced the property and then took his equity and spent it on maintaining a lifestyle, he'd be left with an interest bill that was not deductible. Investors should never draw on equity to fund a lifestyle. It would probably be better for John to sell and pay for his trip out of profits rather than using non-deductible borrowings.

| Table 11 – Rental Income Statement if John Refinances and Spends Money on Lifestyle | |
|---|---|
| Rental income | $14,300 |
| Rental management | ($1,144) |
| Loan interest | ($13,869) |
| Rates etc. | ($2,200) |
| Maintenance | ($1,000) |
| **Total** | **($3,913)** |
| | **JOHN WITH 1 PROPERTY** |
| Salary | $90,000 |
| Property losses | ($3,913) |
| Taxable income | $86,087 |
| Income tax + Medicare | ($28,559) |
| Subtotal | $57,528 |
| Non-deductible interest* | ($5,548) |
| **Total** | **$51,980** |

**\*Note:** The total interest would be ($322,000 x 90%) x 6.7% = $19,417, however, only the portion relating to the property investment ($13,869) would be deductible. The remainder ($5,548) is not deductible as it relates to private rather than investment expenditure.

# FAIRYTALE ASSUMPTIONS

It's just assumed that you'll make money from buying a negatively geared property, provided you can hold on for the long-term and wait for property prices to steadily rise. In times of rapidly rising prices this is great but in times of stagnant or even falling prices, negative gearing is a poor strategy.

It's true that you won't lose unless you sell... if you can hold on for the long-term and ride out any bumps then you should do well because property prices generally trend upwards (meaning that the average property will increase in price over time).

The real losers are investors who buy in the boom and have to sell in the gloom because they can't afford to ride out the storm. If John had purchased five properties and interest rates rose from 6.7% to 10% then the result would have been disastrous. Table 12, below, shows his after-tax remaining cashflow.

| Table 12 – Rental Income Statement if John had 5 Properties and Interest Rates Rose to 10% | |
|---|---|
| Rental income | $65,000 |
| Rental management | ($5,240) |
| Loan interest | ($103,500) |
| Rates etc. | ($10,000) |
| **Total** | **($53,740)** |
| Salary | $90,000 |
| Property losses | ($53,740) |
| Taxable income | $36,260 |
| Income tax + Medicare | ($7,594) |
| **Total** | **$28,666** |

Ouch! John's available cash has just about been crunched. It's no wonder so many property developers went to the wall when interest rates spiked at 17% in the early 1990s. Assuming that interest rates will remain low or that property prices will rise forever are nothing more than fairytale assumptions that are really best-case scenarios.

# THE SEVEN NEGATIVE GEARING TRUTHS!

## Truth #1: Negative Gearing is a Strategy Guaranteed to Lose Money

A negatively geared property is designed to enable you to access an immediate tax deduction arising from the shortfall of rental income failing to cover your property expenses. In other words, negative gearing is a strategy guaranteed to make a loss.

In order for you to afford this loss, you'll have to fund it out of your existing cashflow by working longer hours, or by taking a lifestyle cut. For most people this means going without some of the luxuries they previously enjoyed.

No-one wants to lose money, but it is testimony to the power of effective marketing that smart investors are fleeced out of thousands of dollars by being conned into a concept that only exists to lose money in the short term.

The only way an investor can make money from negative gearing is if any future capital appreciation is higher than the certain cashflow losses which will be immediate. Negative gearing is a valuable profit-making tool in a rising market. It is not a strategy for all investing seasons.

## Truth #2: The Dangers of Depreciation

Buying a property based on depreciation benefits is dangerous and deceptive. Depreciation is an accounting term used to describe the wear and tear of an asset that occurs over time. In practical terms, depreciation on a property refers to the carpet wearing down, the walls becoming chipped or stained and the furniture dating.

In most new properties you're allowed to claim a tax deduction for the depreciation of the fixtures and fittings, and, in certain circumstances, you may also claim a building write-off of either 2.5 per cent or 4 per cent of the property (not land) value too.

Slick marketing companies sell the notion of the taxman paying off your property using depreciation and building write-off deductions, but this sales pitch is quite deceptive because you don't avoid paying tax with depreciation, you just defer it. Commonsense suggests that depreciating an appreciating asset like property will give you a tax deduction today, but you'll have to repay it in the form of capital gains tax at a later date when you sell.

'Bracket-creep' issues can catch out many taxpayers too. If you earn $52,000 when you buy a property you will only be able to claim a deduction for depreciation at 43.5 cents in the dollar, but if your income rises to $62,500 when you sell then you'll need to repay the depreciation at 48.5 cents in the dollar.

If you don't ever plan to sell the property then, at a minimum, you should recognise that your depreciation tax deduction represents the wear and tear on your asset that will need to be eventually refurbished in order to continue attracting quality tenants.

Finally, beware any financial model that allows for depreciation benefits but does not include a maintenance budget. You cannot have depreciation without an expectation of repair costs – even new properties still need tap washers replaced.

## Truth #3: The Deception of Attracting Premium Tenants

A common strategy used to sell negatively geared property is to focus on purchasing a blue-chip property that will attract a premium tenant, since a premium tenant is more likely to be a quality long-term and high-paying occupant. Yet my experience reveals premium tenants are often the most volatile segment of the rental market. When times are prosperous, then premium tenants look for glamorous living in the newest kind of accommodation available with all the modern conveniences.

But when the economy contracts, premium tenants with high paying salaries are at a high risk of being downsized. If this happens, then they will seek cheaper accommodation leaving investors owning expensive property competing for new tenants in a shrinking market. In times of serious recession it's not unusual to expect vacancies of three months or more on premium property, which can make owning negatively geared property an absolute cashflow disaster.

A better strategy would be to attract a quality tenant who is willing to pay between 10 and 20 per cent above the market rate for a well-maintained property and decent landlord service. There will always be demand for a house that the average family can afford to live in. It would be wise for you to focus your attention on purchasing a property that is less prone to market fluctuations, and then seeking to charge above-market rates for a quality property to attract long-term tenants that want to treat your asset like a home.

## Truth #4: Unfair Comparisons

Figures used to substantiate expectations of appreciating property values are in many instances downright deceptive. One common example is the rise in the value of median property prices being applied to the premium real estate market.

In reality property prices can rise and fall in the same market at the same time. To eliminate this variance, statisticians adopt a mathematical snapshot of the market based on the value of median property sold during the period.

Movements in the median property price are certainly not representative of movements in the highly priced end of the market. Attempts to correlate movements in the median property values to highly priced real estate is statistically incorrect at best and potential fraud at worst. Making an assumption that real estate values double every seven to ten years, across all types of property (houses, units, etc.), in all states, is also misrepresentative.

It's very easy to build a financial model and then dismiss the truth via broad assumptions or leave out important information altogether. For example, making no allowance for vacancies after the rental guarantee period has finished or showing after-tax net profit with no allowance for capital gains tax payable when that asset is sold.

One quick way to test the conviction of a sales agent promising capital appreciation is to get him to personally guarantee it in writing. Given the degree of their certainty about rises in property value and considering the massive investment you'll need to outlay to own a blue chip property, a written guarantee simply confirming the underlying assumption isn't too much to ask. Be very wary of the assumptions used in any financial model.

## Truth #5: Who's Really Paying for the Secret Commissions?

If you liked the idea of purchasing property similar to the one that John purchased then you're probably asking "Where can I find such a property?" Enter the free seminar circuit, which is often little more than an elaborate attempt to sell you an overpriced property that meets the finely-tweaked financial models devised by clever marketing agents who are paid a commission to sell real estate on behalf of developers.

It's not unusual for commissions to be five per cent of the sales price, which on the property used in the earlier example amounts to $11,500.

This fee is not paid from the developer's margin. It's a cost added on top and paid for directly by you the purchaser. It can become unnecessarily expensive buying prime property off the plan when there are kickbacks to financiers, fit-out providers and sales agents all funded by you as the purchaser.

Negative gearing is often sold as a strategy that will make you rich in the future, but when you buy a boutique property you'll be making developers and sales agents rich today. Be very wary about letting other people profit at your expense. Remember to always ask "Who gets paid when I buy?"

## Truth #6: The Trap of Trying to Save Tax!

One of the many reasons given for investing in a negatively geared property is that qualified accountants recommend it. Indeed, if you approached most accountants and asked for strategies that legally minimised tax then negative gearing would be one of the first options discussed. But investing in negatively geared property to save tax is a double-edged sword. For every dollar you lose, you'll only ever recoup a maximum of 48.5 per cent back as a tax saving.

While you're waiting for illusive capital appreciation you'll be working longer hours and trying to cut back spending in order to fund the continual cash outflow because your property expenses are always higher than your rental income.

If you're paying your accountant for advice, spend your money searching for strategies that will earn cash profits, not ways that are guaranteed to make a loss.

## Truth #7: How Many of these Properties can You Afford to Own?

As you own more negatively geared property, your after-tax available cash reduces. This is because you only ever recover a maximum of 48.5% in a tax deduction, the remaining 51.5 cents in the dollar comes from your back pocket. It makes sense that as you own more loss making property your real buying power shrinks in ever decreasing circles.

## THE FINAL WORD

I am not totally anti-negative gearing. It's a proven wealth-building strategy during times of rapid price increases; provided you can comfortably afford the negative cashflow and are happy to continue working.

### Is there an Alternative?

The alternative to negative cashflow property is positive cashflow real estate. This is simply property that makes money from day one as it produces more property income than expenses.

But, as the saying goes, it's "horses for courses". Negative gearing is a strategy designed to lose money and in order to fund that loss you will need to continue working. This makes the strategy at odds with the broader goal of financial independence. If your aim is to stop working as soon as possible or to free up more time to do the things you love, then negative gearing is not a wealth building strategy you should implement.

Remember that there's a lot of hype about negative gearing because a huge industry of developers and sales agents make a living by selling property. It's more important than ever that you complete a proper due diligence over a potential property purchase to ensure you can afford the ongoing cash outflow from your property.

# IN A NUTSHELL...

Be very careful about blindly purchasing any kind of property. Be extra cautious when buying something when the outcome is likely to be negative cashflow.

Be extremely careful when buying property that a sales agent or a developer says has tax advantages – this is a red flag that the property is guaranteed to lose money. Making a profit from speculating that property prices might rise while you incur a certain income loss is risky.

Remember that if all you did was make money, then you'd have to make money. If your investments are not making money then something's going badly wrong.

## The Nine Questions to Always Ask

1. What's the end purpose to my investing?

2. Will buying this property bring me closer to, or push me further away from that goal?

3. Am I saving tax or making money?

4.  What is the annual cash injection or cash outflow?

5.  Can I afford to make a sustained loss?

6.  What is my exit strategy if things get tough?

7.  What has to happen in order for my property to make money?

8.  How many of these properties could I afford to own?

9.  Have I checked and double-checked all the figures and sought independent information to ensure the data I have is realistic?

### An Important Note

Please note that depreciation benefits have not been discussed in this analysis of negative gearing since it was assumed that the property that John purchased did not attract any depreciation.

However, in reality, depreciation is an important area that is discussed in an investor briefing titled *Depreciation – Investor Delight or Extreme Danger?* You can access this special free report at www.PropertyInvesting.com/Depreciation.

# Tenant from Hell Stories

These stories have been contributed my members of the www.PropertyInvesting.com community to demonstrate that investing in property comes with occasional surprises.

## Contributed By: Charlie Lear

I've had tenants from hell, only because I didn't know what I was doing as a landlord. If I'd had the experience, they wouldn't have got past the phone interview. As it's sometimes said, good judgement comes from experience and experience comes from bad judgement!

The first was a young couple planning to get married. When the rent came late, or not at all, I took the 'we're-friends, we-can-work-this-out' approach. Things improved for a little while, but not for long.

I sat down with them and was told point blank that *he* had put in his half of the rent, and that what *she* did with hers had nothing to do with him. I blindly ignored the red flashing lights and alarm bells, and extracted a written agreement for the rent to be paid on time and the arrears at $20 per week.

After another couple of missed payments, I called around to find the house empty – sort of. There was furniture scattered about but not enough for it to be livable. The missing bed was a clue that they'd moved out. The holes punched through the walls were a clue that it hadn't been an amicable departure.

I eventually tracked the tenant down at his parent's house. I walked up after dark, knocked on the front door and waited. I heard a rustling sound behind me and I turned around to see the biggest, blackest, most evil looking Rottweiler in the world, front legs braced on the step behind me, and lips curled back in a silent snarl. It gave a low growl and visibly bunched up its muscles, ready to attack. I was going to die. Horribly. Painfully. I did the first thing that came into my head. I stuck my hand in front of its nose.

"Gidday, pup! You being a good guard dog? That's a great set of teeth you've got there. What a good dog!"

The Rottie stopped in mid growl, tipped his head to one side, and looked at me as if I'd just escaped from the loony bin. The door opened and my tenant looked out, obviously surprised to see me. "Where's the dog?"

"Right here," I said, reaching behind and giving the Rottie a pat.

"Jesus! Are you nuts? Didn't you see the sign and the bell push by the gate?"

"Nope. Anyway, I'm here about the rent and the damage to the property."

Turns out they'd split up, he'd taken his furniture and left her to it. He paid me his half of the back rent and the wall damage took care of their bond.

It took four weeks to find her and get her stuff shifted out. I had to promise her parents not to chase her for the rent otherwise they would leave her furniture there for another few weeks. It was only then that I could clean and fix the property and get more tenants.

This time I was more careful. I let the estate agency vet them. I rented the house to a woman who had recently split up from her husband and who had a small baby. The rent wasn't a problem because it was being paid by Social Welfare.

I paid a courtesy call a week later to see if she was happy and the door was answered by another woman. She was a friend who had also moved in, with a couple of small kids, to share expenses. Thanks for asking me!

All three children had colds and were coughing. The house was cold and damp, they hadn't had the heaters going even though it was pouring rain in the middle of winter. I'd bought a dehumidifier for my own house a few weeks before, on a 12-month, interest-free deal. I couldn't see kids suffering like that so I whipped it around and got it going. At least I had the sense to add it to the chattel list on the rental agreement.

Sure enough, rent day came and went. I rang Social Welfare and they said it took a few weeks to go through, and it would be paid as a lump sum. OK. Two more rent days came and went. Social Welfare said it had been paid. I said I hadn't got it. "Oh, we pay it to the beneficiary, they pay it to you!"

I called around, since they hadn't had the phone connected. No sign of my tenant, but the second woman and her kids were there. "Oh, she moved back in with her husband a couple of weeks ago." I agreed to transfer the lease into the second woman's name and she would start payments as of that date.

Two weeks later, no rent, popped around to find the house deserted. Cleaned out. No furniture, no dehumidifier, no curtains. Even the light bulbs and 98¢ plastic light shades had gone. The back door had been kicked in, wrecking the frame and breaking the glass panels.

The police came, spread black fingerprint dust over everything and said that was about all they could do. They phoned a day later to say that they couldn't prove anything, but the word on the street was that the squatter had got back together with her husband, they'd taken everything out of the house and booted the door in to make it look like a burglary. Forget it.

It was kind of hard to forget it when for the next nine months the electricity bill arrived with an amount added for the dehumidifier. Once the door was fixed and the place cleaned, we found tenant number three. Do bad things always come in threes, or would it be third time lucky?

He was around 30, and didn't have any references because he still lived with his parents. I knew enough to make my own checks now, so I spoke to his mother and his boss at work. He was a good clean boy and a valuable sales assistant in the home appliances department. But he had a dog. A smallish, light-brown dog, short-haired and clean. I didn't mind the dog, because we had two of our own, and he promised to keep it outside. And it was clean. What he didn't tell me was that it was a vicious psycho death beast.

Because the rent was being paid on time, every time, and the outside of the place was tidy and the lawns mowed, I didn't bother going around until the six-month inspection was due. "Phone before you come round, I'll put the dog in the garage."

"Sure!"

I wandered around and walked up to the gate. His dog was lying on the path sunning itself, maybe ten feet away. It lay there and looked at me and thumped its tail a couple of times. I leaned over the gate and had my hand on the latch when it struck like a cobra. It just exploded and came up at me like a ginger cannonball. I'd flung myself back but it still sunk its fangs into my hand. If I hadn't moved it would have been my face.

I stood there, white as a sheet, blood dripping onto the concrete. The dog casually walked back to its spot on the path, turned around twice and lay down. It looked at me and thumped its tail a few more times. Just then the tenant walked around the corner of the house. "Oh, you're here. I'll just shut the dog away."

"Ah, thanks, we've already met."

With my hand wrapped up, I checked the grounds. Lawn like a bowling green, zero weeds in the garden, not a single dog poo anywhere. We went inside. You know there's untidy-but-clean, normal clean, and then there's neat-freak clean? Well the inside of the house was scary clean, with just a faint whiff of disinfectant. Not a speck of dust anywhere. None. Not in the bedrooms. Not in the kitchen. Not in the bathroom. Not in the spare room with the leather gear hanging up on the wall, not in the lounge with the huge rear-projection TV and surround sound and bookshelf full of accurately lined up adult videos.

I signed off on the inspection and said I wouldn't be doing anything about the dog, though he'd better put a warning on the gate. I couldn't get out of there fast enough. The rent continued to be paid on time, every time, for the next three years until we sold the property to investors. As far as I know he's still there, quiet, clean, and a good payer... the ideal tenant!

## Contributed By: Jon Stuckey

Our tenant worked at the real estate agency we listed with, so we assumed that she would be OK. And she was. Up until the time she quit working at the agency (which we didn't actually find out until well after she left).

The property was a two bedroom clad cottage in a leafy south-west Sydney suburb. We were achieving a gross weekly rent of $180 per week, and seeing as she worked at the agency, we allowed her to have a dog. Little did we know, that this dog was the 'Hound of the Baskervilles'. It was a very large Rottweiler that didn't mind jumping over 6 ft fences and wore a running line or dusty track along the fence where it paced back and forwards.

Our neighbours kept us informed of the parties that went on etc., but so long as there was no damage, I didn't pursue it. The rental market was also weakening at the time and I didn't want to risk losing a paying tenant. Time went on and our tenant soon had a partner, then the couple had a child and decided to move to a larger house. I was told by the agent that they had moved out a week before the lease expired, so I thought it the ideal time to hop in and clean the place up a bit for the next tenant.

I ended up having to re-turf the ground along the fence and get rid of the remains of a bonfire they decided to have in my back yard. While I was cleaning up, the tenant returned to pick up some cleaning items she had left behind. She warned me that some of her friends were thinking about pinching some of the established plants in the gardens for their own homes.

Anyway, the tenant had advised the agent that the arrears rent could come out of the bond, so I thought it reasonable to add the cost of turf too... until the tenant threatened taking me to the tribunal because I broke the lease agreement by entering the property. What a fright! In the end she paid for 50% of the turf.

Fortunately, a new tenant was found shortly after, with a great dane, who was willing to pay an extra $10 per week for the dog. Now I'm receiving $190 a week in a falling rental market. On top of that, before the new tenant moved in, my neighbour and I knocked down a section of fence between our houses at the rear of the yard. We went in halves to build a new fence which effectively gives my neighbour the back 25 square metres of my yard, and I charge her $10 a week for that. So that brings the rent up to $200 a week.

I discovered the importance of lease agreements, and sticking to the fineprint. I also discovered the importance of your rule to concentrate on a target market and not the property itself. I found the target market of pet owners. My house is quite old, and a bit of extra wear and tear isn't going to hurt. Most investors refuse to have pets, thus shunning a whole group of people, or ending up with pets in the property without knowing. At least I have a clause in my lease where the tenant will pay for any damages caused by the pet.

## Contributed By: Carmel Drovandi

My tenants from hell were two guys – one was a policeman and the other guy ran a store so I thought they sounded very responsible – both late 20s. One of the tenants explained that he had just broken up his marriage and his wife had gone to Queensland leaving him in Sydney with a beautiful dog. He said that if I didn't rent him the house then he'd have to put the dog down. I gave in after he promised it would never go inside (blah, blah, blah...)

Soon after they moved in I received a call saying that an urgent repair was needed after the dog chewed through the telephone wire. Then my neighbour rang to let me in on the secret that my store manager tenant was actually a marijuana dealer and then demanded to know what was I going to do about it. The final straw came when my tenants stopped paying.

When I went to my rental manager to try to sort out the mess I discovered that the office secretary had absconded with funds held in trust and that the records were shoddy too. It was impossible to work out who had paid what.

Things didn't get any better when the agent appointed a new property manager who refused point blank to release any money. My only option was to go to the tenancy tribunal to get the money I thought I was owed.

The wash up is that I changed agents and after they did a property inspection I received a call to say there were five dogs in the backyard, which was by this time totally ruined. I instructed the new agent to evict them, which took four weeks. Now I'm a lot more vigilant about keeping control of my investment.

## Contributed By: Marlene Nothling

My husband and I currently have two houses – one we live in and the other is a rental property. Luckily, although this property started off as a negatively geared investment, today we receive a positive cashflow return as we have paid the loan down over a number of years.

We have spent some time overseas lately and I placed the management of our investment property into the hands of a real estate agent while we were away. After completing their own due diligence, the agent let the property to a tenant who, from the outset, demanded many things.

She wanted to hire a possum catcher, lift up the carpet and polish the floorboards, put hand rails on the three steps leading up to the front door... the list goes on. Strangely, all these requests started after she stopped paying rent.

The property managers investigated but whenever they tried to phone the tenant she'd hang up. When the agent went to the house the tenant told them to get off the property otherwise she would call the police. The neighbours would tell us that the police were called to the house regularly because of domestic fighting, drunken brawls, people lying on the footpath, cars hooning up and down the streets. This went on for five months and still no money had been paid in rent.

Our only option was to end up at the tenancy tribunal to try to seek payment of rent arrears. Our tenant obviously knew the system because she was very familiar with the Residential Tenancy Authority rules and regulations and was attempting to use them to her best advantage. Luckily for us, the Magistrate was not at all sympathetic to her requests and signed an eviction notice. The day before the police were due to enforce the eviction she left of her own accord, presumably to another poor landlord.

When we went to the property to see what condition our tenant had left it in, the place was worse than I'd imagined. She had ripped out the underground sprinkler system and put it on the roof of the house. She had it running day and night so that she could keep cool. The $1,200 water bill for two to three months was a nasty surprise. She had stolen many items in the house including the curtains and handles off the stove, and she had damaged the walls, allowing her child to write all over them with crayon, etc. Luckily for us we were properly insured and recovered most of the damages. However, we still had to cover the loan repayment and expenses until the insurance pay out.

After this tenant was gone the property managers were going to put another tenant into the house. I have experience in debt recovery and am familiar with some of the steps to due diligence. It seems they hadn't even checked that the job of the new prospective tenant was valid. When I pressured them to follow this up, it turned out it was just a friend pretending to be the tenant's employer. I'm now a lot more thorough with my investing and I'm aware of the need to watch my assets carefully.

## Contributed By: Karen Lucas

My husband and I have been lucky with our three investment properties to have good tenants, however, my parents Bob and Julie have not. This is their story.

My parents sold their house and decided to move into their investment property (a four bedroom, two story house) in order to carry out a few renovations and then re-let the property. They painted the place throughout, laid new carpet, fixed up the backyard etc. and then after all the work was done the real estate agent found them new tenants and signed them up on a six-month lease. The tenants moved out before their lease was up and when they left they were eight weeks behind in their rent and the carpet (only four months old and costing over $2,500) was completely trashed. There were coffee and tea stains all up the stairs and their baby must have been toilet training or allowed to roam around the house without a nappy because there were, well, questionable stains everywhere. The child had also drawn all over the newly painted walls and several walls had to be repainted after only four months. It gets worse.

The tenants left some old furniture in the garage which my parents had to pay to have removed and dumped. Finally, they had left their cat and a litter of kittens locked in the garage without any food for two weeks and sadly they all had to be put down. Tenants like these can certainly make you think twice about property investing, but sometimes you need to go through an experience like this to make you realise how important it is to do a thorough due diligence.

## Contributed By: Leslie Howard

This is more a story about a conman from the UK, but he might as well have been a tenant from HELL, the end result was it cost me money.

He came to Australia to visit his lost mother, who he had not had contact with in more than 30 years and had just found. I met this person on the internet and I had a lot of contact with him over a period of two years – so I thought I knew him after many conversations, emails and occasional phone calls. We had formed what I thought was a good friendship

He'd discovered that his mother lived in Australia – in Victoria just outside Melbourne. His newly found mother was having problems and needed to move. I was about to settle on a new property – one thing led to another and I offered the property to him for his mother.

We came to an agreement in writing as to the terms of payment which he was to sign when he arrived on a future surprise visit to see his mother. The terms were a little unusual because he was to build an internet business for me in lieu of rent. However, if this did not materialise within six months then he'd arrange backpayment for the rent owing via a bank transfer.

It came to pass that nothing was happening with the internet business so I asked him for the payment as promised to which he readily agreed to organise via bank transfer. When I questioned why it continually failed to arrive as promised I was told that it had been caught up in the problems surrounding September 11 and that the funds had been frozen. This went on for a period of time. I requested proof to which he sent documentary evidence on bank letterhead supporting the payment.

Needless to say the funds failed to arrive and I placed further pressure on him in order to receive payment by saying that I was going to evict his mother and sister. That's when he exploded and informed me that he would not be threatened and that if I carried out what I said, I would never see a penny in payment. At this stage I began to become suspicious and decided to visit his mother and explain to her what was going on and ask her to vacate the property. Much to my surprise, she was not shocked by what I had to say and agreed to vacate.

I then decided to contact the bank in the U.K. from which the documentary evidence of the transfer was sent. I faxed them copies of all the documents which were supposedly from them for their internal investigation. While agreeing that they were fake, the bank chose to take no further action, however it offered me its support should I wish to take the matter further.

I then contacted my conman acquaintance with the information that the documents were in fact false only to have him accuse me of creating them.

The lesson in all of this is to not let a situation drag on and to always make sure that you follow the proper procedure as, if you're trying to be a nice guy, you may end up being burned.

## Contributed By: Mark Davis

Well, things might have come full circle now since I'm interested in property investing... but in my younger days, while a tenant, I can confess that my mate and I:

▷ Rode our motorbikes into the house, quite often sending the front wheel through the Gyprock.

- ➣ Worked on our car engines in the spare room.

- ➣ Lay on the lounge and shot out the light globes with a slug gun.

- ➣ Scared friends using a black powder rifle. We'd load it up with powder only, point to the roof and let her rip. What a mess!

- ➣ Spread graffiti all over the house, inside and out.

- ➣ Repainted the house for inspection using a compressor and spray gun for the inside.

- ➣ Poisoned all grass with Roundup to save mowing.

- ➣ Used the driveway as a skid pan.

- ➣ Accidentally burnt down the back fence.

- ➣ Accidentally blew up the outside furnace using small compressed gas cylinders.

It's possible that I epitomised the tenant from hell.

# Index

# HERE'S YOUR V.I.P. INVITATION!

*Join me and other top investors at the next Property Masterclass and discover more about how you can create wealth in today's turbulent property market.*

 The real estate market is always rapidly changing. It's now more important than ever to re-equip yourself with the latest techniques to ensure you're not using ineffective, outdated strategies.

For example, in the world of real estate it's just as important to know when to sell as it is when to buy. However, most investors have no idea how to read the market and instead hang on forever in the hope of avoiding tax. If prices fall then losses will follow.

If you're looking for the investing edge then I'd like to invite you to attend one of my Property Masterclasses – seminars quite unlike any others you might have been to. The simple aim of these unique events is to help you build a financial position that ensures you're primed to profit no matter what happens in the market.

There'll be no hype and no fuss – just intensive training as I join with other seasoned investors and work as hard as we can to not only reveal the techniques we're using to profit, but to also discuss the way we're 'financially sandbagging' our positions for safety.

What I'm offering is the chance to spend a full day with several investors, who own or control multimillion dollar property portfolios. This is not an event for academics who want to argue theory all day long – only people who want exposure to real-life investing talent that has been forged on the back of successful investing should attend.

Some of the topics on the agenda (at the time of writing) include:

- Positive cashflow hotspots – what's hot and what's not in the world of positive cashflow.

- How you can unlock profits, even when paying full price in blue-chip locations, by understanding and profiting from 'The 11 Second Solution Mark II'.

- The six 'rules of thumb' when it comes to buying property, which I apply to quickly and cost-effectively tell the difference between a good deal that is primed to make money and a bad deal that might become a financial nightmare.

- 'Take 4 to Profit!', our effective and convenient new four-stage process that allows any deal to be evaluated by even the most mathematically challenged investor.

- And much more ...

### Money Back Guarantee

Enjoy peace of mind with our no 'BS' policy that allows you to stay up until morning tea and, if you're not totally satisfied, hand in your course notes to receive a full 100% refund of your purchase price.

### Your Special VIP Offer

The full retail price to attend this event is $695, which is quite cheap when you take into account the professional nature of the seminar, the information on offer and the access you'll have to successful investors. However, to thank you for buying and reading this book, I'm able to slash a massive $200 off, meaning you can attend for just $495 – and this price includes GST, course notes and a working lunch!

### The Next Event ...

I usually run the Masterclasses once a quarter on a rotating basis at venues around Australia. To find out more information about upcoming dates, or to have your questions answered, please visit:

www.PropertyInvesting.com/Masterclass

Alternatively, if you don't have access to the internet then you can call toll-free (within Australian for non-mobile callers) on 1800 660 630.

### In Closing

Thanks again for buying and reading this book. I hope to see you at the next Property Masterclass and to meet you personally!

Sincerely,

*Steve McKnight*

*IMPORTANT: To take advantage of the special VIP offer of a massive $200 off the admission price you MUST enter in or quote the following discount code at the time of ordering:*

### MSTCLS

# Also by Steve McKnight

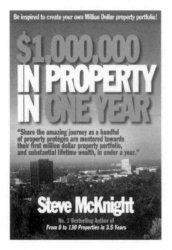

If you enjoyed this book then be sure to grab a copy of Steve's latest book – *$1,000,000 in Property in One Year*.

The title is derived from the Millionaire Apprentice Program ('MAP') – a private mentoring project author Steve McKnight ran for a small group of investors which began in August 2003 and finished a year later.

Coming from diverse backgrounds with varying degrees of experience, the MAP participants ('MAPPERS') were put through an intensive training regimen with the goal of acquiring a (gross) million dollar property portfolio in 12 months. Not just any property would do though – it had to be purchased according to a plan for it to make money immediately.

Without wanting to spoil the ending, a significant number of MAPPERS managed to achieve the stated goal despite the deteriorating investing climate, proving that the right person with the right training and investing system can achieve massive results in a short amount of time, even when the odds are stacked against them.

Steve's three goals for writing this book were to provide the reader with:

1. A comprehensive understanding of how to make positive cash flow profits

2. The practical context in which to apply the theory so you can find and profit from deals in any market anywhere in the world

3. The motivation to attempt something new.

This book is available from bookstores or online at www.PropertyInvesting.com.